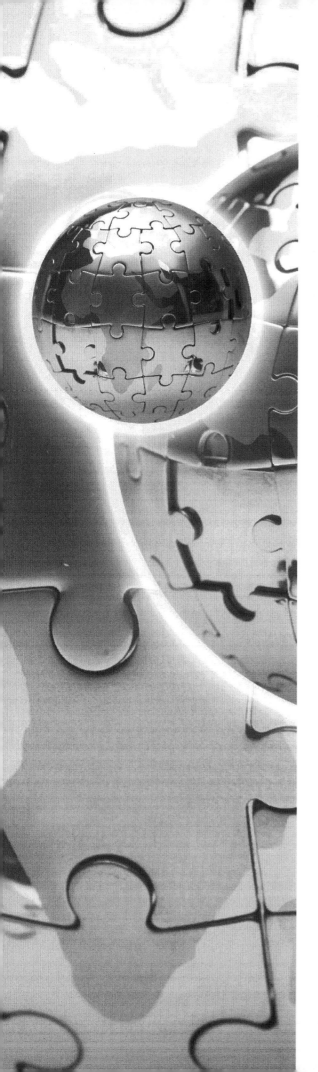

CW00520619

Investment Operations Programme

Global Securities Operations

Edition 14, April 2018

This learning manual relates to syllabus
version 13.0 and will cover examinations from
1 July 2018 to 30 June 2019

APPROVED WORKBOOK

Welcome to the Chartered Institute for Securities & Investment's Global Securities Operations study material.

This workbook has been written to prepare you for the Chartered Institute for Securities & Investment's Global Securities Operations examination.

Published by:
Chartered Institute for Securities & Investment
© Chartered Institute for Securities & Investment 2018
20 Fenchurch Street
London
EC3M 3BY
Tel: +44 20 7645 0600
Fax: +44 20 7645 0601

Email: customersupport@cisi.org
www.cisi.org/qualifications

Author:
Kevin Petley, Chartered FCSI

Reviewers:
Stephen Lacey, Chartered MCSI
Henrietta Wu

This is an educational workbook only and the Chartered Institute for Securities & Investment accepts no responsibility for persons undertaking trading or investments in whatever form.

While every effort has been made to ensure its accuracy, no responsibility for loss occasioned to any person acting or refraining from action as a result of any material in this publication can be accepted by the publisher or authors.

A learning map, which contains the full syllabus, appears at the end of this workbook. The syllabus can also be viewed at cisi.org and is also available by contacting the Customer Support Centre on +44 20 7645 0777. Please note that the examination is based upon the syllabus. Candidates are reminded to check the Candidate Update area details (cisi.org/candidateupdate) on a regular basis for updates as a result of industry change(s) that could affect their examination.

The questions contained in this workbook are designed as an aid to revision of different areas of the syllabus and to help you consolidate your learning chapter by chapter.

Workbook version: 14.1 (April 2018)

Learning and Professional Development with the CISI

The Chartered Institute for Securities & Investment is the leading professional body for those who work in, or aspire to work in, the investment sector, and we are passionately committed to enhancing knowledge, skills and integrity – the three pillars of professionalism at the heart of our Chartered body.

CISI examinations are used extensively by firms to meet the requirements of government regulators. Besides the regulators in the UK, where the CISI head office is based, CISI examinations are recognised by a wide range of governments and their regulators, from Singapore to Dubai and the US. Around 50,000 examinations are taken each year, and it is compulsory for candidates to use CISI learning workbooks to prepare for CISI examinations so that they have the best chance of success. Our learning workbooks are normally revised every year by experts who themselves work in the industry and also by our accredited training partners, who offer training and elearning to help prepare candidates for the examinations. Information for candidates is also posted on a special area of our website: cisi.org/candidateupdate.

This learning workbook not only provides a thorough preparation for the examination it refers to, it is also a valuable desktop reference for practitioners, and studying from it counts towards your continuing professional development (CPD).

CISI examination candidates are automatically registered, without additional charge, as student members for one year (should they not be members of the CISI already), and this enables you to use a vast range of online resources, including CISI TV, free of any additional charge. The CISI has more than 40,000 members, and nearly half of them have already completed relevant qualifications and transferred to a core membership grade. You will find more information about the next steps for this at the end of this workbook.

It is estimated that this manual will require approximately 80 hours of study time.

What next?
See the back of this book for details of CISI membership.

Need more support to pass your exam?
See our section on Accredited Training Partners.

Want to leave feedback?
Please email your comments to learningresources@cisi.org

Chapter One
Securities

This syllabus area will provide approximately 10 of the 50 examination questions

1. Securities Investment

Companies periodically need to raise funds to finance new developments in their business. To do so, they have a range of options open to them.

One method that a company can use to raise new money is to take out a loan from a bank. The company will subsequently be required to pay back the principal on the loan (ie, the sum initially borrowed), plus an agreed rate of interest, at an agreed date in the future.

It may be cheaper, and more in keeping with the strategic objectives of the company, to raise these funds through the capital markets.

Capital markets bring together companies looking for money with investors who have money to invest. Companies need development money to finance research, to buy new equipment, to take on and train new staff, to modernise their infrastructure and to finance the acquisition of other companies. To access this investment capital, companies may issue securities in the name of the company which they then sell to the investor community.

One technique for doing so is for the company to issue and sell **shares** in the company, a strategy known as equity financing. A person who buys shares (a **shareholder**) becomes a part-owner of the company. In return for investing money in the company, the shareholder shares both in the risks borne by that company (in a limited way) and in the profits that it generates. Shares represent a security in the company and can be sold to other investors, either via a **stock exchange** (exchange-traded) or through direct communication between investors themselves or agents acting on their behalf, commonly known as over-the-counter (OTC) or off-exchange trading, or via multilateral trading facilities (MTFs) or **systematic internalisers**.

Another way that a company can generate funds through the capital markets is to sell debt in the company by issuing **bonds** and other debt-related securities (debt instruments). In simple terms, the company (the issuer) issues an IOU that it sells to investors (the bondholders) in return for cash. These loans will typically be established for an agreed period of time and the issuer will repay (redeem) the loan on a specified date when the loan matures (the **redemption** date). However, the investor is not required to hold the IOU until it is repaid. If the investor wants to realise money before this point, they may sell this IOU to another investor. These loans may pay a fixed or variable rate of interest to the bondholders on agreed dates throughout the period of the loan.

Governments, municipal authorities and other public bodies also borrow money to finance development projects (ie, to build schools, roads, hospitals) or to manage their daily running costs. These bodies may also issue bonds and other debt instruments to raise this finance (eg, government bonds, municipal bonds). However, since they are not companies, governmental bodies do not issue shares.

Companies regularly employ investment banks to help them to issue equity and bonds that are carefully tailored to investors' needs. Investment banks may also underwrite securities issues to ensure that the issuer is able to raise the amount of capital that it needs. In order to raise finance through the capital markets, the securities issue must be appealing to the investor community, offering an instrument that will be appropriate for the investors' investment objectives and financial circumstances. Issuers are creating increasingly sophisticated types of financial instrument, designed to offer an attractive return at a level of risk that the investor is prepared to bear.

1.1 Why Do Investors Buy Securities?

The fundamental goal from an investor's standpoint is to optimise the level of return generated from its investments at a level of risk that the investor is willing to accept. This risk/return balance is integral to the investment process. Commonly, investments that hold greater potential for generating sizeable returns also carry higher risk that the investment will lose money, or may need to be written off altogether.

A number of factors make securities investments attractive:

- **Superior performance** – as a long-term investment, securities may deliver higher returns than holding money in a bank cash deposit account. However, securities are not guaranteed to outperform cash investments, and investors must make an informed decision about the projected rates of return that will be delivered by **equities**, fixed-income securities, property and other potential asset classes over the term of their investment.
- **Diversification** – investing in a diverse range of securities (eg, different types of equities issued by companies in different economic sectors and different markets, a spread of government and corporate debt instruments with different times to **maturity**), alongside other categories of investment (eg, property, precious metals, commodities and collectibles, such as fine art), allows the investor to spread risk across the investment portfolio. Because not all parts of the economy deliver the same level of performance at the same time, exposure to a range of different sectors enables the investor to diversify their investment risk, providing a broad spread of growth and income opportunities as the economy grows. Spreading risk further across a range of global markets adds increased diversity to the asset portfolio.
- **Regulatory oversight** – securities markets globally are usually closely regulated, affording protection to the investor against malpractice and **systemic risk**.
- **Liquidity** – the market in many securities is relatively liquid, meaning that a buyer can be found without either delay or a significant effect on market price when the investor wishes to sell a security, and vice versa. If an investor feels that the market for certain securities is likely to move up or down, it is important that the investor can increase or reduce the size of their securities holdings without delay in response to these market trends.
- **High volume, low relative costs** – many securities trade in high volume in securities markets on a daily basis. Consequently, the costs of securities trading can be relatively low compared with trading in some other categories of investment.

1.2 Sources of Investment Return

Equities and fixed income products offer two principal avenues for generating return on investment:

1. **Capital appreciation** – if the price of the security rises, the investor has an opportunity to sell the asset in order to realise a profit. The principle of buying and selling securities is in many ways similar to buying and selling used cars, gold coins, or other tradeable items: the investor aims to buy securities at market price and later sell for a higher price in the hope that they will be able to realise a capital gain on their investment. If the company is generating strong profits, then the share price is likely to rise as demand for the stock increases. For example, if the investor buys 100 shares in a company called ABC Manufacturing Company at £0.80 per share, and later sells these shares when the price has risen to £1.60 per share, the investor will have realised a profit (or capital gain) of £80, ie,

$$\text{Capital gain} = (100 \times 1.60) - (100 \times 0.80) = 160 - 80 = £80.$$

2. **Income payments** – investors may be paid an income (ie, **dividends** or interest) on the securities that they have bought.
   - Equities investors (ie, ordinary shareholders) may be entitled to a share of any profits that the company has made through a dividend payment that is approved at the company annual general meeting (AGM).
   - Bondholders will usually be paid a fixed rate of interest (known as the **coupon**) at fixed intervals throughout the period of the loan.

1.3 Who Invests in Securities?

For the sake of simplicity, we have referred so far to an individual investor who has purchased stocks and bonds in order to realise an income and a potential capital gain on their initial investment. However, pension schemes, life insurance companies, mutual funds and other **institutional investors** also invest widely in securities markets in order to generate returns on the investments that they hold on behalf of their members.

Members and sponsors of pension funds, for example, will pay into the scheme throughout their working life and will expect to receive an income from the pension scheme on retirement. These monies will be invested by the pension scheme in a range of financial instruments, including equities and fixed income instruments, to meet the liabilities that the pension scheme will have to pay to its members when they retire.

Governments and sovereign wealth funds may also invest in international capital markets to optimise investment return and to provide a diversified portfolio of assets that will afford protection against movements in global markets.

Investment management companies (often known also as asset managers or fund managers) will invest in securities markets, either:

1. to generate investment returns for investors (eg, **private investors**, pension funds) who have paid money into the funds that they manage, or
2. to generate returns on the company's own account by investing its own money. This situation, where the investment company acts as principal for the invested funds, is known as a proprietary investment.

Investment banks have traditionally been high-volume players in global securities markets, trading both as principal in order to generate investment returns on their own accounts, and as agency traders, placing trades on behalf of third-party clients. Investment banks historically have not catered directly for the retail investor, but have concentrated on providing services to corporations, governments and other financial institutions. In some cases, however, they may also provide investment services to wealthy private banking clients, often known as high net worth individuals (HNWIs).

Having provided a brief introduction to the world of securities investment, and to the functioning of capital markets, we will now look more closely at the characteristics of some of the broad range of securities available to the investor.

2. Shares (Equities)

All listed companies issue **ordinary shares**, but some may also issue **preference shares** and **deferred shares**.

2.1 Ordinary Shares

Learning Objective

1.1.1 Understand the characteristics of ordinary shares: ranking in liquidation; dividends; voting rights/non-voting shares; deferred shares; registration; bearer/unlisted securities; transfer restrictions

Equity is the residual value of a company's assets after all its liabilities have been taken into account. The equity of a company is the property of the ordinary shareholders. Hence, ordinary shares are often known as equities. The money that a company raises by issuing ordinary shares and selling them to investors is called equity capital.

Unlike debt capital, which is borrowed money, equity capital does not need to be repaid since it represents continuous ownership of the company. In return for investing in the company, ordinary shareholders are part-owners of the company and have rights to:

- attend and vote at shareholder meetings, including the AGM and any extraordinary general meeting (EGM)
- receive the annual report and accounts
- share in the company's profits by receiving a dividend paid on each share that the investor holds (although in some circumstances the directors may elect not to pay a dividend)
- participate in the appointment and removal of company directors
- share in the remaining assets of a company if it goes into **liquidation**
- receive a **capitalisation**, or bonus issue in proportion to their existing holdings
- participate in **rights issues** or other offers of new shares
- be consulted in special circumstances (eg, when a merger is proposed)
- additional benefits, or perks (eg, eligible shareholders in a construction company may be offered a discount on the price of a new property, and eligible shareholders in a train company may be offered discounts on the price of rail travel – typically, the company will specify a minimum number of shares that must be held to qualify for these benefits).

In some instances, a company may issue ordinary shares that do not carry voting rights (known as non-voting shares). Holders of this type of share will not be entitled to vote on company resolutions at any AGM or EGM.

Deferred shares are part of the ordinary capital of a company and offer holders the same rights as ordinary shares, with the exception that they do not rank for a dividend until specified conditions are met, at which time they are then said to rank **pari passu** with the ordinary shares. For example, a dividend may not be paid until a specified date has been reached, or until the company has reached a specified level of profitability.

2.1.1 Share Registration

In the UK and many other major markets, the shareholder's name and address will be recorded in the issuer's register of shareholders. In the UK, the issuer register is in two parts: the physical share register, maintained by the issuer **registrar**, and the dematerialised part of the register maintained in the **CREST** system, the securities settlement system of Euroclear UK & Ireland. CREST passes the dematerialised part of the register to the issuer registrar to ensure the registrar holds a complete copy of the register for public inspection. The dematerialised part of the register in CREST provides a legal record of title, representing the primary legal record determining share ownership (see chapter 2, section 3.3).

Some countries place restrictions on the sale or transfer of certain categories of shares to non-resident investors (see section 2.1.4).

In some jurisdictions, takeover regulations require that a shareholder makes an open offer to acquire shares from all remaining public shareholders when his/her holding reaches a specified threshold limit (eg, in the UK, this threshold is currently 30% of a company's issued capital).

2.1.2 Listing

Listed securities are those that have been accepted for trading on a recognised investment exchange (RIE, a stock exchange or securities exchange offering listing services and trading in a range of securities and, in some cases, a selection of other instruments). To list their securities, issuing companies must, typically, fulfil conditions specified under the listing requirements of the RIE concerned.

In the UK, the term 'listed securities' refers to securities which are:

*   admitted to trading on a specified recognised investment exchange, and
*   included in the official UK list maintained by the **Financial Conduct Authority (FCA)** (in its capacity as the UK Listing Authority) or are officially listed in a qualifying country outside of the UK in accordance with provisions corresponding to those generally applicable in European Economic Area (EEA) states.

The listing process may offer a number of benefits to the issuer and the holder of the security:

*   The security is traded in a regulated and orderly marketplace.
*   The exchange can provide a liquid market for the security – those wishing to sell the security can find potential buyers, and vice versa.
*   The exchange will provide regular reporting on sales and purchases of listed securities.
*   Disposal of shares by company directors and associated persons must be publicly disclosed.
*   Companies wishing to list on an RIE will typically be subject to a detailed investigation, designed to safeguard the integrity of the exchange and to offer a degree of protection to investors that they are buying securities in a bona fide company. Listing is also subject to regulatory approval.
*   The liquid nature of exchange trading can facilitate price determination – typically, prices of listed securities will move up and down according to supply and demand across potential buyers and sellers active on the exchange.

Unlisted securities are those that are not listed on an RIE. These securities will be traded off-exchange or **over-the-counter (OTC)** (see section 10 for further detail).

2.1.3   Bearer Securities

Historically, new issues of equity resulted in the issue of **share certificates** in the name of the shareholder. Some markets continue to issue and process certificated securities. If the security is unregistered, legal title will rest with the investor who physically holds the security (the bearer). This is known as a **bearer security**. A bearer security is a security where no registration of ownership is required and proof of ownership lies in physical possession of the security certificate, which will typically be held in safe custody with a specialist custodian bank (see chapter 2, section 2.1). The investor's name does not appear on the security and, thus, anyone who presents the certificate has the right to receive the cash value. Dividends are normally claimed by detaching coupons from the certificate.

Bearer securities are often used by Eurobond and other international issuers but they are rarely seen physically these days, due to the high risk of loss and/or misappropriation. Few UK companies issued bearer shares and after a phasing-out period they were abolished. The main reasons bearer shares were phased out were to improve transparency of ownership and because of drives to dematerialise shares. Such drives have been replicated across most jurisdictions.

2.1.4   Transfer Restrictions

In some jurisdictions, and for certain securities, restrictions may be applied on how, and to who, securities may be transferred. For example:

1. In some instances, securities may not be sold to foreign investors, or foreign investors may be restricted from holding more than a specified percentage of the total issued capital in specified companies, or must report to the regulatory authorities, the exchange and/or the depository when the size of their holding exceeds a specified percentage of the total issued shares in a company.
2. In some circumstances, securities holders may be restricted from selling or transferring securities in quantities of less than 1,000, or some other specified block/lot size.
3. Restrictions may be placed on the transfer of securities when the issuer is subject to bankruptcy or legal proceedings.
4. Issuers in some jurisdictions may place restrictions on the transfer of securities for a given period after issuance, conversion or other form of change in status, without the issuer's explicit consent.

2.2   Preference Shares

Learning Objective

1.1.2   Understand the characteristics of preference shares: ranking in liquidation; dividends; voting rights/non-voting shares; cumulative/non-cumulative; participating; redeemable; convertible

By issuing preference shares, companies may raise **share capital** without diluting the ownership rights of ordinary shareholders. Preference shares are part of the company's total share capital, but do not represent part of the company's equity share capital. Consequently, preference shareholders do not have a share in the rising profitability of the company.

Characteristics of preference shares are:

- Preference shareholders have no voting rights.
- Preference shareholders are paid a fixed dividend per share, which is established at the time of issue and does not increase with rising profits of the company.

Example

Consider the following preference share: 3% preference dividend £0.40.

This is a preference share with a nominal value of £0.40 per share that carries a dividend of 3%. Hence, it will pay a dividend income of 3% of £0.40 every year for every share issued. If a company has issued 100,000 of these shares at nominal value then it will have received:

$$100,000 \times 0.40 = £40,000 \text{ from shareholders on issue.}$$

It will pay a total annual dividend of:

$$40,000 \times 3\% = £1,200 \text{ each year.}$$

Preference shares do offer some important benefits over ordinary shares:

- Holders of preference shares take preference over the ordinary shareholders for dividend payments and payments following liquidation. If the company were to go into liquidation with sufficient funds available, preference shares will be repaid at nominal value (or par value, namely £0.40 in the example above) before any repayment is made to ordinary shareholders (see figure 1).

Figure 1: Payment of Obligations after Liquidation

If a company goes into liquidation, or is wound up, the assets are generally sold and the proceeds will be paid out in the following order:

1. Fixed-rate loans and bonds secured on the assets of the company.
2. Preferential creditors.
3. Floating rate loans and bonds secured on the assets of the company.
4. Unsecured loans and bonds and other unsecured creditors.
5. Subordinated loan stocks.
6. Preference shares.
7. Ordinary shares.

- Preference shareholders may be entitled to a fixed dividend even when no dividend is paid to ordinary shareholders. A preference shareholder is not guaranteed a dividend every year, since the company may decide not to pay a dividend at all. However, if the company does decide to pay a dividend, preference shareholders have the right to receive their dividend before the ordinary shareholders in all circumstances – hence the term preference.

Preference shares may be cumulative or non-cumulative. If a dividend is not paid, cumulative shareholders receive the dividend carried over, and the company must pay these shareholders before it can pay any other dividends. In the example above, if the £1,200 for 2018 is missed, then preference shareholders will receive £2,400 in 2020 (assuming the company is in a position to pay a dividend in 2020). Non-cumulative shareholders simply lose the dividend if it is not paid, as a normal shareholder would.

A preference share may be redeemable, which means that at some time in the future, the company will buy it back. Redeemable shares usually look like this:

3% cumulative preference share of £0.40, 2020

This indicates that the £0.40 per share preference share carries an entitlement to a 3% dividend and will be redeemed in 2020.

If a preference share is a participating preference share, then the shareholder has the right to participate in, or receive, additional dividends over and above the fixed percentage dividend discussed above. The additional dividend is usually paid in proportion to any ordinary dividend declared.

Preference shares may be convertible. If the shares are convertible then the shareholders have the option, at some stage, of converting them into ordinary shares.

3.   Debt Instruments

Learning Objective

1.1.5   Understand the characteristics of fixed-income instruments: corporate bonds; eurobonds; convertible bonds; government bonds; discount securities; floating rate notes; coupon payment intervals; coupon calculations (may be tested by the use of simple calculations); accrued interest calculations (may be tested by the use of simple calculations) (actual/actual, 30/360); clean and dirty prices; mortgage-backed securities, asset-backed securities; index-linked bonds

Debt instruments are (generally) interest-bearing securities issued when a borrower wishes to raise a specified amount of cash in a specified currency. As with equities, an issuer (ie, a company, government or government agency) sells bonds to investors in order to raise capital. However, unlike with equities, the borrower promises to:

- repay the capital to the investor at an agreed date in the future (except in the case of perpetual or undated bonds), and
- make periodic interest payments (known as the coupon) to the investor throughout the loan period (except in the case of **zero coupon bonds**).

Corporate bondholders (ie, holders of debt instruments issued by a company) typically bear a lower risk in the company than shareholders. Hence, in the long-term, returns on equities may be higher than on bonds (though bonds may outperform equities for more prolonged times during this period). This additional return generated on equities, compared with bonds, is known as the equity risk premium.

Bonds typically carry lower risk than equities because of the following factors:

• Bondholders have a prior claim on the company's assets relative to shareholders. Hence, if the company goes into liquidation, shareholders will face a higher likelihood that they may lose their money than bondholders.

• The return that the bondholder will usually receive is fixed at the time of issue and will be predictable if the bond is held until the redemption date. Specifically, the bondholder will receive an interest payment at fixed intervals throughout the period of the loan and will be repaid the par value of the bond at maturity. In contrast, shares have no fixed maturity and the shareholder's return will be dependent on the company's profitability and a number of other factors. In lean years, the company may pay no dividend on ordinary shares. However, it will still be required to pay interest on bonds and other debt securities.

Example

Take as an example an investor who is prepared to lend £1,000 to a company for five years and assume that interest rates are 7% per annum. In return for that loan, the company issues the lender with a bond. The bond is a legal acknowledgement of the debt and, under the terms of the bond, the company makes a number of promises to the lender.

The two main promises are:

• To pay interest on the bond at 7% a year. This interest payment is called the coupon and, in this case, will be 7% x £1,000 = £70 a year.

• To repay the capital of £1,000 in five years' time. The repayment value of £1,000 is called the nominal value of the bond.

Graphically, the cash flow will be as follows:

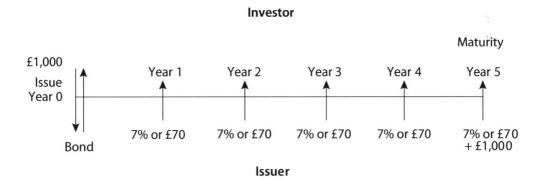

From the perspective of a company issuing bonds:

• bond issues typically allow the issuing company to obtain fixed-term finance at lower cost than it could via a bank loan,

• bondholders do not represent part of the company's equity share capital. Hence, issuing bonds do not dilute the ownership of the company,

• bondholders do not share in the rising profitability of the company, nor do they carry other corporate ownership privileges held by shareholders.

The term coupon comes from the traditional feature of bond certificates where coupons were attached to the certificate. These were cut off and submitted to the company in order to claim interest entitlement. Most bonds are now dematerialised (that is, paper certificates have been eliminated and bonds are held and registered electronically, with transfer of legal title also taking place electronically) or immobilised (where the global certificate is held by a central depository and, again, transfers and legal title are registered electronically), but the term coupon is still used to denote the periodic interest payment.

The coupon rate is the rate of interest paid on the nominal value (also known as the face value, par value or redemption value) of the bond.

The coupon may be paid every six months or annually. Referring back to the example above, if the bond pays a semi-annual coupon, then £35 will be paid every six months. UK government bonds (known as gilts) and US government Treasury bonds both pay a semi-annual coupon. Occasionally a bond may pay a quarterly coupon, eg, some **floating-rate notes**.

With some bonds, the coupon is paid without tax being withheld. This is termed a gross payment. Other bonds pay the coupon with tax withheld. This is termed a net payment. Whether payments are made gross or net depends on the tax legislation of the country concerned, but the coupon rate in the title of the bond will always be the gross amount.

When the bond reaches its redemption date, it is said to mature and the bond is then redeemed. In the example, the bond was issued with a five-year maturity. After one year has elapsed, it will have a four-year maturity. The repayment of the principal of the loan at maturity is not usually subject to **withholding tax**, although it may be subject to capital gains tax or income tax.

Bonds are typically classified as short, medium and long maturity. The UK Debt Management Office (DMO), for example, which issues UK gilt securities (ie, UK government bonds), categorises gilt maturities as follows:

- Short: 0–7 years.
- Medium: 8–15 years.
- Long: 15+ years.

Gilts with a maturity of less than three years are sometimes labelled ultra-short. Gilts with a 50-year maturity, which have been issued by the DMO since 2005, are sometimes labelled ultra-long.

The coupon reflects the interest rate payable on the nominal amount. However, an investor will have paid a different amount to purchase the bond, so a method of calculating the true return is needed. The return, as a percentage of the cost price, which a bond offers is often referred to as the bond's yield. The interest paid on a bond as a percentage of its market price is referred to as the flat or running yield. This is calculated by taking the annual coupon and dividing by the bond's price and then multiplying by 100 to obtain a percentage.

Risk of Default

The price of a bond will reflect interest rates. It will also reflect the risk that the issuer of the bond will fail to meet the two promises to pay interest and to repay the capital on maturity. This is known as **default risk**.

It is difficult to quantify default risk with the same precision as yields, but the investor must draw on as broad a range of risk measures as possible in order to evaluate the expected return on a bond investment against the associated risks borne in holding this instrument.

For large issues of bonds, such as those taking place in the **eurobond** market (see section 3.1.4), there are specialist rating agencies (for example, Standard & Poor's, Moody's, Fitch), which give each bond issue a credit rating that reflects the agency's assessment of the likelihood of default. The most secure bonds are given a AAA rating, referred to as triple A, according to Standard & Poor's. Bonds that are less secure will have a lower price, and thus a higher yield, than a triple A-rated bond. Bonds with a Standard & Poor's rating of BB or below are considered to be speculative/junk/high-yield/sub-investment grade rather than investment grade.

3.1 Types of Fixed Income Instrument

Bonds are typically labelled according to who issues the bond, which market they are issued in, and any defining characteristics that differentiate the instrument from a standard fixed-interest bond.

3.1.1 Government Bonds

The bonds issued by politically stable and traditionally economically strong governments, such as the US, Germany and the UK, are typically among the most secure marketable investments in the world. The risk of default on sovereign debt (as government debt issues are generically known) in more volatile developing economies, and some struggling European economies, is significantly higher.

Governments may issue debt instruments denominated in their domestic currency or in a foreign currency. Whereas governments rarely default on domestic currency government debt, default on foreign currency government debt is more common. Sovereign risk is the name given to the risk that a government will fail to honour its debt obligations to creditors.

Widely traded government bonds include:

- US – Treasury bonds or Treasury notes
- UK – Gilt-edged securities (or gilts)
- Japan – Japanese government bonds (JGBs)
- Germany – Bunds, Bobl and Schatz
- France – OATs and BTANs.

3.1.2 Domestic Bonds

This is a bond issued by a borrower resident in the country of issue, denominated in the local currency and regulated by the regulatory authority of the jurisdiction concerned. For example, a bond issued by a US company, denominated in US dollars and regulated by the US Securities and Exchange Commission (SEC), is a US **domestic bond**.

3.1.3 Foreign Bonds

A **foreign bond** is one issued by a foreign issuer in the local currency in the local market. For example, a US dollar bond issued in the US by a non-US company is a foreign bond. Foreign bonds are often given colloquial names:

Name	Currency	Issuer	Market
Yankee	US Dollar	Non-US	US
Samurai	Yen	Non-Japanese	Japan
Bulldog	Sterling	Non-UK	UK
Matador	Euro	Non-Spanish	Spain

3.1.4 Eurobonds

A eurobond is a bond issued by a company and sold to investors outside the country where the currency is employed. For example, a US-denominated bond sold outside the US (designed to borrow US dollars circulating outside of the US) would typically be referred to as a eurodollar bond. This may, for example, represent a dollar-denominated **debenture** issued by a Dutch company through an underwriting group consisting of a syndicate of investment banks (eg, Dutch, UK and US investment banks). Coupon payments on eurobonds are subject to the tax legislation of the country where the payment is effected. Interest on bonds held in a recognised clearing system is typically paid gross. For more about eurobonds, see section 8.4.

3.1.5 Convertible Bonds

A **convertible bond** is a bond that gives the holder the right, but not the obligation, to convert the bond into a specified number of underlying shares (normally ordinary shares) of the issuing company on terms that are set out at the time of issue of the bond. Convertible bonds commonly pay lower interest than straight bonds, but provide greater opportunity for capital gain if the price of the underlying shares of the company appreciates during the loan period. In the same way as regular bonds, holders of unconverted bonds at maturity retain the right to redeem the bonds at nominal value.

The conversion rate is the number of shares that are received for each bond unit. For example, an investor exercising a convertible bond with a conversion rate of two will receive two shares for each bond unit exercised.

An exchangeable bond is a hybrid security consisting of a bond and a conversion option to exchange the bond for the shares of a company other than the issuer (usually a subsidiary or related company).

Contingent convertible bonds (also known as CoCos) are very similar to traditional convertible bonds. The key difference, however, is that a price is set, which the underlying equity share price must reach before conversion can take place (ie, conversion is contingent on the ordinary shares attaining a certain market price over a specified period of time).

3.1.6   Discount Securities

A discount bond is a bond issued at a price that represents a discount to the redemption price at maturity. Zero coupon bonds represent one form of discount security. This type of bond does not pay interest, but the price paid by the investor to acquire this bond at the time of issue is at a discount to the capital redemption price at maturity. As such, the investor receives no coupon income, but receives a capital gain at redemption.

This type of issue may be attractive for companies wishing to borrow money to finance a project that has a long development time. As such, they do not wish to be paying out coupon payments throughout the loan period when income generated by the project may be low, but would prefer to repay a capital lump sum at redemption, when it is hoped that the project will be well established and generating sizeable returns.

Discount securities may also be attractive to investors because of, for example, tax considerations and the timing of cash flows.

3.1.7   Floating-Rate Notes (FRNs)

A floating-rate note (FRN) is like a bond, except that its coupon is linked to a floating interest rate. For example, an FRN might pay a semi-annual or quarterly coupon linked to a reference or benchmark rate, such as the London Interbank Offered Rate (LIBOR). This is the rate of interest at which banks will lend to one another in London and is often used as a basis for financial instrument cash flows.

A company might issue an FRN if it believes that interest rates will fall in the future and it does not want to lock into a high fixed coupon rate; or it may wish to issue an FRN if it has floating-rate receipts in order to match the interest rate basis of its receipts and payments, thereby hedging against unexpected and/or adverse changes in interest rates.

3.1.8   Asset-Backed Securities (ABSs)

Asset-backed securities (ABSs) are issued against a pool of loans – which may be credit card debt, student loans, automobile loans, property loans or other types of loan contract. They can sometimes be issued against other types of expected future cash flows, eg, royalties.

In creating an ABS, the originator of the loan will typically sell a pool of its outstanding loans to a third party. The buyer may elect to securitise this package of loans by issuing securities – underpinned by cash flows from the pool of underlying loans – which can be bought and sold by investors just like any other tradeable securities. On purchase, the ABS holder will acquire the right to a share of the cash flows resulting from loan repayments, but will also take on the risk of potential default by borrowers on their repayments.

3.1.9   Mortgage-Backed Securities (MBSs)

A **mortgage-backed security (MBS)** is a type of ABS (see section 3.1.8) that uses a single mortgage, or a pool of mortgage loans, as collateral. Investors receive payments derived from the interest and principal of the underlying mortgage loans.

3.1.10 Index-Linked Bonds

Index-linked bonds (variable or floating rate) are fixed-income securities where the coupon payment (ie, the income) and the principal (the price at which the bond will be redeemed) are adjusted to take into account movement in retail prices. In the UK, this adjustment may be made according to movement in the Retail Prices Index (RPI), for example.

Example

Assume that an index-linked bond is issued at its par value of £100, with a 2% coupon.

Consider that, over a five-year term, retail prices rise by 25%. As a result, the bond will be redeemed at £125.

The interest paid on these bonds will also increase by 25% over this five-year period, such that the bond pays a real interest rate of 2%. Thus, the interest paid across the five-year term will be 2% on the revised redemption value of £125 (which is equivalent to 2.5% on the original £100 nominal value).

3.2   Clean and Dirty Prices

Interest entitlements on UK gilt-edged securities, and on many other fixed income securities, are paid twice per year. During the period leading up to the next value date for a coupon payment, interest will accrue on a daily basis. If the security is sold during this period, the seller typically has an entitlement to any interest that has accumulated since the last coupon date. Market convention dictates that the buyer will normally compensate the seller for this **accrued interest** at the time of **settlement**. Hence, the accrued interest due to the seller will be added to the buyer's purchase cost and forwarded to the seller.

In many jurisdictions, the transaction price actually quoted for the debt security must exclude the accrued income. This is known as the **clean price**.

Under UK tax law, for example, the clean price and accrued interest must be quoted separately for accounting and tax declaration purposes. The capital value (as valued on the transaction date by the clean price) will be subject to capital gains tax rules, whereas any accrued income will be taxed under income tax rules.

When a price is quoted for a debt security that includes the accrued interest, this is known as the **dirty price**.

3.3   Calculating Accrued Interest on Bonds

When a bond is sold, the accrued interest will need to be calculated and added to the clean price that the buyer pays the seller.

If the trade settlement date is after the **record date** (see chapter 4, section 5.5), the coupon will be paid to the seller and the accrued interest then subtracted from the clean price.

The first of these is known as a cum-interest transaction and the second is known as an ex-interest transaction.

Example: Cum-Interest Transaction

A cum-interest transaction is agreed. £200,000 5% Treasury 2020 are traded on 3 March for settlement on 4 March. Graphically:

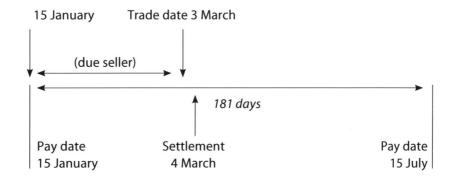

The interest due to the seller can be calculated by the following formula:

$$\text{Accrued interest} = \text{nominal value} \times \text{coupon for the period} \times \frac{\text{days of accrual}}{\text{days in coupon period}}$$

The days of accrual will be between the day of the most recent coupon payment (15 January) and the day before the transaction settlement date (3 March), both days included, which is 48 days, and there are 181 days in the coupon period.

More generally, it will be annual coupon/number of coupons in the year. This would give:

$$\text{Accrued interest} = \frac{\text{nominal value}}{\text{number of coupons}} \times \frac{\text{annual coupon} \times \text{days of accrual}}{\text{days in coupon period}}$$

The accrued interest is added to the clean price.

Example: Ex-Interest Transaction

An ex-interest transaction is agreed. £200,000 5% Treasury 2020 are dealt on 10 July for settlement 11 July. Graphically:

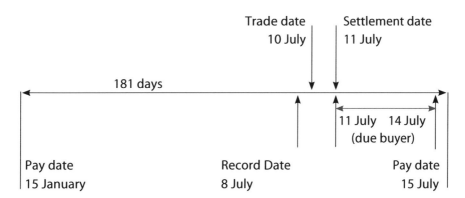

The accrued interest on an ex-interest transaction is called rebate interest. The rebate interest is deducted from the clean price.

The days of accrual are the days from the day of the transaction settlement date (11 July) through to the day before the next coupon payment (14 July), both days inclusive, which is 4 days.

3.3.1   Accrual Conventions

There are four common methods of calculating the interest payable on interest-bearing bonds. These are called interest rate conventions. Some bonds will use a **30/360** convention, while others will use the actual number of days in the month or year. Each convention differs slightly in the assumptions about the calculation of the period over which interest is payable. The conventions change depending on the market, for instance:

*   UK corporate bonds pay interest based on actual/365-day convention,
*   US corporate bonds pay interest based on actual/360-day convention,
*   eurobonds generally pay interest based on the 30/360 day convention, and
*   most government bonds pay interest based on the actual/actual convention.

30/360

This case assumes and bases the calculation on there being 30 days in each and every month and 360 days in a year.

For example, if XYZ bonds are acquired on settlement date 1 April and sold for settlement day 2 July, the buyer will receive all the interest accrued during the period 1 April to 1 July (ie, the day before settlement date). The settlement process is calculated as follows:

1 April–30 April	=	30
1 May–31 May	=	30
1 June–30 June	=	30
1 July	=	1
		91 days

Number of days in year is: $12 \times 30 = 360$.

$$\text{Accrued interest} = \text{nominal} \times \frac{\text{interest}}{100} \times \frac{\text{number of days in period (assuming 30 days in month)}}{360}$$

Actual/Actual

The calculation for actual/actual is the same as above, except that the number of days is:

1 April–30 April	=	30
1 May–31 May	=	31
1 June–30 June	=	30
1 July	=	1
		92 days

This convention assumes the number of days in the year is equal to the calendar days in the interest period, multiplied by the number of interest periods in the year.

Accrued interest =

$$\text{nominal value} \times \text{annual coupon (\%)} \times \frac{\text{calendar days in period}}{(\text{calendar days in period}) \times (\text{number of interest periods in year})}$$

Actual/360-Day Convention

This case assumes and bases the calculation on a 360-day year.

$$\text{Accrued interest} = \text{nominal value} \times \text{annual coupon (\%)} \times \frac{\text{actual days in period}}{360}$$

Actual/365-Day Convention

This case assumes and bases the calculation on a 365-day year.

$$\text{Accrued interest} = \text{nominal value} \times \text{annual coupon (\%)} \times \frac{\text{actual days in period}}{365}$$

Example

Question

Investor X holds $1 million corporate bonds of ABC ltd with a coupon of 6%. Interest is paid quarterly and the interest periods are:

- 1 January–31 March,
- 1 April–30 June,
- 1 July–30 September,
- 1 October–31 December.

Calculate the amount received by the investor per period and in total for each of the four interest rate conventions.

Answer

The interest rate periods are 90 days, 91 days, 92 days and 92 days respectively.

Actual/360-Day Convention:

Q1: Interest paid = $1m x 0.06 x 90/360 = $15,000
Q2: Interest paid = $1m x 0.06 x 91/360 = $15,166.67
Q3: Interest paid = $1m x 0.06 x 92/360 = $15,333.33
Q4: Interest paid = $1m x 0.06 x 92/360 = $15,333.33

Total interest received = $60,833.33

Actual/365-Day Convention:

Q1: Interest paid = $1m x 0.06 x 90/365 = $14,794.52
Q2: Interest paid = $1m x 0.06 x 91/365 = $14,958.90
Q3: Interest paid = $1m x 0.06 x 92/365 = $15,123.29
Q4: Interest paid = $1m x 0.06 x 92/365 = $15,123.29

Total interest received = $60,000.00

30/360-Day Convention:

Q1: Interest paid = $1m x 0.06 x (3x30)/360 = $15,000
Q2: Interest paid = $1m x 0.06 x (3x30)/360 = $15,000
Q3: Interest paid = $1m x 0.06 x (3x30)/360 = $15,000
Q4: Interest paid = $1m x 0.06 x (3x30)/360 = $15,000

Total interest received = $60,000.00

Actual/Actual Convention:

Q1: Interest paid = $1m x 0.06 x 90/(90x4) = $15,000
Q2: Interest paid = $1m x 0.06 x 91/(91x4) = $15,000
Q3: Interest paid = $1m x 0.06 x 92/(92x4) = $15,000
Q4: Interest paid = $1m x 0.06 x 92/(92x4) = $15,000

Total interest received = $60,000.00

Example

On 22 July, purchaser X buys £100,000 bonds at 98.125% from seller Y. These bonds have a coupon of 6%, which is paid semi-annually on 1 April and 1 October. Interest is calculated on actual/365-day convention basis.

What is the total amount payable to seller Y, assuming that the trade settles on a T+3 basis and that accrued interest is calculated up to the day prior to the settlement date?

Price = 98.125%, therefore the principal amount is £98,125.00

On settlement date minus one (24 July) the bonds have accrued 115 days interest since the last payment date of 1 April.

Accrued interest = £100,000 x 6% x 115/365 = £1,890.41

Total amount payable = £98,125.00 + £1,890.41 = £100,015.41

Exercise 1

£100,000 7% bonds are purchased for settlement on 1 April and sold for settlement date 28 June. If the investor receives all the interest accrued during this period, calculate accrued interest using:

a. 30/360 convention,
b. actual/365 convention.

The answers can be found at the end of this chapter.

Exercise 2

£200,000 8% bonds are traded cum-interest. Interest is calculated on actual/365-day convention basis. How much interest will the buyer pay to the seller if there are 100 days of accrued interest?

The answer can be found at the end of this chapter.

Exercise 3

£100,000 7% bonds are traded ex-interest. Interest is calculated on actual/360-day convention basis. How much interest will the seller pay to the buyer if there are 175 days of accrued interest and the coupon period is 180 days?

The answer can be found at the end of this chapter.

4. Warrants

Learning Objective

1.1.4 Understand the characteristics of warrants and covered warrants: what are warrants and covered warrants; how they are valued; effect on price of maturity and the underlying security; purpose; detachability; exercise and expiry; benefit to the issuing company and purpose; issue by a third party; right to subscribe for capital

A **warrant** gives the holder the right, but not the obligation, to subscribe to an ordinary share or a bond at a specified price on or before a specified date. In other words, they give the holder the right to purchase the underlying share or bond.

Warrants are bought and sold on exchanges in the same way as equities and bonds. However, they pay no income to the warrant holder. Thus, the warrant holder will not be eligible for dividends paid on the underlying shares (unless the warrant is exercised).

The amount that the investor pays for the warrant is called the **premium**. This is commonly a fraction of the price of the underlying asset.

Example

An investor buys a warrant at a strike price of £1 and pays a premium of 20p per warrant.

- If the warrant expires without the underlying share price going above £1, the investor will make a loss of 20p (the premium). A warrant is said to be **out-of-the-money** if the underlying share price is lower than the strike price.
- If the underlying share price rises above £1, the investor has the right to buy the shares at £1, sell them on the market at the higher price and keep the difference. A warrant is said to be **in-the-money** if the underlying share price is higher than the strike price.

Plotting profit/loss against share price gives:

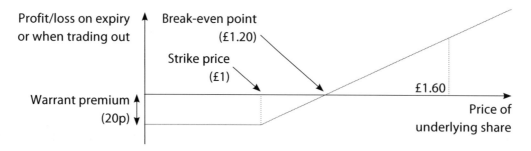

If the price of the share goes up as far as £1.20, the investor will break even. The investor can buy the shares at £1 as per the warrant, and then sell them to the market at £1.20. He/she will make 20p on this transaction, which will offset the 20p paid for the warrant. Any further increase in the price of the share is profit.

If the price rises as far as £1.60:

Profit per warrant   =   Price of underlying share – strike price – warrant premium
                 =   £1.60 – £1 – 20p
                 =   40p

The investor, therefore, has a limited loss – the 20p paid – but, potentially, an unlimited profit.

Hence, we note that the warrant provides a degree of gearing to the investor. A 20p initial investment in the warrant has translated into a 40p profit. This profit will increase further if the share price continues to rise.

The price that the warrant trades at in the market will be related to the current share price, but also to the expectation of what the share price will do before the warrant expires. A range of variables can shape how the price of a warrant will move, including the price of the underlying instrument, the exercise price of the warrant, time left to expiry date, the volatility of the underlying instrument, interest rates and dividend expectations for the underlying share.

A company may have a variety of reasons for issuing warrants. For example, it may issue warrants when raising capital through issuing stock. It may also issue warrants alongside the share issue in order to improve the attractiveness of the stock issue and, ultimately, to raise more capital for the company. For example, a company may issue 500,000 shares at £20 per share, thereby raising £10 million in capital. However, it anticipates that it may raise further capital from investors if it also issues 100,000 warrants, each sold at a premium of £2.00 and with an exercise price of £16. An investor holding the warrant will have the right to exercise the warrant with a specified period in which to purchase the ordinary share (ie, providing the warrant is in the money). By doing so, the company may raise further capital from investors that had been unwilling to subscribe to the original share issue at £20 per share.

Companies may issue warrants, for example, as a 'sweetener' for a bond or preferred stock offering. By adding the warrants, the company aims to improve the terms on which it can raise capital through issuing bonds or preference shares. Moreover, warrants represent a potential source of equity capital in the future and can thus offer a capital-raising option to companies that cannot, or prefer not to, issue more debt or preferred stock.

For example, a company may sell a corporate bond with a face value of US$2,000 with warrants attached, entitling the holder to buy 200 ordinary shares in the company at US$10.00 per share during the next two years. If the share price rose to US$15.00 per share during this period, the holder could exercise the warrants, purchasing 200 ordinary shares at US$10.00 each. If the investor sold shares immediately in the open market at US$15.00 per share, it would realise a gain of:

$$200 \times (15\text{-}10) = US\$1,000$$

Thus the minimum value of each warrant at this point in time would be US$1,000 / 200 = US$5 per warrant.

In practice, some investors may be willing to pay more than US$5 per warrant, believing that the share price would rise higher than US$15.00 during this two-year period. If an investor anticipated that the share price might rise to US$20.00, for example, it may be willing to pay:

$$200 \times (20\text{-}10) / 200 = US\$10$$

ie, it may be willing to pay up to US$10 for the warrant.

More broadly, companies may issue warrants for a number of other reasons, which include the following:

- It may issue warrants to staff as part of their staff benefits or remuneration package; or through an agreement with a trade union in recognition, for example, of a change of working practice or staff rights.
- During the global financial crisis, several US companies were required to issue warrants to the US government in exchange for receiving financial assistance from the government.
- In some circumstances, a law court may instruct a company to issue warrants as part of a settlement when a class of litigants has brought legal action against the company.

A covered warrant has similar behavioural characteristics to those outlined for a warrant above. However, a warrant is issued by a company over its own underlying shares. When the warrant expires, the company will deliver the requisite quantity of shares to the warrant holder. In contrast, a covered warrant is a synthetic product structured by an investment bank or another financial institution over a range of possible underlying assets, which may be a share in a company, a share price index, a commodity, a currency or a basket of currencies.

All UK covered warrants are cash-settled rather than stock-settled. This means that the issuer pays a cash sum for the intrinsic value of the warrants at the expiry date, or on exercise. In other words, although the terms of warrants are usually expressed as a right to purchase the underlying share(s), a covered warrant is more accurately a right to receive a cash payment equivalent to the difference between the exercise price and the value of the underlying asset at expiry.

Example

An investor holds 5,000 covered warrants with the right to buy one share at 100p. At final maturity date, shares close at 140p.

Cash settlement = (share price – exercise price) x number of covered warrants.

Cash settlement = (140 – 100) x 5,000 = £2,000.

The terms 'European-style' and 'American-style' are sometimes used to describe the different ways that warrants may be exercised. The distinction is:

- **American-style** means the warrants can be exercised at any time on or before their expiry date.
- **European-style** means the warrants may only be exercised on the expiry date of the warrant.

Further characteristics of warrants and covered warrants are summarised in the following table:

Traditional warrants	Covered warrants
Issued by a company over its own company shares	Issued by an investment bank or institution over other assets, which may be a share in a company, a share price index, a commodity, a currency or a basket of currencies
New shares issued upon exercise	No new shares issued on exercise; an equivalent value payment is made to the warrant holder in cash
Maturities typically several years	Shorter maturities – typically one or two years

Source: London Stock Exchange

Warrants are sometimes used to make an issue of **loan stock** more attractive to potential investors. During periods of high inflation, investors may be cautious about buying or subscribing for loan stock. In such circumstances, the issuer may also offer equity warrants to subscribers of the bond issue. For example, they may be offered one warrant for each £3.00 of loan stock, thus increasing the loan stock's appeal.

If the share price of the company rises above the warrant strike price, this will enhance the returns accruing to the investor. When warrants are issued in this manner, they are commonly traded separately from the loan and are said to be detachable.

In the UK, an attraction of cash-settled covered warrants is that they are exempt from the 0.5% transaction tax duty levied on share transfers.

Exercise 4

An investor buys 50 warrants for a premium of £0.20 each and a strike price of £1.25. To what level will the share price need to rise if the investor is to make a profit of £30.00?

The answers can be found at the end of this chapter.

5. Depositary Receipts (DRs)

Learning Objective

1.1.3 Understand the characteristics of depositary receipts (DRs): American depositary receipts (ADRs); global depositary receipts (GDRs); depositary interest; transferability/registration/transfer to underlying; how created/pre-release facility; rights; stamp duty and conversion fees

Depositary receipts (DRs) are financial instruments that mirror the shares of a foreign company. For example, an investor may buy a DR in a Russian company that is traded on the German market. The DR represents the underlying shares in the Russian company, but it is denominated in euros and can be bought and sold on the German market, trading either OTC or, if it has satisfied exchange listing requirements, on a stock exchange or MTF. Any dividends or other entitlements due on the underlying share will be paid in euros on the DR.

There are several steps to creating a DR. Consider, for example, that a foreign company registered and listed in Country A will create a DR in Country B. Typically, a **broker** from Country B will buy a quantity of shares in the company in its home market (A). These shares will be deposited with a depository bank in Market A. The depository bank will then create DRs in Market B. The depository bank will set the ratio of DRs per underlying share. The DR can be freely traded in the **secondary market** in Country B and will be subject to Country B's market regulations and tax requirements. The price of the DR – denominated in currency B – should mirror the price of the underlying shares (denominated in Country A's currency) held by the depository bank.

DR holders usually have a right to convert their DRs into underlying shares. In some instances, a DR programme may be terminated, potentially at the request of the issuer company or the depository bank. DR holders will typically be notified in advance and will have the right to exchange their DRs for underlying shares.

5.1 American Depositary Receipts (ADRs)

A common type of DR is an **American depositary receipt (ADR)**. ADRs are issued in the US in US dollars and provide a mechanism through which US investors can reduce the costs and risks associated with investing in non-US companies (see example below).

ADRs must comply with various SEC rules, including the full registration and reporting requirements of the SEC's Exchange Act.

Example

A US investment bank, NYC, purchases ten shares in UK company BHM on the London Stock Exchange (LSE). NYC then registers the shares with the SEC, the US regulator, in order to issue and market ADRs in BHM. When approval has been granted, NYC applies to the New York Stock Exchange (NYSE) to list and trade BHM ADRs on the exchange.

In essence, the BHM ADR is a repackaged BHM share, backed by BHM ordinary shares that are owned by NYC. The ADRs are valued in US dollars and trade like any other ordinary share on the NYSE.

NYC will set up an arrangement with a custodian bank for the latter to act as the depository bank for the ADRs (the Bank of New York Mellon, Citi and J.P. Morgan Investor Services hold the largest market share for this service in the US).

The underlying shares will be deposited with the depository bank in the UK market (or with the depository bank's local agent, or sub-custodian, in the UK market – see chapter 2, section 2.1).

Dividends paid by BHM are received by the depository bank and distributed to BHM ADR-holders in US dollars in direct proportion to their ADR holding. If BHM withholds tax on dividends before this distribution, then the depository bank will withhold a proportional amount before distributing the dividend to ADR holders.

Subsequently, holders of the BHM ADR may trade the ADR in the secondary market, either via an exchange transaction or OTC, just like any other US-listed security. The ADR holder is entitled to instruct NYC to cancel the BHM ADR at any point and to convert this back into the underlying BHM ordinary share.

NYC, as investment bank, will typically receive a commission or management fee for overseeing the ADR issuance and marketing process, and the custodian depository will also receive fees. Indeed, typically, holders of an ADR will be required to pay a conversion fee to the manager of the ADR programme when wishing to convert the ADR to the underlying share. Similarly, holders of the underlying ordinary shares will be subject to a conversion fee when wishing to convert these shares into an ADR.

To summarise, DRs overcome a number of problems facing investors wishing to hold a foreign company's shares.

The following table uses ADRs as an example:

Characteristics of Holding American Depositary Receipts Compared with Holding a Company's Ordinary Shares in a Foreign Market

Issue	Holding Foreign Shares	Holding an ADR
Foreign ownership restrictions	Some countries do not allow foreign ownership of local companies.	As a US security, the ADR is not subject to local ownership restrictions.
Settlement procedures	Ordinary shares traded in the local market may be subject to extended settlement cycles and inefficient settlement procedures.	ADRs settle according to a T+2 settlement cycle, just like any other US-listed share.
Foreign exchange (FX)	Shares have to be paid for in the foreign currency, requiring an FX transaction.	ADRs settle in US dollars.
Dividend payments	Dividends are paid in foreign currency, requiring periodic FX transactions.	ADRs pay dividends in US dollars.
Rights	Shareholders have the right to vote and to participate in rights issues.	ADRs typically provide the holder with the right to vote, but not to participate in rights issues. Shareholders receive the proceeds of the sale of the rights (if any). However, this may vary according to the terms of the depository agreement.
Liquidity	There may be a lack of liquidity in the foreign market.	ADRs trade on US stock exchanges and OTC. Consequently, they can be more liquid than underlying shares.
Legal framework	The legal framework in the foreign country may offer limited protection to the investor. Local legal procedures may be difficult to interpret in the case of a dispute.	ADRs comply with US securities legislation and accounting principles.

5.2   Pre-Release Facility

In certain circumstances, a depository may issue DRs before the underlying shares have been deposited. This is called the pre-release of DRs. The underlying shares must be delivered within a specified time period, usually three months.

Typically the depository will only pre-release DRs when:

1.   the DR issuer verifies in writing to the depository that it owns the underlying equity shares to be deposited,
2.   the pre-release is fully collateralised with cash or other acceptable collateral,

3. the depository is able to close out the pre-release within a specified notice period,
4. other indemnities required by the depository are provided.

The DR pre-release can be closed out by presenting either the underlying equities or the pre-released DRs to the depository.

5.3   Global Depositary Receipts (GDRs)

Global Depositary Receipts (GDRs) allow issuers to raise capital in two or more markets simultaneously, thus broadening their shareholder base. They can be settled outside their market of issue. Many GDRs settle in Euroclear Bank or Clearstream Banking.

GDRs may be widely used by companies in emerging and frontier markets to extend their reach to global investors. Acer, a Taiwanese computer company, has a GDR quoted in euros and dollars, for example.

Companies are also increasingly attempting to achieve this goal by listing their shares on multiple exchanges. The GDR offers the advantage that requirements to list a GDR are often much less demanding than those for listing an ordinary share on an exchange.

5.4   Depositary Interest (DI)

A depositary interest (DI) is a depositary receipt issued against foreign securities.

When shares in a company are traded in a foreign market, a DI (rather than the underlying share) may be settled and held at the local **central securities depository (CSD)**. A DI issuer will issue DIs in respect of the underlying shares. These DIs may then typically be held electronically at the local CSD and transferred via its real-time settlement system. For example, transactions in the shares of companies that are incorporated outside the UK but traded in London are normally settled in the form of a DI held in CREST (the electronic settlement system operated by Euroclear UK & Ireland, the CSD for UK and Irish equities).

In the UK, transfers of DIs are exempt from stamp duty reserve tax (SDRT) for foreign securities.

5.5   Stamp Duty Reserve Tax (SDRT) in the UK

Prior to 2012, Her Majesty's Revenue & Customs (HMRC) charged SDRT at a rate of 1.5% of the share value when shares are converted into DRs. This principle was subject to legal review during 2012 and was found to be contrary to EU law. Subsequently, this point of UK tax law has been changed, such that the 1.5% SDRT is no longer applicable to new issues of UK shares to a DRs system (whereby the investor is then issued with DRs).

6. Collective Investment Vehicles

Learning Objective

1.1.6 Know the uses of: exchange-traded products; mutual funds; tax transparent funds; hedge funds; investment trusts; real estate funds; private equity

In addition to investing directly in the financial instruments outlined above, investors can invest money in a range of collective investment vehicles. A collective investment is an investment fund that takes money from a number of investors and pools it together. A professional fund manager will then use their skill to make investments designed to increase the value of the funds under management. Unit trusts, open-ended investment companies (OEICs) and investment trusts are examples of collective investment vehicles.

Actively managed funds are a category of collective investment funds whereby the fund manager attempts to outperform their peer group (ie, other funds of the same type) through the excellence of their research, stock-picking skills and market timing (ie, predicting when to buy and sell assets in order to optimise levels of return). The selling point for actively managed funds is that the fund manager's skill can generate a higher level of returns than an investor could secure by investing in a passive fund that tracks an index in that sector. However, actively managed funds generally involve higher charges (typically an initial charge when the investor first buys units or shares in the fund and an annual management fee) than passive funds.

Index-tracking funds (also known as passive funds) attempt to track the performance of an index (eg, FTSE 100) by investing in all the shares in that index or in an index-based financial instrument in their relevant proportions.

6.1 Mutual Funds/Unit Trusts

A unit trust is a trust formed to manage securities on behalf of investors that offers the combined benefits of diversification and sufficient weight of assets to ensure cost-effectiveness.

- A fund will use its investors' money to buy shares or other financial instruments. The fund will then issue units in this underlying portfolio.
- A unit trust is open-ended; this means that the manager can create new units when new investors subscribe, and can cancel units when investors cash in their holdings. Units can be sold back to the fund at any point.
- The daily price of the units will vary depending on how the underlying portfolio is performing, ie, based on the net asset value (NAV) of the underlying constituents (NAV = assets of fund minus liabilities of fund divided by the number of shares/units issued in the fund).
- The fund managers will either sell the units on to other investors, or, if no other investors are willing to buy, they will sell underlying shares and use the cash to meet the cost of redemptions.
- The fund managers will charge a commission on units sold. Hence, the price at which a fund manager sells a unit to a retail investor (the **offer price**) will typically be higher than the price at which a fund manager will buy a unit from a retail investor (the **bid price**).

6.2   Open-Ended Investment Companies (OEICs)

Open-ended investment companies (OEICs) are another type of collective investment vehicle, and these have many similar characteristics to unit trusts. However, OEICs are companies, not trusts, and consequently they issue shares rather than units.

Like unit trusts, the price per share in an OEIC is calculated on the basis of assets that the OEIC owns. However, the OEIC quotes a single price for buying and selling shares, rather than a separate bid and offer price as is the case for a unit trust.

The term open-ended means that, as investor money flows into or out of the fund, the fund manager can create new shares or cancel existing shares in order to meet investor demand. In contrast, in a closed-ended fund such as an investment trust (see section 6.4), only a finite number of shares or units are issued in the fund.

OEICs or mutual funds registered in France, Belgium or Luxembourg are commonly known as SICAVs (Sociétés d'Investissement à Capital Variable).

Undertakings for Collective Investment in Transferable Securities (UCITS) are harmonised fund products that can be established in all EU member states, providing a robust and consistent level of investor protection, independent of where the UCITS product is manufactured. Since the launch of the original UCITS directive in 1985, UCITS have provided an important tool through which asset management companies can market fund products internationally to eligible retail and institutional investors.

6.3   Exchange-Traded Products (ETPs)

An exchange-traded product (ETP) is an investment fund with specified objectives which is traded on many global stock exchanges in the same manner as a typical share. An ETP holds assets, such as stocks or bonds, and trades at approximately the same price as the net asset value (NAV) of its underlying assets over the course of the trading day.

In general, ETPs can be attractive as investment vehicles because of their low costs, tax-efficiency, and equity-like features.

Types of ETPs

Exchange-traded funds (ETFs) allow an investor to buy an entire basket of stocks through a single security that tracks the returns of a stock market index. Investors can buy an ETF, for example, that will track global indices such as the FTSE 100 or S&P 500.

ETFs are a special type of index mutual fund, but they are listed on an exchange and trade and settle like equities. As such, they are designed to combine the diversification benefits offered by mutual funds with the simplicity of holding shares. ETFs typically have lower costs than conventional mutual funds or unit trusts and are often more tax-efficient.

ETFs also differ from mutual funds in the following ways:

*   ETFs trade on a major exchange throughout the day, just like ordinary stocks, and are priced intra-day. In contrast, transactions in OEICs and unit trusts only occur once per day at the market's close and units are repriced daily.

- Because ETFs trade on an exchange, their prices are determined by market demand for the ETF shares. Hence, ETF shares may be bought at a discount or a premium to the value of the underlying assets if trading conditions push their price up or down. By contrast, mutual funds (unit trusts) take their price from the net value of assets owned by the fund.

Exchange-traded notes (ETNs) are senior, unsecured, unsubordinated debt securities issued by an underwriting bank. Similar to other debt securities, ETNs have a maturity date and are backed only by the credit of the issuer.

- When an investor buys an ETN, the underwriting bank promises to pay the amount reflected in the index, minus fees upon maturity. Similar to equities, they are traded on an exchange and can be shorted. Similar to index funds, they are linked to the return of a benchmark index but, like debt securities, ETNs do not actually own anything they are tracking.

- Investors must evaluate the credit risk of an ETN issuer. It is important to know that uncollateralised ETNs are fully exposed to the credit risk of the issuer. Many investors will determine that ETNs do not correspond to their risk appetite and investment objectives.

Exchange-traded commodities (ETCs) are investment vehicles that track the performance of an underlying commodity index, including total return indices based on a single commodity. Similar to ETFs, and traded and settled exactly like normal shares, ETCs have liquidity provided by **market makers**, enabling investors to gain exposure to commodities, **on-exchange**, during market hours.

6.4 Investment Trusts

An investment trust, despite its name, is not a trust but a company whose business is to invest in the shares of other companies. Like unit trusts and OEICs, investment trusts pool investors' money and employ a professional fund manager to invest in the shares of a wider range of companies than most retail investors could practically invest in themselves.

Investment trusts have a number of features that differentiate them from unit trusts and OEICs:

- **Closed-ended** – investment trusts raise money for investing by issuing shares. Generally, this happens just once, at the launch of the fund. This makes investment trusts closed-ended: the number of shares the trust issues and, therefore, the amount of money it raises to invest, is fixed at the start. Knowing this amount of money is fixed enables fund managers to plan ahead. Unit trusts and OEICs, by contrast, are open-ended: they expand or contract as people invest in or leave the fund.
- **Pricing methodology** – the price of shares in an investment trust is established by the stock market. Hence, the price of investment trust shares may be above or below the value of the underlying assets, expressed as the NAV per share. By contrast, the prices of OEICs and unit trusts are calculated on the basis of the value of their underlying assets (ie, by dividing the value of the investment assets held by the fund by the number of issued shares/units in the fund).
- **Different share classes** – some investment trusts issue different classes of shares to meet different investors' needs. These are called split capital investment trusts (splits). Different classes of shares have varying rights and entitlements within the trust. Some split shares aim to pay regular dividends for investors who want an income. Others aim to pay out only a capital amount at the end of the trust's life.

- **Independent boards of directors** – investment trusts are companies listed on the stock market. This dictates that they must have independent boards of directors, whose duty it is to look after the interests of the shareholders, to whom the directors are answerable. The shareholders may challenge the actions of the directors, call for changes in company strategy, and vote for or against issues at the AGM and any other special shareholder meeting called during the year.
- **Gearing** – investment trusts, being companies, can borrow to purchase additional investments. This is called gearing or leverage. This allows an investment trust to increase the risk that it takes in its investment strategy in search of additional return.

6.5   Hedge Funds

Hedge funds come in many shapes and sizes. The precise definition of what is, or is not, a hedge fund is widely debated.

Like the other fund types described above, hedge funds pool investors' money and employ a professional hedge fund manager to invest this money through a diverse range of strategies and instruments.

Hedge funds may employ a range of investment strategies to make money in rising or falling market conditions. In this respect, they differ from conventional equity or mutual funds (unit trusts), which are generally 100% exposed to market risk (ie, investors make money when markets rise and lose money when markets fall). One strategy widely employed by hedge fund managers is **short selling**. In simple terms, short selling can be explained as the opposite of a conventional securities purchase trade.

In a conventional long trade, the investor buys an investment in anticipation that its price will rise. If it does, the investor will sell the instrument at the higher price to realise a profit (ie, the difference between the lower purchase price and the higher sale price).

In a short position, an investor sells an instrument on the premise that it is overvalued or bad news is expected and its price will fall. If the price goes down, the investor can then buy the security back at the lower price to realise a profit (ie, the difference between the higher sale price and the lower purchase price).

Short selling is a practice that has been employed by hedge funds in anticipation that market valuations might fall, and as a means of hedging risk in long-only portfolios. However, financial regulators in many countries have introduced rules that forbid short selling without the trader first borrowing or owning the security concerned – so-called naked short selling. Some regulatory authorities have also introduced disclosure requirements, demanding that firms report net short positions to the appropriate supervisory body. The EU introduced a Regulation on Short Selling in November 2012. The aims of this Regulation are to:

- increase the transparency of short positions held by investors in certain EU securities,
- reduce settlement risks and other risks linked with uncovered or naked short selling,
- reduce risks to the stability of sovereign debt markets posed by uncovered (naked) credit default swap (CDS) positions,
- ensure EU member states have clear powers to intervene in exceptional situations to reduce systemic risks and risks to financial stability and market confidence arising from short selling and CDSs, and
- ensure co-ordination between member states and the European Securities Markets Authority (ESMA, a body that promotes co-operation and alignment between securities regulators and across financial sectors in the EU, working closely with regulators in the areas of banking, insurance and occupational pensions) in addressing the above issues.

Other investment strategies employed by hedge funds include the following:

- **Distressed securities** – a hedge fund manager buys equity or debt at big discounts in companies facing bankruptcy or restructuring. The hedge fund manager aims to profit from the market's limited appreciation of the true value of the deeply discounted securities and to take advantage of the fact that many institutional investors cannot own securities with a credit rating below investment grade, or go short. Consequently, this will create a wave of forced selling by institutional investors that will push the price of the asset downwards.
- **Special situations** – a hedge fund manager invests in event-driven situations such as mergers, hostile takeovers, reorganisations or leveraged buy-outs. They may simultaneously purchase stock in companies being acquired and sell stock in the acquiring company, hoping to profit from the spread between the current market price and the ultimate purchase price of the company. As in many other styles of hedge fund, they may also use **derivatives** to leverage returns and to hedge out interest rate, currency and/or market risk.
- **Arbitrage** – the hedge fund manager seeks to exploit specific inefficiencies in the market, taking advantage of pricing discrepancies and/or anticipated price volatility by trading a hedged portfolio of offsetting long and short positions. It is by carefully pairing individual long positions with related short positions that the hedge fund manager seeks to significantly reduce, if not remove, market-level risk. Arbitrage strategies employed include:
    - **Convertible arbitrage** – buying and selling different securities of the same issuer (eg, the ordinary shares and convertible bonds). By buying the security that is deemed undervalued and selling the security that is overvalued, the hedge fund manager seeks to profit from the anticipated correction in the spread between the instruments.
    - **Fixed income arbitrage** – exploiting interest rate opportunities by taking offsetting positions in fixed income securities and their derivatives.
    - **Statistical arbitrage** – by using quantitative criteria, the hedge fund manager selects a long portfolio of temporarily undervalued stocks and a roughly equal-sized short portfolio of temporarily overvalued stocks. This is also sometimes referred to as pairs trading.

Recent years have also witnessed a dramatic rise in investment in funds of hedge funds (FOHFs). FOHF managers attempt to select and invest in a range of individual hedge funds that will offer positive returns to investors, while providing the diversification needed to ensure that investors are not over-exposed to the risks associated with any individual hedge fund or investment strategy.

Many hedge fund strategies, particularly arbitrage strategies, are limited as to how much capital they can successfully employ before returns diminish. These are often termed capacity constraints. As more investment money flows into the fund, the opportunities to profit from that investment idea progressively become exhausted. As a result, many successful hedge fund managers limit the amount of capital they will accept into their funds.

6.6   Real Estate Funds

Real estate investment trusts (REITs) are listed investment trusts (see section 6.4) through which investors purchase exposure to investments in the real estate sector. A pool of investors' money will thus be invested in property assets and shares issued to underlying investors.

Tax will typically not be levied on rental or capital gains earned within a REIT, provided that at least 90% of its income is distributed to investors via dividends.

Listed real estate trusts have been available on the Australian Stock Exchange since the 1970s. REITs have also attracted strong money flows in recent years in the US (in parallel with the unlisted property fund marketplace), Hong Kong, Japan, Taiwan, the Netherlands and a range of other jurisdictions. REITs have also been available in the UK market since 1 January 2007. Prior to this, investors had the opportunity for a number of years to invest in property through property unit trusts (PUTs). These unlisted collective investment vehicles have often been registered in offshore tax domiciles such as Jersey and Guernsey, Luxembourg (as a self-managed investment company with variable capital, SICAV) or the Cayman Islands.

The unlisted property fund market has attracted strong investment flows in the US market for many years. Luxembourg also continues to attract strong investment flows into real estate investment funds (REIFs) – closed-ended or open-ended investment funds that invest in property.

Note that REITs and PUTs bear the characteristics of investment trusts and unit trusts outlined in sections 6.4 and 6.1. As unlisted vehicles, PUTs trade in parallel with their underlying value. As a listed share, REITs may trade at a premium or discount to underlying valuations, depending on demand for the share within the stock market.

6.7   Private Equity Funds

Private equity firms invest in unlisted assets that are not publicly traded on a stock exchange or MTF, or in some instances they may purchase publicly traded assets with the intention of taking these private.

Typically, a private equity firm will raise funds from a group of investors. These pooled funds will be used to purchase assets that it believes will rise in value (this may be a distressed company, for example, when it believes that improved management and a more favourable business climate may provide the opportunity to return to strong profitability in the future).

Also, these funds may be invested in ventures that it believes will generate attractive cash flow (this might be, for instance, investment in public-private partnerships to build schools, hospitals, airports, or other infrastructure projects).

Usually, the private equity firm, as general partner, will be responsible for management decisions relating to the investment of these pooled funds and for management of the assets that it purchases (eg, by changing the management structure in a company that it has acquired). The investors, as limited partners, provide start-up and operating funds but are not responsible directly for day-to-day management of the fund, or the assets that it purchases. Moreover, typically, they will only be responsible for any losses sustained by the partnership up to the amount of their investment.

Like other types of asset management company, private equity groups may specialise in specific types of investment strategy that they employ to optimise return for themselves and for their investment partners. A buy-out fund, for example, may specialise in purchasing privately owned companies, improving their profitability and then realising a financial return through their exit strategy – the point when it elects to sell the firm to other private investors, or to float the company through an **initial public offering (IPO)**.

A venture capital fund may finance the development of promising emergent companies, whether by taking an equity stake in the business (which it expects to rise in value as the company grows and its profitability increases), or by committing loan capital, thereby generating interest income on its loan commitment.

Private equity funds, along with hedge funds, real estate funds and some other categories of investment funds, such as infrastructure funds, form part of a broad category of investment vehicles known as alternative investment funds.

6.8 Tax Transparent Funds (TTFs)

Tax transparent funds (TTFs) were introduced on 1 July 2013 to bring the UK in line with other European Fund centres. Investors in the TTF pooled investment vehicle are expected to be mainly UK-authorised unit trusts, OEICs, pension funds and insurance companies, and similar European investors. TTFs have the option to be based in the UK rather than in competing European domiciles, such as Luxembourg and Ireland.

UK tax law allows investors in TTFs to be treated for CGT as owning an interest in the fund, rather than underlying assets. There are also certain stamp duty and VAT exemptions.

7. Securities Identification Numbers

Learning Objective

1.1.7   Know how securities are identified: International Securities Identification Number (ISIN); Committee on Uniform Security Identification Procedures (CUSIP); Stock Exchange Daily Official List (SEDOL); tickers

To enable securities to be clearly identified during transaction-processing and asset-servicing procedures, each security is given its own unique identification code number.

An **International Securities Identification Number (ISIN)** is a unique international code issued to identify a security. This numbering convention was introduced by the **International Organization for Standardization (ISO)** to harmonise the array of country-specific numbering systems that had grown up at the domestic level (see below). The Association of National Numbering Agencies (ANNA), acting on behalf of ISO, is responsible for appointing a national numbering agency in each country that bears responsibility for allocating a unique security identification number to each security.

The ISIN consists of a total of 12 characters. The first two characters represent the ISO two-letter country code. The next nine characters represent the local number of the security concerned, with a final check digit so that systems can validate the number.

In the case of depositary receipts such as ADRs, the instrument takes its country code from the organisation that issued the receipt, rather than the one that issued the underlying security. For example, the Acer Taiwan stock mentioned earlier has an ISIN of TW0002306008 for the Taiwanese share and GB0057226440 for the GDR.

The local securities identifier number allocated to a security is based on numbering conventions that have evolved within individual markets. For example:

- A Committee on Uniform Security Identification Procedures (CUSIP) number is used to identify securities issued in the US and Canada. The CUSIP number is allocated by the CUSIP Service Bureau. The CUSIP Service Bureau is operated by Standard & Poor's, on behalf of the American Bankers' Association (ABA). The code is a nine-digit alphanumerical code.
- A **Stock Exchange Daily Official List (SEDOL)** number is a securities identifier issued by the LSE and Irish Stock Exchange to provide unique identification of instruments traded in the UK and Ireland and on a global basis. This code forms the basis of the ISIN code for UK securities and consists of a seven-digit alphanumeric code, allocated by the master LSE file service. So too, the Irish Stock Exchange issues SEDOL codes for Irish securities. Until 5 January 2004, SEDOL codes had a seven-digit numeric format. However, given the number of requests for new SEDOL codes, and concerns that the seven-digit numeric format was reaching its capacity, a decision was taken to move to the new seven-character alphanumeric code. The LSE is the National Numbering Agency for the UK market.

Other national conventions include:

- SVM code, employed in Belgium.
- WKN code, employed in Germany.
- Valoren code, employed in Switzerland.
- ASX code, employed in Australia.

Once a local identifier has been allocated, it is possible to derive the global ISIN identifier, using the convention outlined above. (For a UK SEDOL code, which is only seven digits, the ISIN consists of the prefix GB00, followed by the SEDOL, followed by a single check digit.)

A stock ticker is an identifier code used to identify a security when it trades on a stock market or in the OTC market. For example, the stock ticker for UK-listed telecoms Vodafone Group plc is VOD, the ticker for StatPro Group plc is SOG, and the ticker for the iShares DJ Euro STOXX MidCap ETF is DJMC.

Stock tickers can have an additional identifier which indicates the stock exchange or MTF on which they are traded. For example, IBM, which has a primary listing on **NYSE Euronext**, has a ticker IBM-N. Qualcomm, which is listed on NASDAQ-OMX, has a ticker QCOM-Q. Blackberry, which is listed on the Toronto Stock Exchange, has a ticker BB-T.

Note: ticker can also refer to a running feed of current pricing and trading volume for a given security, alerting the investor to the sale price and quantity of recent transactions in a specified instrument.

A **market identifier code (MIC)** is a unique identification code used to identify securities trading exchanges, regulated trading venues and non-regulated trading venues. The MIC is a four alpha character code defined by the International Organization for Standardization under ISO Standard 10383. For example, trades that are executed on the US National Association of Securities Dealers Automated Quotations (NASDAQ) market are identified by the MIC XNAS. Trades on BATS Chi-X Europe typically have the MIC BCXE.

Legal Entity Identifiers (LEIs)

The **Legal Entity Identifiers (LEIs)** programme for financial contracts establishes a universal standard for identifying any organisation involved in a financial transaction worldwide. By establishing a distinct identifier for each legal entity, the global LEI system helps financial regulators to improve their supervision of financial institutions and the transactions these institutions conduct with their financial counterparties across products and markets.

The importance of creating such a system of legal entity identifiers has been highlighted in statements from (among others) the Financial Stability Board, the **International Organization of Securities Commissions (IOSCO)** and the G-20 finance ministers. In the US, the Dodd-Frank Act has established a requirement for each financial entity to have its own standard LEI, and the US Treasury's Office of Financial Research has driven the implementation of this initiative. In Europe, a parallel commitment has been established under the supervision of the ESMA.

The International Organization for Standardization created a new draft standard, ISO 17442, which provides a template for the LEI. The LEI is a 20-character alphanumeric code. The first four characters represent the Local Operating Unit (LOU) who issued the code. The fifth and sixth characters are '00' and the seventh to eighteenth characters are unique to the entity. The final two characters are check digits. The Global Legal Entity Identifier Foundation (GLEIF) delegates this responsibility for issuing LEIs to LOUs. The **Society for Worldwide Interbank Financial Telecommunications (SWIFT)** is serving as LEI registration authority, coordinating allocation of LEIs to financial companies according to this draft standard. The Depository Trust & Clearing Corporation (DTCC) has been appointed facilities manager, collecting requests for LEIs, storing reference data associated with each LEI, and maintaining and updating the LEI reference database.

By creating a unique ID associated with each legal entity, financial regulators are confident that LEIs will allow more consistent procedures to be set in place for identifying parties to a financial transaction. In turn, this will help financial regulators to maintain a consistent and integrated view of any firm's exposures and to identify at an early point any risk concentrations that may present grounds for concern.

8. Issue Methods in the UK

Learning Objective

1.1.8 Understand how securities are issued: equities (offers for subscription; offers for sale; introductions; placing; offer to tender); government bonds (auction; tap; tranche); eurobonds (lead manager; syndicate; underwriting)

8.1 Equities: Listing

A private company may reach a stage in its development where it feels that, in order to raise the capital that it needs to carry its business forward, it may be beneficial to obtain a stock exchange quotation in order to make a public issue of shares.

Companies wishing to list on a recognised stock exchange will typically be subject to detailed investigation designed to safeguard the integrity of the exchange and offer a degree of security to investors that they are buying shares in a bona fide registered company.

Listing activity in the UK market is regulated via the FCA. The UK Listings Authority (UKLA), which is a division of the FCA, exists to ensure a transparent and efficient listing process and safe and efficient operation of securities markets. It does so by:

- monitoring market disclosures by issuers and through enforcing compliance with the FCA Disclosure and Transparency Rules,
- reviewing prospectuses published by issuers of securities and through enforcing the FCA Prospectus Rules,
- operating the UK listing regime, which requires issuers of listed securities to comply with the FCA Listing Rules.

This set of provisions is designed to provide confidence to investors that issuers of listed securities adhere to high standards of governance and investor protection. The UKLA's Official List provides the definitive record of whether a company's securities are officially listed in the UK. This will also indicate whether a particular security has been suspended from trading.

Securities that have been listed on a RIE may also be admitted for trading on other execution venues (ie, on other recognised exchanges, MTFs or other types of trading venue).

To list shares on a recognised exchange, a company must fulfil listings criteria which typically include the following:

Trading Record

In general, a company applying to list on a recognised exchange must have an established trading record. On NYSE Euronext or the LSE, for example, a company must have published annual financial statements for the preceding three financial years. The Australian Stock Exchange (ASX) specifies that companies must meet minimum standards of quality, size, operations and disclosure. Some types of companies, such as scientific research-based companies and fast-growing innovative technology businesses, may be allowed to list with a shorter trading record provided that they meet specified additional criteria. Typically, these stocks will not be listed on the Main Market, but on a designated segment for new and emerging companies (such as the Alternative Investment Market (AIM) – the LSE's international market for smaller growing companies).

Sponsor

In the UK, every company applying for a listing must be represented by a sponsor, which will usually be an investment bank, stockbroker, law firm or accountancy practice. The sponsor, which must itself meet certain qualifications, provides the link between the company and the UKLA, and guides the company through the listing process. Companies listed on the AIM are subject to continuous oversight from the issuer's **underwriter**, known as a nominated adviser (NOMAD). The NOMAD is both an adviser and a regulator to the AIM company, providing guidance on how the company should meet its obligations as a securities issuer listed on the AIM.

Shares in Public Hands

A specified minimum percentage of shares should be distributed to the public. On NYSE Euronext or the LSE, for example, at least 25% of outstanding shares must be made available to persons not connected with the company. The exchange may also require that the company's **market capitalisation** exceeds a specified minimum (on the LSE this is currently £700,000 for companies listed on the Main Market).

Prospectus

The company and its advisers must publish a prospectus that complies with the Listing Authority's rules. The prospectus provides potential investors with the information that they need to make an informed decision on the company and its shares. It will typically include independently audited financial figures, details of directors' salaries and contracts, and information on major shareholders.

Continuous Disclosure Requirements

Once the company's shares have been listed and admitted to trading, the company must fulfil a number of obligations on a continuing basis. These include producing half-year and independently audited full-year financial reports within a set timeframe, and notifying the market of any new price-sensitive information. Typically, these financial reports must be compliant with recognised International Financial Reporting Standards (IFRS) accounting standards.

8.2   Procedure for a Public Issue of Shares

A public company seeking to raise capital by issuing shares will circulate a prospectus, inviting potential investors to apply for shares. The successful applicants will be granted shares in return for payment, which may either be in full or in instalments, depending on the conditions of the share issue.

If demand for shares exceeds the number of shares available, then application money will be refunded to unsuccessful applicants. Oversubscription can also lead to scaling down and partial refunds of application monies (see overleaf) or to allocation of shares via a ballot.

The share issue may proceed through a number of methods, as follows:

Offer for Subscription

The issuing company invites applications from, and sells shares directly to, the public. The share offer is not underwritten by an investment bank or other sponsor. In some circumstances, the offer for subscription will only proceed if a minimum number of shares are purchased. If there are insufficient applications, all applications may be rejected, the submissions cancelled and application money returned.

Offer for Sale

The issuing company offers a specified number of shares for sale to the public at a specified price. These shares may be sold to the public directly, or via an investment bank or other body that agrees to sponsor the share issue. The steps are as follows:

1. The company sells this specified number of shares to the sponsor (the issuing house).
2. The issuing house will then sell the shares to the public and will end up holding any shares that the public does not buy.
3. Hence, the issuing house underwrites the share issue. The company has received the capital it set out to raise directly from the issuing house. The latter bears the cost of any shares that do not sell.

4. The issuing house will, typically, (a) charge a fee to the issuer to provide this sponsor/underwriting service and/or (b) extract a commission on shares sold (by purchasing shares from the company at a discount to the price at which it sells them to the public).

If the issue of new shares is oversubscribed, the issuing house will determine how the shares are to be allotted. This may be done via a ballot, or by allocating a quota of shares to each applicant, up to a specified ceiling.

Offer to Tender

In a variation on the above procedure for an offer for sale at a fixed price, the issuing house may specify a minimum price for the share offer and invite offers (tenders) from investors at prices of their own choosing. When the application deadline has passed, the sponsor will fix a sale price (the strike price). All investors that have offered the strike price or above are likely to receive shares, which will be sold to them at the strike price.

Placing (or Private Placements)

Like offers for sale, the issuing company will typically sell shares directly to an investment bank or another sponsor. The latter will then sell shares to its preferred clients (commonly institutional investors and investment managers), but there will be no general sale to the public. For the issuing company, private placements can yield substantial cost savings when compared to the public offers described above, since it will eliminate a layer of administration and publicity costs demanded when a company, via an issuing house, sells shares to retail investors.

Introductions

In the UK, an introduction is typically employed when a company already has a broad spread of shareholders and seeks authorisation to list shares on an exchange. Introductions do not involve the immediate raising of capital or issue of shares, but are designed to meet the conditions required to allow a company to do so in the future. As per the requirements for a full listing detailed above, at least 25% of the company's shares should normally be owned by people unconnected to the business.

Introductions are used, for example, when:

*   a company wishes to move from the AIM, the LSE's international market for smaller companies (see section 9.1.1), to the Main Market,
*   a company that is already listed on the exchange wants to divide into two or more separate companies – the new companies may obtain a quotation via an introduction,
*   an overseas company is already listed in another market but wishes to establish a UK stock exchange listing as well.

8.3   Government Bond Issues

For government bonds issued by auction, competitive bids (where the bidder specifies a price and quantity of issue for purchase) will be ranked in descending order of price and bonds will be sold to applicants whose competitive bids are at, or above, a minimum price (the lowest accepted price) established by the issuing authority. Successful bids above the minimum price will be satisfied in full at the bid price. Bids made at the minimum price may be satisfied in full or only in part.

Any unsold bonds will be retained by the issuing authority and may be offered for resale at a later date. This is known as **tap stock**. In exceptional circumstances, if it considers bids to be unacceptably low, the issuing authority may opt not to allot all of the stock on offer at a conventional or index-linked auction.

Some government issues are structured such that the full quota of bonds is not made available to investors in a single sale, but is sold in blocks (commonly known as tranches or tranchettes) at times when the issuing authority (ie, the DMO in the UK or the Bureau of Public Debt in the US) feels it is appropriate. Like tap stocks, tranches offer the issuing authority a means of fine-tuning market liquidity and raising public funds in smaller quantities than is practical through tender or auction.

In some markets, competitive bids are typically placed by registered agents (eg, gilt-edged market makers [GEMMs] in the UK, primary government dealers in the US) on behalf of smaller institutional investors and individual investors.

Individuals may be permitted to make non-competitive bids at auction. In a non-competitive bid, no bid price is specified and the bids are allotted at the weighted average price of successful competitive bids.

To provide some illustration of the above, US Treasury securities (T-bills, notes, bonds, Treasury inflation-protected securities or TIPS) are sold by the US government's Bureau of Public Debt by auction in the **primary market**. Investors may place competitive or non-competitive bids, with a minimum purchase amount of US$1,000 specified for all Treasury securities. In a single auction, an investor may bid non-competitively for up to US$5 million in any particular security.

The US Treasury (Treasury or department) also maintains a legacy Treasury Direct system designed for investors that buy Treasury securities when they are issued and plan to hold them until they mature. The investor purchases securities directly from the US government and holds these in an account with the government, rather than with a bank or broker.

In Japan, the Japanese government's Ministry of Finance issues ten-year Japanese government bonds (JGBs) through syndicate underwriting. The government will purchase any JGBs that remain unsold by syndicate members. Competitive auction bidding and non-competitive tender by the syndicate determines 60% of the issue. The remaining 40% is allocated in fixed share to each syndicate member at the average price of the auction. JGBs with maturities of 2, 4, 5, 6, 15, 20 and 30 years are issued by public auction. Successful bidders, and the terms of issuance, are determined by multiple price auction, where bids are accepted from the highest price downwards until the issue is fully subscribed.

In France, government bonds (OATs and BTANs) and **Treasury bills** (BTFs) are issued primarily through competitive auction (where bids are accepted from the highest price downwards until the issue is fully subscribed), but partly by tap.

In the UK, government bonds' (or gilts') market liquidity is preserved by GEMMs, serving as competing market makers that have a commitment to make, on demand and in all market conditions, effective two-way prices on gilts that they are contracted to deal in. This arrangement is designed to encourage investor demand for UK government bonds and, consequently, to minimise the government's borrowing costs.

GEMMs are the only institutions eligible to submit a competitive bid by telephone directly to the DMO. All other market participants wishing to bid at a gilt auction must route their orders through a GEMM. GEMM firms are entitled to submit non-competitive bids for a 10% share of the total amount of stock on offer at a gilt auction. In conventional auctions, this 10% allowance is split evenly amongst all GEMM firms, whereas in index-linked auctions each firm's individual allowance will be determined by its successful purchases at the three previous auctions.

8.4   Eurobonds

As explained in section 3.1.4, a eurobond is an international bond issued in markets outside the domestic market of the issuer. Key participants in supporting a eurobond issue include the following:

Lead Manager and Syndicate

The lead manager is a financial institution (commonly an investment bank) that assumes responsibility for managing the entire issue process. The lead manager will advise the issuer on the structure and timing of the issue, and it will appoint the syndicate, a group of investment banks that will market, sell and underwrite the issue.

Underwriter, Advisers, Trustees and Paying Agents

The underwriter to an issue typically agrees to purchase any unsold securities at a specified price (see section 8.2). Typically the underwriter will be paid a commission for providing this service, ensuring that the issuer raises the quantity of capital intended through the eurobond issue. However, the underwriter will bear the risk of covering the cost of securities that remain unsold.

Legal advisers are responsible for conducting due diligence on the issue process and the parties involved, as well as drafting and validating the listing details and accompanying documentation posted to investors, the stock exchange and regulatory authorities.

Trustees act on behalf of the investors, ensuring that the issuer adheres to conditions set out in the bond sale and ensuring that the rights and entitlements of bondholders are protected and met in full.

The paying agent is responsible for receiving coupon payments from the issuer and distributing this income to the bondholders.

Issuance Methods

While methods for eurobond issuance vary from market to market, typical methods include:

- **Bought offer** – the lead manager purchases the full quantity of bonds issued at a predetermined price and then places these securities with its own clients.
- **Fixed price re-offer** – the lead manager distributes the bonds to the syndicate. This group of investment banks then places the securities with their own clients at a fixed price. They may only sell at below this price when the syndicate has been disbanded by the lead manager. This will generally not occur until most of the bonds have been placed.

9.   Principles of Trading

Learning Objective

1.2.1   Know the characteristics of the regulated markets and multilateral trading facilities (MTFs)

9.1   Regulated Markets and Multilateral Trading Facilities (MTFs)

The **Markets in Financial Instruments Directive (MiFID)** was implemented in November 2007 and represents a central component of the European Parliament's ambition to create a single market in financial services for the European Economic Area (EEA). Under MiFID, investment firms are required to take all reasonable steps to deliver best execution to their customers, taking into account factors including speed, cost and certainty of execution and settlement. The directive aims to promote competition between trading venues based on market transparency and a regulatory level playing field. Under MiFID, key execution venues include:

- **Regulated markets**, referring to regulated stock exchanges such as NYSE Euronext, the LSE's Main Market and the Frankfurt Stock Exchange, operated by **Deutsche Börse**.
- **Multilateral Trading Facilities (MTFs)** – sometimes referred to as alternative trading systems, MTFs are registered execution venues which bring together purchasers and sellers of securities. Subscribers can post orders into the system and these will be communicated (typically, electronically via an electronic communication network [ECN]) for other subscribers to view. Matched orders will then proceed to execution.

9.1.1   Regulated Markets

The regulated markets and their equity-trading systems in the selected markets are as follows:

United Kingdom

The Stock Exchange Electronic Trading System (SETS) is the LSE flagship electronic order book, trading FTSE 100, FTSE 250 and the FTSE Small Cap Index constituents, as well as some other liquid securities. The Exchange also operates a modified version of SETS for the trading of covered warrants and other structured products.

The LSE's Main Market is its flagship market for the listing and trading of equity, debt and other securities. AIM is a share trading market established principally for small companies; classified as a MTF (see section 9.1.2). It is regulated by the LSE but it has less demanding listing rules.

SETSqx (Stock Exchange Electronic Trading Service – quotes and crosses) is a trading platform for securities that are less liquid than those traded on SETS. SETSqx combines a periodic electronic auction book with stand-alone non-electronic, quote-driven market making. Electronic orders can be named or anonymous.

SEAQ is the LSE's trading platform for the fixed-interest market and AIM securities that are not traded on either SETS or SETSqx.

BATS Chi-X Europe, which became a RIE in May 2013, is the largest European equities exchange by market share and value of securities traded. It was formed as a result of the acquisition of Chi-X Europe by BATS Europe in 2011 – Europe's two largest pan-European MTFs. BATS Chi-X Europe, which is a brand name of BATS Trading Ltd, is the first MTF to make the transition to full RIE status.

BATS Chi-X Europe offers trading in more than 3,600 securities, across 15 major European markets via a single trading platform and a single rule book. In addition, BATS Chi-X Europe's smart order routing service allows customers to access 13 other recognised exchanges, as well as a range of MTFs.

United States

The largest securities exchanges are:

- NYSE – the NYSE Hybrid Market is an **order-driven market** model that attempts to integrate the best aspects of the auction market with automated trading. In April 2007, NYSE formalised a merger with Euronext (see below) to form NYSE Euronext.
- NASDAQ OMX – Nasdaq is the world's largest exchange company. Matched orders are executed.
- In October 2008, NYSE Euronext acquired the American Stock Exchange (Amex), renaming the exchange NYSE Amex Equities.

Japan

The Tokyo Stock Exchange is the main exchange for equities trading. Its equities trading system is known simply as the TSE trading system.

Europe

Euronext, the integrated exchange for trading equities on the French, Belgian, Dutch and Portuguese markets, has merged with NYSE to form NYSE Euronext. Equities trading on NYSE Euronext is via the Nouveau Système de Cotation (NSC), the exchange's integrated electronic cash market trading platform. It is an order-driven market.

Germany

FWB, the Frankfurt Stock Exchange, is the largest of the seven regional German securities exchanges. FWB is managed by Deutsche Börse AG, which provides the **Xetra** electronic trading system and which also owns and manages Clearstream Banking and **Eurex**, the German derivatives exchange. Some of the other regional stock exchanges also use Deutsche Börse's systems.

Spain

Equities trading in the Spanish market is conducted on the Barcelona, Bilbao, Madrid and Valencia stock exchanges, which form part of the **Bolsas y Mercados Españoles (BME)** holding group.

Hong Kong

Equities trading on the Hong Kong Stock Exchange (HKEx) is via the HKEx trading system.

Singapore

Equities trading on the Singapore Exchange (SGX) is via the SGX trading system.

India

Equities are traded on the Bombay Stock Exchange (BSE) and the National Stock Exchange (NSE) (both located in Mumbai), as well as on 23 smaller regional exchanges.

Brazil

Equities are traded on B3 (formerly Bovespa), the São Paolo-based exchange for cash equities and derivatives trading.

South Korea

Equities are traded on the Korea Stock Exchange (KSE).

China

Equities are traded on the Shanghai Stock Exchange and Shenzhen Stock Exchange.

9.1.2 Multilateral Trading Facilities (MTFs)

With the implementation of MiFID, we have witnessed the emergence of two principal categories of MTF, namely:

- Open order book type venues that provide publicly displayed liquidity. These open order book type MTFs handle predominantly small-ticket, high-volume trading with trading typically cleared via a central counterparty (CCP) (see chapter 2, section 2.2). For example, Chi-X Europe has been live since April 2007. Turquoise, a pan-European equity-trading MTF, with initial backing from nine leading investment banks, went live in August 2008 and was acquired by the LSE in December 2009. BATS Europe has offered trading in leading European equities markets since October 2008. BATS Global Markets acquired Chi-X Europe in December 2011 to establish BATS Chi-X Europe, Europe's largest MTF. In May 2013, BATS Chi-X Europe was accorded full stock exchange status (as a recognised exchange) by the UK regulatory authorities. It is now Europe's largest stock exchange for share trading.
- Dark liquidity pools that provide anonymous trading. These execution venues do not display order details publicly, thereby preserving the anonymity of trading parties and minimising the degree to which their trading activity can impact the market. These dark pool MTFs typically support large ticket-size trades at lower trading volume – and in many cases they will not employ a CCP structure, with the broker standing as **counterparty** to the trade and a global settlement agent employed to provide trade settlement. Examples of dark pool MTFs include Euronext Block and LiquidNet.

10. Exchange-Traded and Over-The-Counter (OTC) Transactions

Learning Objective

1.2.2   Understand the differences between: on-exchange/Multilateral Trading Facilities (MTF) and over-the-counter (OTC)

Although many financial instruments are traded 'on-exchange' (ie, on a recognised exchange or MTF), there are times when an instrument may be traded privately away from a recognised exchange or other type of execution venue. In this case, it will typically be traded off-exchange or OTC. Some derivatives products are widely traded OTC.

Exchange-traded	OTC
Instruments generally have high liquidity and can be traded on to other buyers.	Less liquid instruments may trade off-exchange (ie, OTC).
The exchange regulations and governing body specify trading procedures and detail actions to follow in case of dispute.	Any legal agreements that are set in place around an OTC trade must typically be negotiated directly between the trade counterparties involved. Master legal agreements between trade counterparties may specify basic terms that will apply to all transactions. In case of dispute, trading parties may need to seek resolution through the law courts, subject to the contractual terms that they have set in place.
Participants dealing on a recognised exchange normally benefit from clearing through a CCP.	Trades made with an OTC counterparty may have a higher risk as there may be no central clearing counterparty and exposure is directly related to the OTC counterparty chosen. However, some OTC transactions may be forwarded to a CCP for central clearing.
Exchange provides a price discovery mechanism. Hence, pricing of exchange trades is typically relatively transparent.	Pricing is more complex. When the OTC market for an instrument is still immature, investment banks can often make large profits by exploiting the lack of an effective price formation mechanism and the resultant difficulties faced by counterparties in pricing instruments accurately. To help them, trading parties may employ the services of an independent valuation agent that specialises in providing mark to market pricing for OTC traded instruments. As the market develops, and price-discovery mechanisms become more mature, spreads tend to narrow. As trading activity in the instrument grows, there may be benefits to bringing the instrument on-exchange.
Trading participants are typically required to publish the price, volume and time of securities traded on a recognised stock exchange within a specified timeframe after a transaction.	In some jurisdictions, OTC trades may be subject to more lenient post-trade reporting requirements than those conducted on a recognised stock exchange. However, under MiFID, trading participants are required to report price, volume and time of trades in listed shares, even if executed outside a regulated market (for EEA countries). Note that in some jurisdictions (for example, the UK and Ireland), OTC trades in local instruments are conducted subject to the rules of the stock exchange.
Trading limited to specified trading hours of the stock exchange or MTF.	Trading may take place 24 hours a day between trading counterparties.

11. Order-Driven and Quote-Driven Markets

Learning Objective

1.2.3   Understand the main characteristics of: order-driven markets; quote-driven markets; principal trading; agent trading; systematic internalisers; dark pools

1.2.4   Know the roles of: market makers/liquidity providers; sales traders; proprietary traders

The price discovery mechanisms provided by a stock exchange will differ slightly depending on whether a market is order-driven or quote-driven. The main characteristics of order-driven and quote-driven trading are outlined below:

- **Order-driven**
  - The buyer and the seller of shares each have a broker acting on their behalf as an agent.
  - The broker's job is to find a matching buyer for his seller's shares, or vice versa. This matching might take place either on the floor of an exchange, via a computerised system or both.
  - The broker makes a profit by charging his clients commission for arranging the deal.
  - The movement in price on an exchange is governed by the demand for a share and the availability of supply. The disadvantage of an order-driven market for large orders is that the order itself may move the price. Computerised trading (eg, the LSE's SETS system) can reduce this effect by making the buyer or seller anonymous and allowing the order to be placed in small amounts. By placing an 'Iceberg Order', a trading firm may split its order into a visible component, which is displayed to other trading parties, and an invisible component, which is not displayed. When the visible component of the order is matched and executed, a new part of the hidden order will then be displayed to other trading parties.
  - A market needs to have good liquidity if it is to become order-driven, otherwise there are problems with filling orders and pricing.

- **Quote-driven**
  - Liquidity is provided by a market maker (these are also known as 'specialists' in some markets), whose role is to quote prices at which they will buy and sell securities above a specified minimum volume. In the UK, the market maker must maintain a two-sided quote (bid and offer) at normal market size (this is based on 2.5% of the security's average daily turnover during the preceding year) or greater at all times. This will ensure that there is a buyer for a sell order and a seller for a buy order at any time.
  - Market makers always quote a price for buying and a price for selling (known as the spread) and they make their profits through such dealing.
  - Buyers and sellers may still have brokers acting on their behalf, but, instead of trying to find a matching counterparty, the broker arranges the transaction with a market maker. As in the order-driven market, the broker makes a profit by charging a commission to the client.
  - Examples of **quote-driven markets**, where market makers publish quoted prices on computer screens, are Nasdaq in the US, SEAQ in the UK, and the eurobond market. Trade execution may be electronic, or by manual media such as fax or telephone.

When a securities house deals in the market it is acting either as principal or as an agent.

Principal trading is when an instrument is bought or sold through a firm's own account (rather than on behalf of a client), with the view that the price will move up or down and the instrument can later be traded on for profit. The price does not always have to move up for the firm to make a profit. A falling share price can create a profit if the firm has invested in an appropriate derivatives-based instrument (refer back, for example, to comments on short selling earlier in this chapter).

Agency trading is when a firm acts as an intermediary, or agent, on behalf of a client. This arrangement is commonly employed when the client does not have its own trading capability, or does not have direct access to a market (ie, it may not be a member of the local stock exchange).

A **crossing network** is an electronic network (eg, MTF) that matches orders for execution without routing the order to a registered exchange.

In an **agency cross**, a broker matches an order between two of its own clients on its own books, rather than going via the market. Although the broker will typically charge a commission to both clients, this arrangement will save clients the need to pay all of the spread charged by market makers. Agency cross-trades are tightly regulated to ensure that brokers do not give preferential treatment to favoured customers. Under MiFID, implemented on 1 November 2007, all brokers are required to demonstrate that they are delivering best execution (ie, executing trades on the most favourable terms, taking into account price, costs, speed, likelihood of execution and settlement, size and other considerations relevant to the execution of the order) for all clients that they service.

Riskless principal is a transaction in a security that involves two orders, with execution of one contingent on the execution of the other. If a trader receives a sell order from a customer, it would be required to execute an identical sell order in the market (ie, identical in size, in the same security at an identical price) on a principal basis.

So if a **broker-dealer** receives a customer order to purchase 100,000 ordinary shares in ABC corporation at US$1.00 per share, it would immediately buy 100,000 shares in ABC from another seller at an identical price. Since both trades were executed at the same price (excluding commissions), this would be classified as a riskless principal transaction.

MiFID-classified trading venues fall into three explicit categories:

1. **Regulated markets** – referring to regulated stock exchanges such as NYSE Euronext, the LSE and the Frankfurt Stock Exchange.
2. **MTFs** – sometimes referred to as 'alternative trading systems', MTFs are typically registered non-exchange trading venues which bring together purchasers and sellers of securities. Subscribers can post orders into the system and these will be communicated (usually electronically via an electronic communication network, [ECN]) for other subscribers to view. Matched orders will then proceed for execution.
3. **Systematic internalisers (SIs)** – an investment firm that, on an organised, frequent and systematic basis, deals on its own trading account by executing clients' orders outside a regulated market or MTF. This practice is broadly synonymous with agency crossing (above), whereby a crossing network electronically matches orders for execution without routing these to an exchange or MTF.

Under a series of amendments and updates to MiFID (contained in the **MiFID II** Directive), the European Union (EU) has introduced a new category of trading venue known as organised trading facilities (OTFs). OTFs are able to trade non-equity instruments, including bonds, structured products, derivatives and emission allowances.

Execution of orders on an OTF will be conducted on a discretionary basis. The OTF operator will be allowed to exercise discretion regarding: (i) whether it decides to place or retract an order that has been submitted to the OTF; (ii) whether it decides to match a client order with another client order (or orders) to create a matched trade. Given this freedom, the OTF operator may facilitate negotiation between trading parties and bring together two or more trading parties that may potentially be compatible in order to make a trade. The task of operating an OTF is deemed under MiFID II to be an investment service and, thus, only firms licensed as investment firms under MiFID will be permitted to run an OTF.

OTF operators will not typically be permitted to trade using their own proprietary capital. However, an exception is made for sovereign bonds for which there is no liquid market, and in a small number of other specified cases when an OTF operator may trade on a proprietary basis.

Market makers are firms that maintain a firm bid and offer price in a given security, making themselves available to buy or sell a specified list of securities at publicly quoted prices, within a specified quoted trade size. The bid price is the price at which the market maker is prepared to purchase a security from another investor. The offer price is the price at which the market maker is prepared to sell that security to the counterparty. By providing such a service, market makers promote a liquid market in the trading of specified securities (thereby serving as liquidity providers), ensuring that a buyer is available when a firm wishes to sell and a seller is available when a firm wishes to buy. Examples of quote-driven markets, where market makers publish quoted prices on computer screens, are NASDAQ in the US, SEAQ in the UK, and the eurobond market. Trade execution may be electronic, or by manual media – such as telephone.

Stock exchanges and/or regulators commonly impose strict rules that firms must adhere to in order to act as market makers within the exchange. This may include the times each day at which the firm must publish the bid/offer prices for securities in which they trade, and the means through which these prices should be published. They may also require, for example, that a specified number of market makers are active in each stock listed in the system.

Sales traders are broadly responsible for managing the agency trading relationship with a client, offering market advice, providing analysis and taking and placing orders for instruments. Given the importance of stock picking to an investor in optimising the balance of return and risk through investments, advice provided to the investor regarding which stocks are likely to move up or down may be an important element of the sales relationship. For highly structured and complex OTC products, developed on a bespoke basis for individual clients, sales traders may play a key role in communicating with clients regarding the specific needs and specifications that such an instrument must fulfil. As noted earlier, all brokers are required under MiFID to demonstrate that they are delivering best execution for all clients that they service.

Proprietary traders are responsible for buying and selling securities for a firm's own account (see principal trading, above). Additionally, proprietary traders may receive orders from the agency sales team and execute these in the market, commonly using electronic order placement facilities, but still in some instances communicating by telephone, especially for OTC trading. Sophisticated order routing systems are employed to ensure that purchase orders are relayed to the trader promptly, and once the order is filled, the agency sales team can inform the client of the price obtained without delay.

In some smaller firms, agency trading and **proprietary trading** may be conducted off the same trading desk.

For MTFs and dark pools, see section 9.1.2.

12.   Programme and Algorithmic Trading

Learning Objective

1.2.5   Know the principles of programme trades, algorithmic trading and high-frequency trading

1.2.6   Understand the impact of high-frequency trading on the market

12.1   Programme Trades

Fund managers that offer index-linked funds will typically need to purchase blocks of shares that mirror the composition of the index they are tracking. Rather than purchasing shares in each of the companies that make up the index on a trade-by-trade basis, it is commonly more efficient to buy or sell the whole block or basket of shares through what is known as a programme trade.

Programme trades are communicated electronically through an order generated by the fund manager or trader. This will place a buy or sell order for a block of trades that, for example:

- mirrors a financial market index such as the FTSE 100, S&P500, the Nikkei 225,
- represents a specific basket of shares put together by the fund manager to track, for example, ethical stocks.

It may also place a programme trade when, for example, selling off a large block of shares in one company and simultaneously replacing these with a large block of shares in another.

Settlement procedures are similar to those for single shares, but note the following points:

- It may be difficult to obtain or dispose of all shares in the market on the same day.
- **Trade confirmation** typically occurs after the complete order has been filled. Therefore, the time from execution in the market to trade confirmation may be longer for some shares in a programme trade than it would be had they been executed individually.

The choice of a counterparty for programme trading is typically based on its credit rating and its ability to provide access to all markets and sectors covered by the trade. This is important in large trades. The choice will also be influenced by price, likelihood of execution, cost of execution and settlement efficiency.

Some programme trades may be sufficiently large to have an impact on the price of the securities that the investor is trying to buy or sell. For example, when a large buy order arrives for a particular security (or basket of securities), it may have the effect of pushing up the price. Consequently, much effort has been dedicated to developing trading procedures and systems that ensure, as fully as possible, that the block trade remains invisible to the market. These are sometimes known as iceberg trades.

12.2 Algorithmic Trading

Algorithmic trading involves using computer-based mathematical models, or algorithms, to support decision-making around how a trade, or blocks of trades, should be executed. Typically, this may involve splitting a trade into multiple small orders to minimise its market impact (ie, the impact on the share price of placing a sizeable trade) and its visibility to others trading in the market. The trade may subsequently be executed automatically (hence this practice is commonly labelled black box trading) according to a set of pre-set rules which, when satisfied, trigger the order placement.

Similarly, **high-frequency trading (HFT)** employs powerful computers, high-speed connections and sophisticated trading algorithms to identify trading opportunities and to execute multiple orders in a short time frame in order to take advantage of these opportunities.

Indeed, the speed of trading has increased dramatically from seconds to milliseconds and now to microseconds. The term 'high-frequency trading' is still evolving and has not been clearly defined. However, it is commonly used to refer to professional traders acting in a proprietary capacity who engage in strategies that generate a large number of trades on a daily basis. These traders might, for example, be a proprietary trading desk of a multi-service broker-dealer or they might be a hedge fund. Firms engaged in HFT may share a number of other characteristics:

1. Use of high-speed, sophisticated computer programs or algorithms for generating, routing and executing orders.
2. Use of very short timeframes for establishing and liquidating trading positions.
3. Submission of trade orders in high quantity, many of which may be cancelled before execution.
4. Use of co-location services and individual data feeds offered by exchanges or third-party service providers to minimise network delays and to facilitate high speed trading.
5. Use of arbitrage strategies to drive trading profits. These strategies may be complex and may take many different forms. For example, these may (to provide two heavily simplified examples):
   a. attempt to exploit small pricing differences for a quoted instrument across different trading venues,
   b. attempt to capture liquidity rebates made available to firms that post liquidity to a particular execution venue. Some venues will offer rebates to market makers (liquidity providers) that post liquidity, and will charge those who take this liquidity (liquidity takers). Rebate arbitrage strategies are employed by HFT firms in order to draw maximum benefit from these 'maker/taker' pricing models.

By using co-location services, a trading firm will seek to locate its computer server as near as possible to the trading platforms upon which these trades are executed. Given that trade order messages take a finite time to be transported from the trading firm's computer server to the execution venue's matching engine, there is an advantage for HFT firms in making this distance as short as possible. Co-location is a service offered by execution venues or by third-party providers, providing rack space to the trading firm that enables the latter to situate its server in close physical proximity to the execution venue's order management system and matching engine.

Financial regulators in a number of jurisdictions have been monitoring closely how co-location services are marketed and used – particularly to ensure that co-location services are offered on a non-discriminatory basis and at fees which are fair and reasonable, such that certain firms are not excluded (eg, by virtue of being small trading firms that are unable to pay high co-location fees) from the potential advantages that HFT may offer.

To maximise their effectiveness, HFT firms will focus not only on minimising delays (or 'latency') in order placement, but also in ensuring they have fast access to trade data needed to support their trading strategies. In larger trading markets, a consolidated data feed (often known as a 'consolidated tape') may be available providing the best-priced quotes for a given instrument across a wide range of possible trading venues. However, the task of preparing this consolidated data feed – sourcing price information from multiple execution venues, processing this data and communicating this to trading parties – itself takes a finite time. HFT firms may gain a competitive advantage from sourcing individual data feeds directly from relevant execution venues and processing this internally. The US Securities and Exchange Commission (SEC) has estimated that the average latency in building the consolidated data feed is just a few milliseconds. However, these small margins can be vital to HFT firms seeking to gain trading advantages through maximising their speed to market (for further information, see Securities and Exchange Commission, Concept Release on Equity Market Structure, Release No. 34-61358; File No. S7-02-10).

MiFID II will introduce a range of provisions designed to ensure that HFT does not have a negative impact on market quality or integrity. These include controls on:

- **Order to trade ratios (OTRs)** – trading venues will be required to set limits on the maximum number of order messages that a market participant can send relative to the number of transactions they execute.
- **Minimum tick sizes** – equity exchanges in Europe voluntarily set minimum increments, or 'tick sizes', by which prices can change. MiFID II will establish minimum tick sizes in shares and other selected financial instruments.
- **Venue pricing** – there will be controls on the fees charged by trading venues to HFT firms to ensure that these fee structures are transparent, fair and non-discriminatory.
- **Market making** – HFT firms that use market making strategies on trading venues will be required to sign market making agreements with these venues to ensure they provide liquidity on a consistent basis.

13. Multi-Listed Shares

Learning Objective

1.2.7 Understand the principles of multiple listed shares

A share has historically been listed on only one exchange. However, increasingly, companies that are active in more than one market may list their shares in a number of exchanges. One name for these shares is **globally registered shares (GRSs)**. Here are some of the main features:

- An investment bank may list on the Swiss Exchange (SIX Swiss Exchange) and in New York.
- Most of the trading takes place on the SIX Swiss Exchange, and so this generally sets the price for the day. At the time when both exchanges are open, the price will adjust to be the same on both exchanges.

- Any price differences are reduced to zero by firms using arbitrage. Arbitrage is possible when a share (or any tradeable instrument) is quoted in more than one market. It will be cheaper in one market than another, even if only fractionally and temporarily. A firm can therefore make money by buying in one market and selling in the other. Normally, the price differences are so small that a large volume of shares has to be traded to make it worthwhile. Specialist firms tend to do this and fulfil the function of equalising the price between the markets.
- Arbitrage also eliminates differences in price due to any FX movements.
- Liquidity is typically higher as the share is available in more than one market. The issuer benefits as it has access to a larger investment community than is the case for a single listed share. Investors have the option of buying in one market and selling in another.
- Traders involved in arbitrage trading will need to maintain stock in multiple locations and conduct regular stock realignment to ensure that working stock is available, when required, for trades to proceed to settlement. Some organisations (eg, SIS [SegaInterSettle], the Swiss CSD) have established a third-party service that allows traders to hold stock in a single securities account and for the intermediary to realign the stock on the trader's behalf.

With increasing consolidation of, and cooperation between exchanges, companies are exploring the opportunity of listing their shares on multiple exchanges rather than issuing ADRs. This is particularly true of multinational companies whose revenue streams are received in multiple currencies. However, companies that are looking to multi-list shares must assess the costs involved against the potential benefits offered by this strategy. The significant costs involved have caused some companies to cancel multi-listings in recent times. For example, the company will typically incur listing fees on each stock exchange on which it wishes to list its stock. Also, multiple listing can add cost and complexity to the task of disseminating shareholder information, scheduling shareholder meetings and processing voting entitlement, or in managing income distribution, rights issues or other corporate events across shareholders in multiple jurisdictions.

More broadly, multiple listing can have a negative impact on the liquidity of the issuer's stock in its home market. If an issuer's primary listing is in a developing market (eg, Latvia, Czech Republic), a decision to dual-list its stock on a large international stock exchange (eg, NYSE Euronext, LSE) may cause the stock's liquidity to decline on the domestic exchange with different rules and conventions.

These are some of the key characteristics of DRs and GRSs:

- **Depositary Receipt (DR)**
  - Shares are listed on a single exchange in a single currency, but DRs can be listed on multiple exchanges in multiple currencies.
  - DRs are generally not transferable across markets (although they can be converted).
  - The listing requirements for a DR on a particular exchange are typically less stringent than for a share.
  - A DR does not necessarily require the co-operation of the underlying company.
  - Increases the size of the potential investor community.

- **Globally Registered Share (GRS)**
  - Listed on multiple exchanges in multiple currencies.
  - Can be transferred across markets.
  - Has to meet the listing requirements of each exchange on which it is listed.
  - Creation is driven by the issuing company.
  - Increases the size of the potential investor community. Extends the global reach and global reputation of the issuing company.

14. Settlement Periods for Equities and Bonds in the Selected Markets

Learning Objective

1.2.8   Know the settlement periods for equities and bonds in the selected markets

Australia	Equities: T+2 (CHESS) Bonds: T+2 (Austraclear)
Brazil	Equities: T+3 (CBLC) Corporate debt: T+0 (CETIP) Government debt: T+0 (SELIC)
France	Equities and bonds: T+2 (Euroclear ESES)
Germany	Equities and bonds: T+2 (Clearstream Banking Frankfurt)
Hong Kong	Equities: T+2 (HKSCC) Debt: T+0 (CMU)
India	Equities and debt: T+2 (CDSL or NSDL) Government debt: T+2 (Reserve Bank of India)
South Korea	Equities: T+2 (KSD) Debt: T+0 (KSD)
Japan	Equities: T+3 (JASDEC) Government debt: T+3 (Bank of Japan) (to migrate to T+1 during 2018)
UK	Equities and corporate debt: T+2 (CREST) Gilts: T+1 (CREST)
US	Equities and corporate debt: T+2 (DTC) Government debt: T+1 (Federal Reserve)

Answers to Exercises

Exercise 1

a. Number of days of accrued interest under 30/360 convention for period 1 April (settlement date for purchase) to 27 June (settlement date – 1 for sale):

1 April–30 April	=	30
1 May–31 May	=	30
1 June–27 June	=	27
	=	87 days

Accrued interest = nominal x interest/100 x number of days of accrued interest (assuming 30 days in month)/360

	=	100,000 x 7/100 x 87/360
	=	£1,691.67

The investor will receive £1,691.67 in accrued interest under 30/360 convention.

b. Number of days of accrued interest under actual/365 convention

1 April–30 April	=	30
1 May–31 May	=	31
1 June–27 June	=	27
	=	88 days

Accrued interest = nominal x interest/100 x number of days of accrued interest/365

	=	100,000 x 7/100 x 88/365
	=	£1,687.67

The investor will receive £1,687.67 in accrued interest under actual/365 convention.

Exercise 2

Days of accrued interest due to seller = 100

Accrued interest = nominal value x annual coupon rate/annual divisor x days of accrual

Accrued interest = 200,000 x 8/100 x 1/365 x 100 = 4,383.56

Buyer will pay £4,383.56 in accrued interest to seller.

Exercise 3

Days of accrued interest due to seller = 175

Days of accrued interest due to buyer = 5

Accrued interest = nominal value x annual coupon rate/annual divisor x days of accrual

Accrued interest due to buyer = 100,000 x 7/100 x 1/360 x 5 = £97.22

Seller will pay £97.22 in accrued interest to buyer.

Exercise 4

Profit per warrant = price of underlying share – strike price – warrant premium (1)

Rearranging this equation:

Profit per warrant + strike price + warrant premium = price of underlying share (P) (2)

To make an overall profit of £30.00, the buyer will make a profit of 30.00/50 = £0.60 per warrant.

Thus, from (2):

£0.60 + £1.25 + £0.20 = P

£2.05 = P

Therefore, the buyer will make a profit of £30.00 if the share price rises to £2.05.

End of Chapter Questions

Think of an answer for each question and refer to the appropriate section for confirmation.

1. What is the nominal value of a bond?
   Answer Reference: Section 1

2. What is equity?
   Answer Reference: Section 2.1

3. What are the rights held by ordinary shareholders?
   Answer Reference: Section 2.1

4. What are the advantages and disadvantages to an investor of holding preference shares relative to ordinary shares?
   Answer Reference: Section 2.2

5. List the order in which obligations will be paid out if a company goes into liquidation or is wound up.
   Answer Reference: Section 2.2

6. What are the advantages to a company of issuing a bond over issuing shares?
   Answer Reference: Section 3

7. What are the characteristics of a eurobond?
   Answer Reference: Section 3.1.4

8. What is the clean price and the dirty price of a debt security?
   Answer Reference: Section 3.2

9. What is a warrant? What are the characteristics of covered warrants?
   Answer Reference: Section 4

10. What is a depositary receipt? How are depositary receipts issued? What are the benefits of holding depositary receipts rather than the underlying shares?
    Answer Reference: Section 5

11. What is a unit trust? What is bid price and offer price? Why are these different prices quoted?
    Answer Reference: Section 6.1

12. What are the characteristics of an ETF?
    Answer Reference: Section 6.3

13. What is an ISIN and what purpose does it serve?
    Answer Reference: Section 7

14. What is:
    a. a CUSIP?
    b. a SEDOL?
    Answer Reference: Section 7

15. List the qualification criteria that a company must typically satisfy to list its shares on a registered stock exchange.
    Answer Reference: Section 8.1

16. Who are the main parties involved in the issuance of a eurobond?
    Answer Reference: Section 8.4

17. What are the differences between on-exchange and OTC transactions? What are the advantages and disadvantages of each type of trading?
    Answer Reference: Section 10

18. What are the characteristics of an order-driven and quote-driven market? Give two examples of each.
    Answer Reference: Section 11

19. What are the functions performed by:
    a. a market maker,
    b. a proprietary trader,
    c. an agency trader?
    Answer Reference: Section 11

20. What is a programme trade?
    Answer Reference: Section 12

21. What are the advantages to a company of issuing multi-listed shares?
    Answer Reference: Section 13

Chapter Two
Main Industry Participants

This syllabus area will provide approximately 11 of the 50 examination questions

1.   Participants

Learning Objective

2.1.1   Know the characteristics of the following types of participant: individual; institutional; investment manager; prime broker; broker; inter-dealer broker (IDB); investment bank; central bank

1.1   Investors

As we noted in chapter 1, a range of different types of investors buy and sell securities in search of optimal returns at an appropriate level of risk.

Investors fall into a number of categories:

1. **Individual investors** put their own money at risk in the hope that this will increase in value. They invest on their own account, rather than on behalf of a company or institution. Individual investors may decide on their investment strategy, or may draw on the services of a financial adviser to finalise how their money is allocated (the asset allocation process) across different investment types. Having decided on which asset classes to invest in, they will commonly employ one or more investment management companies to manage the money invested in these investment vehicles.

    A professional investor (sometimes known as a sophisticated investor) is one that is deemed sufficiently knowledgeable to have a sound understanding of the risks and potential returns associated with the instruments in which they invest. In the UK, certified sophisticated investors are persons holding a certificate issued in the past three years by an FCA-approved authority, confirming that they have this required level of investment knowledge.

    A wider body of investors with recent professional experience may register themselves as self-certified sophisticated investors (for example, a person who in the past two years:
    ◦ has been a director of a company with an annual turnover of at least £1 million, or
    ◦ has been employed in the private equity sector or has provided finance for small- and medium-sized enterprises, or
    ◦ has made at least one investment in an unlisted company during this period).

    The term high net worth individual (HNWI) is used to refer to individual investors with substantial sums to invest. In the UK, certified HNWIs are persons who, during the preceding 12 months, have had an annual net income of at least £100,000 or net assets valued at £250,000 or more (not including the value of the person's primary residence).

2. **Institutional investors** are institutions (rather than individuals) that invest in financial markets, channelling the investments of a number of smaller investors or themselves, so that there is a pooling of the investments of these individual members. Institutional investor is a generic term that broadly includes pension funds, insurance and life assurance companies and pooled funds/collective investment schemes. Endowments and hedge funds are sometimes also classified as institutional investors.

    Institutional investors may manage their portfolio of investments internally, or may employ the services of one or more investment managers to manage these assets on their behalf.

    An institutional investor would not commonly be the principal beneficiary of any investment performance. Rather, its function will be to serve as a transparent vehicle through which other investors may channel their investments, in order to spread investment risk and to achieve economies of scale.

3. **Investment managers** are people or organisations that manage the investment assets of any individual or institutional investor. This involves buying and selling investments, stock-picking and, in some instances, directly aiding the client with asset allocation decisions. An investment management company may also invest its own company's money, acting as principal with regard to assets under its management.

   When managing investments on behalf of investor clients, the investment manager may offer a discretionary service through which the investor will delegate day-to-day management of its portfolio (or specific sections of its portfolio) to the investment manager. The latter will make investment decisions on the investor's behalf, managing holdings in line with the investor's objectives and risk tolerance, while providing reporting on investment performance and levels of risk exposure.

   Often, investment management companies have specialist expertise in managing specific categories of investment (eg, UK equities, corporate bonds, technology funds, emerging markets, absolute return funds). Consequently, an investor may employ a number of investment managers to optimise the investment performance delivered by different sections of its investment portfolio.

4. **Brokers** execute trades on an agency basis on behalf of their clients (which may be institutional or retail investors), find buyers for securities that their clients wish to sell and vice versa. A broker-dealer firm is licensed to trade on an agency basis for its clients (as above), or on a proprietary basis (ie, on its own behalf).

5. **Inter-dealer brokers** act as intermediaries between market-maker firms, meeting the latter's need for the securities that they require to support their trading requirements. Inter-dealer brokers provide a liquid source of a wide range of securities that may be difficult to access in quantity, and at competitive prices, in public exchanges. They also enable dealer firms to buy and sell securities without revealing their identities – reducing the risk that they transmit key information about their trading strategies to competitors and trigger price movement of the securities concerned within the market.

5. **Investment banks** are financial institutions that serve as intermediaries between securities issuer and investor, offering a wide range of investment services which may include organising and underwriting the issuance of securities (see chapter 1, section 8), providing market making and agency brokerage services, eurobond dealing and the FX provision of services. An investment bank may assist companies in managing mergers and acquisitions, and in raising capital to finance a range of possible development activities.

   Some investment banks may also employ prime brokerage arms, typically providing execution services for securities and derivatives, clearing and settlement, **securities lending**, credit services and research, predominantly to hedge fund customers.

   Investment banks may employ specialist financial analysts that provide investment research to investors. This research may be purchased as a stand-alone service, or as part of a bundled package that may include a selection of the other functions outlined above.

   Investment banks traditionally service a predominantly institutional customer base and tend not, specifically within their investment banking divisions, to specialise in administering retail deposits/current accounts, nor in providing a wider array of investment services targeted specifically at the retail public.

1.2 Central Banks

A central bank is a banking institution that sits at the heart of a country's financial and monetary system, playing a key role in promoting monetary and financial stability and in encouraging stable economic growth. The functions of the central bank may include controlling monetary policy and overseeing money market operations, managing the national currency, exchange and gold reserves, serving as lender of last resort to commercial banks, and providing banking services to government. In some countries, the central bank may serve as a regulatory authority, supervising the functioning of the financial system and the activities of institutions and individuals operating within this system. In some countries also, the central bank may deliver specific market infrastructure functions, eg, operation of the payments system, design of the **TARGET2-Securities (T2S)** platform for centralised settlement of euro-denominated (and some non-euro) securities in the EU (see section 3.5). Typically the central bank will be state controlled, but increasingly, central banks are being accorded independent status, in order to separate key central bank functions from political influence and day-to-day party politics. In an economic and political union such as the EU, a supranational central bank (eg, the European Central Bank [ECB]) may co-ordinate the monetary policy and financial operations of national central banks within that union.

1.3 Client Categories

The Markets in Financial Instruments Directive (MiFID) (see chapter 1, section 9.1) identifies two main categories of client (retail clients and professional clients), and a distinct third category (known as eligible counterparties) that is applicable to a limited range of businesses. Different levels of regulatory protection apply to clients within each of these categories:

- **Retail clients** are afforded the most regulatory protection.
- **Professional clients** are considered to be more experienced, knowledgeable and sophisticated and are able to assess their own risk. Thus, they are afforded fewer regulatory protections.
- **Eligible counterparties (ECPs)** are investment firms, credit institutions, insurance companies, asset management companies and other regulated financial institutions. MiFID provides a lighter regulatory regime when investment firms engage in transactions with ECPs.

2. Investment Administration and Operations: Custody

When an investor invests in an asset, it may employ a **custodian** to keep the assets secure and to administer the assets on its behalf. Why does it do so? Because the investor feels that its resources and time are best dedicated to what it specialises in: namely selecting, buying and selling investment assets. Its primary goal is to optimise the investment returns and risk on these invested assets (acting either for itself or for investor clients that it represents). The investor may not have the systems and expertise internally to provide custody for its assets.

However, when the investor buys investment assets (these may be equities, bonds or a range of the other instruments described in chapter 1), it must ensure that the assets are secure; that its transactions and any rights and benefits to which the investor is entitled are processed effectively; that correct tax is paid; and that regulatory reporting requirements, and a host of other responsibilities, are discharged effectively. In short, the investment process does not just involve picking stocks and waiting for the investment returns to roll in. Holding assets generates a host of administrative obligations that must be handled safely and effectively. If the investor fails to do so:

- its assets may be under threat due to loss, theft, fraud or counterfeit
- the investor may miss out on income (ie, dividends, interest payments) and other benefits that they are entitled to, and they may have the wrong level of taxation applied to their income
- inefficiencies in transaction-processing and asset servicing may generate high costs or losses that compromise the returns generated on invested assets
- inefficiencies in the management of a client's cash flows may add to costs and compromise returns on investment. The investor may be subject to penalties/fines and face potential disqualification from investing in the market if they fail to comply with regulatory requirements and legal obligations.

With these points in mind, the risks and costs involved with holding and servicing securities can be substantial, even when an investor is holding assets in just one market. Given that institutional investors, and some HNWIs, invest across a wide range of instruments in many different markets, it frequently makes sense for them to appoint a specialist custodian to provide safekeeping and asset servicing duties for their global portfolio of assets, as well as to manage language issues and to provide close links to financial regulators, key infrastructure entities and other vital contacts in the local market.

2.1 Custody Services

Learning Objective

2.1.2 Understand the advantages, disadvantages and purposes of the following types of custodian: global; sub-custodian

When an institutional investor invests in securities, it will commonly employ the services of a custodian to administer these securities by:

- providing safekeeping of the investor's assets in the local market
- making appropriate arrangements for delivery and receipt of cash and securities to support settlement of the investor's trading activities in that market
- providing market information to the investor on developments and reforms within that market
- collecting dividend income, interest paid on debt securities and other income payments in the local market
- more broadly, managing the client's cash flows
- monitoring and managing entitlements through **corporate actions** and voting rights held by the investor in the local market
- managing tax reclaims and other tax services in the local market
- ensuring that securities are registered and that transfer of legal or beneficial title on securities transactions proceeds effectively
- efficient reconciliation of assets according to best practice and regulatory standards
- maximising portfolio return by engaging in stock lending programmes
- ensuring that reporting obligations to the regulatory authorities, and to other relevant bodies, are discharged effectively.

The primary responsibility of the custodian is to ensure that the client's assets are fully protected at all times. Hence, it must provide robust safekeeping facilities for all valuables and documentation, ensuring that investments are only released from the custodian's care in accordance with authorised instructions from the client.

Importantly, the client's assets must be properly segregated from those of the custodian and appropriate legal arrangements must be in place to ensure that financial or external shock to the custodian does not expose the client's assets to claims from creditors or any other party.

The investor may manage its custody arrangements in foreign markets in which it invests by:

- appointing its own local custodian in each market in which it invests (often referred to as direct custody arrangements)
- appointing a global custodian to manage custody arrangements across the full range of foreign markets in which it has invested assets, or
- making arrangements to settle trades and hold securities and cash with central securities depositories (CSDs) within each market, or to go via an international central securities depository (ICSD) (see section 3.1).

2.1.1 Global Custodians

A global custodian provides investment administration for investor clients, including processing cross-border securities trades and keeping financial assets secure (ie, providing safe custody) outside the country where the investor is located.

The term global custody came into common usage in the financial services world in the mid-1970s, when the Employee Retirement Income Security Act (ERISA) was passed in the US. This legislation was designed to increase the protection given to US pension fund members. The act specified that US pension funds could not act as custodians of the assets held in their own funds. Instead, these assets had to be held in the safekeeping of another bank. ERISA went further to specify that only a US bank could provide custody services for a US pension fund.

Subsequently, use of the term global custody has evolved to refer to a broader set of responsibilities, encompassing settlement, safekeeping, cash management, record-keeping and asset servicing (eg, collecting dividend payments on shares and interest on bonds, reclaiming withholding tax, advising investor clients on their electing on corporate actions entitlements), and providing market information.

Some investors may also use their global custodians to provide a wider suite of services, including investment accounting, treasury and FX, securities lending and borrowing, collateral management, and performance and risk analysis of the investor's portfolio.

Some global custodians maintain an extensive network of branches globally and can meet the local custody needs of their investor clients by employing their own branches as local custody providers.

2.1.2 Subcustodians

In locations where a global custodian does not have its own branch, or in situations where it may find advantage by looking outside of its proprietary branch network, a global custodian may appoint an external agent bank to provide local custody services.

Similarly, investment banks and global broker/dealers (for example, Morgan Stanley, Goldman Sachs and UBS) will also typically employ a network of agent banks to meet their needs for clearing, settlement, asset servicing and cash management in markets around the world where they have investment activities.

A subcustodian effectively serves as the eyes and ears of the global custodian in the local market, providing a range of clearing, settlement and asset servicing duties.

It will also typically provide market information relating to developments in the local market, and will lobby the market authorities for reforms that will make the market more appealing and an efficient target for foreign investment.

In selecting a subcustodian, a global custodian may:

- appoint one of its own branches, in cases where this option is available,
- appoint a local agent bank that specialises in providing subcustody in the market concerned,
- appoint a regional provider that can offer subcustody to the global custodian across a range of markets in a region or globally.

Single Market Providers

Agent banks that specialise in providing sub-custody in their home market are sometimes known as single market providers. Stiff competition from larger regional or global competitors has meant that these are becoming a dying breed. However, some continue to win business in their local markets, often combining this service with offering global custody or **master custody** for institutional investors (eg, local pension and insurance funds) in their home markets. Examples include Bank of Tokyo-Mitsubishi UFJ (due to be renamed MUFG Bank ltd in April 2018), Mizuho Bank and Sumitomo Mitsui Banking Corporation in Japan and Maybank in Malaysia. United Overseas Bank also offers custody services in Malaysia, Fondaco in Luxembourg and Intesa Sanpaolo in Italy.

A principal selling point is that the providers above are local market specialists and that is what they do – hence, they can remain focused on their local business without spreading their attentions broadly across a wide range of markets. A local specialist bank may be attractive in a market in which local practices tend to differ markedly from global standards, or where a provider's long-standing relationship with the local regulatory authorities and/or the political elite leaves it particularly well placed to lobby for reforms on behalf of its cross-border clients.

Reciprocal arrangements may be influential in shaping the appointment of a local provider in some instances. Under such an arrangement, a global custodian (A) may appoint the local provider (B) to deliver subcustody in its local market (market B). In return, the custodian (A) may offer subcustody in its own home market (market A) for pension and insurance funds in market B which use provider B as their global custodian.

Global and Sub Custodian Reciprocal Arrangements

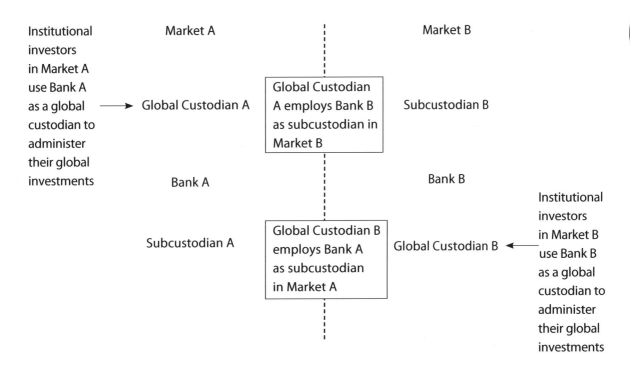

In summary, the advantages of a local provider may include:

- They are country specialists (especially on taxation).
- They act as the eyes and ears of the global custodian or global broker/dealer in the local market.
- They will have regular dealings with financial authorities and local politicians, and may be well placed to lobby for reforms that will improve the efficiency of the local market.
- They will have expert knowledge of local market practice, language and culture.
- They often have a long track record in the local market.
- They may offer opportunities for reciprocal business.

A local custody bank may be perceived to have the following disadvantages when compared with a regional custodian:

- Its credit rating may not match up to requirements laid down by some global custodians or global broker/dealers.
- It cannot apply developments in its technology and client service across multiple markets (unlike a regional custodian) – hence, product and technology development may lag behind the regional custodians with which it competes.
- It may not be able to offer the price discounts that can be extended by regional custodians offering custody services across multiple markets.
- For the global custodian or global broker/dealer client, it will be necessary to conduct due diligence, performance and risk reviews across a host of single-market custodians within its global network. As we see next, appointing a regional custodian can sometimes reduce the administrative burden that this involves.

Regional Providers

A regional custodian is able to provide agent bank services across multiple markets in a region.

For example, Standard Chartered Bank and HSBC have both been offering regional custody and clearing in the Asia-Pacific and South Asian region for many years, competing with Citi, Deutsche Bank and some strong single-market providers for business in this region. In Central and Eastern Europe, Unicredit, Deutsche Bank, Raiffeisen Bank International and Citi each offer a regional clearing and custody service.

Employing a regional custodian may offer a range of advantages to global custodian or global broker/dealer clients:

- Its credit rating may be higher than for a single market custodian.
- It can cross-fertilise good practice across multiple markets – lessons learned in one market may be applied, where appropriate, across other markets in its regional offering.
- It can leverage innovation in technology, product development and client service across multiple markets – delivering economies of scale benefits.
- It can offer standardised reporting, management information systems and market information across multiple markets in its regional offering.
- Economies of scale may support delivery of some or all product lines from a regional processing centre – offering potential cost savings and efficiency benefits.
- Its size and regional importance, plus the strength of its global client base, may allow a regional custodian to exert considerable pressure on local regulators, political authorities and infrastructure providers. This may be important in lobbying for reforms that support greater efficiency and security for foreign investors in that market.
- Using a regional custodian may help in resolving language barriers for individual countries as they are likely to be multilingual.
- The global client may be able to secure price discounts by using a regional custodian across multiple markets.

In some situations, a regional provider may be perceived to have certain disadvantages when compared with a local custody bank:

- A regional custodian's product offering may be less well attuned to local market practice, service culture and investor needs than that of a well-established local provider.
- A regional custodian may spread its focus across a wider range of clients and a wider range of markets than a single market provider. Hence, a cross-border client may not receive the same level of attention, and the same degree of individualised service as may be extended by a local custodian.
- Some regional custodians may lack the long track record, customer base and goodwill held by some local custodians in their own market.

2.2   Custody and Subcustody Agreements

Learning Objective

2.1.3   Understand the purpose and provisions of custody and sub-custody agreements

2.1.5   Understand the requirements of a service level agreement (SLA) between an investor and its custodian

2.2.1   Custody Agreement

To formalise the custody arrangements outlined in section 2.1, it is standard for the institutional investor and the global custodian to sign a custody agreement that details:

- the legal conditions under which the investor's assets are held by the global custodian, and are protected and segregated from the assets of the global custodian,
- the responsibilities and obligations required of the global custodian under the custody relationship,
- the authority for the custodian to accept instructions from fund managers, in instances where an institutional investor employs investment managers to manage assets on its behalf.

The global custodian will negotiate a separate custody agreement with each institutional investor with which it conducts business. Given that these institutions may have markedly different investment strategies, allocating their assets across a different range of markets and investment instruments, the structure and content of the legal agreement may differ significantly from client to client. However, each custody agreement is likely to address the following:

- the method through which the client's assets are received and held by the global custodian,
- reporting obligations and deadlines,
- guidelines for use of CSDs (see section 3) and other relevant use of financial infrastructure,
- business contingency plans to cope with systemic malfunction or disaster,
- liability in contract and claims for damages,
- standards of service and care required under the custody relationship,
- a list of persons authorised to give instructions,
- actions to be taken in response to instructions,
- actions to be taken without instructions,
- default **options** for corporate action elections,
- specification of **contractual settlement date accounting (CSDA)** or **actual settlement date accounting (ASDA)** where relevant (see chapter 3, section 3.5 for further detail).

Institutional investors and global custodians are required to adhere to the legal framework prevailing in the countries in which assets are invested.

The custody agreement will typically include provision on the part of the investor to conduct periodic reviews of the custodian's internal control environment, in order to ensure that it has effective procedures in place to monitor and manage risk. These controls should ensure that the investor's assets are held securely and that procedures for accepting and acting on authorised instructions are in place.

The custody agreement will commonly detail the level of indemnity that the global custodian will provide to the client in instances of error or negligence on its own part, or on the part of sub-custodians that it employs. It will also define the level of indemnity, if at all, that it will provide to clients against catastrophic events, default by a CSD or **clearing house** or counterparty, theft or fraud, and a wide range of other contingencies.

2.2.2   Subcustody Agreement

When the global custodian employs a subcustodian to provide custody on its behalf in a foreign market, it will sign a legal agreement with the subcustody provider that will detail:

*   the legal conditions under which client assets are held by the sub-custodian, and are protected and segregated from the assets of the subcustodian
*   the responsibilities and obligations required of the sub-custodian by the global custodian under the custody relationship.

A subcustodian, global custodian and its foreign investor clients are bound by the legal regulations prevailing in the overseas market. Hence, while many provisions of the subcustodian agreement will resemble those appearing in the example investor-global custodian agreement outlined above, these provisions will be amended in certain instances to comply with local regulatory requirements and legal practice.

2.2.3   Service Level Agreement (SLA)

Detailed specifications pertaining to the standards of service required by an investor from its custodian are spelled out in a service level agreement (SLA). This lays down required standards for service areas, including:

*   record-keeping and maintenance of accurate and up-to-date documentation,
*   settlement (exchange, MTF and OTC)
*   communication and reporting
*   corporate actions processing
*   income processing
*   tax services
*   cash management
*   management information systems
*   stock lending and borrowing
*   market information and market knowledge
*   standards of service expected from account officers and relationship managers that represent primary points of contact with the investor.

2.3   Selecting a Custodian

Learning Objective

2.1.4   Understand the purpose of a request for proposal (RFP) in the selection of a global custodian by an investor

2.1.6   Understand how legislation can affect the appointment of custodians

When selecting a global custodian, an institutional investor will typically invite statements of interest from suitable candidates. The investor may ask for further detail of services offered by applicants via a request for information (RFI). Eligible candidates will typically then be asked to complete a detailed request for proposal (RFP) submission as a preliminary stage in the appointment process. An RFP is a tendering process for buyers of global financial services. Although the size and scope of the RFP will vary slightly from client to client, this will generally represent a lengthy questionnaire that will request background information on the custodian's staffing and IT capacity, its track record and experience in the custody area, the strength of its existing client base and assets under custody, its creditworthiness and its record of recent losses.

The RFP should be viewed as an early stage in the selection process, rather than a selection process in its own right. Typically, it will be used to screen out candidates that do not meet the client's selection criteria, and then to provide a springboard for further investigation at the site visit and/or interview stage.

The core elements typically addressed in an RFP are mapped out in the following table:

Service Element	Information Typically Required in an RFP
Background of custodian	Including the number of years the custodian has been in the business, number/type of existing clients, assets under custody held on behalf of these clients, clients won and lost in previous three years, credit rating.
Service capacity	Including name and biographical details of persons responsible for managing the custody account, their level of experience and total account load, level of back-up support available, strategy for servicing the client's account.
Account, reporting and settlement processing	Including details of the custodian's accounting and reporting system: report formats, electronic reporting capacity, frequency of reports, quality checks to ensure reporting accuracy, deadlines for settlement instructions, mechanisms for dealing with exceptions and failed trades.
Safekeeping	Including procedures for segregating assets and ensuring security of assets, reconciliation procedures, procedures for income collection, procedures for processing mandatory and voluntary corporate actions, tax services.
Cash management and FX	Requiring details on account overdraft policy, instruction deadlines for cash movements, policy for maintaining single currency and multi-currency accounts, overnight sweeping of cash balances.

Subcustodian network	List of subcustodians in network and length of relationship, procedures for appointing subcustodians, review procedures, content and structure of SLA, indemnities in place in case of subcustodian failure/error or failure on part of a third party used by the subcustodian, frequency and format for providing market information, messaging procedures.
Pricing structure	Including the range of service provided in the custodian's **core** package, pricing schedule for services incurring additional charges, billing frequency and format.
Value added services	Including stock lending, fund accounting and performance measurement.

Given the weight of RFPs that custodians are required to complete in bidding for new mandates, investors are advised to be clear about their objectives before finalising and sending the RFPs to interested parties.

The RFP process should draw attention to issues that will be key for the investor client in formulating its choice of custodian. Importantly, these selection priorities should be communicated clearly to the candidates. This will help prospective custodians to structure their responses in such a way that will simplify the selection process for the investor.

Legislation governing the responsibilities held by pension fund trustees and other fiduciaries can be important in shaping the procedures through which custodians are appointed and standards of service monitored. For example, standards of fiduciary conduct laid down in the US in ERISA Section 404 and the 1995 UK Pensions Act require pension fund trustees to be directly responsible for the appointment of custodians. This makes trustees liable for civil penalties if they rely on the skill or judgement of any person who is appointed (other than by the trustees) to exercise a prescribed function. To put it simply, this requires that pension fund trustees should have a direct legal relationship with their custodian, not an indirect one via the investment manager or any other appointed intermediary. Trustees must take full responsibility for appointing and monitoring the actions of custodians acting on behalf of their fund.

In their capacity as fiduciaries, pension fund trustees are generally required to uphold the following prudential standards:

- They must demonstrate that they have the necessary familiarity with the structure and aims of their pension scheme and have an appropriate level of training and skill to carry out their responsibilities to scheme members effectively.
- Fiduciaries have a responsibility to monitor and review the tasks that they delegate to third parties (including custodians and investment management companies) in order to ensure that these tasks are discharged effectively.
- The duty of loyalty demands that trustees administer their pension scheme solely in the best interests of the scheme members.
- Trustees must avoid undue risk in the way that scheme assets are managed and appoint intermediaries to manage or administer scheme assets on the scheme's behalf.

Also, legislation guiding safekeeping of client assets requires that a firm that holds safe custody investments with a custodian must have effective and transparent procedures in place for custodian selection and for monitoring performance. The frequency of these risk reviews should be dependent on the nature of the market and the types of services that the custodian delivers to the client.

3. Central Securities Depositories (CSDs) and International Central Securities Depositories (ICSDs)

3.1 The Role of Depositories

The main functions of a depository are typically to:

1. enable members to hold book-entry accounts for dematerialised securities
2. settle transactions between members on a **delivery versus payment (DvP)** basis, often in central bank funds
3. provide basic custody services.

The types of instruments typically eligible to be deposited in a CSD or ICSD include equities, government bonds, corporate bonds and money market instruments.

CSD systems can be classified as direct holding systems or indirect holding systems, or a combination of the two. In some CSDs, securities may be held in book-entry form in the name of an intermediary (or **nominee**) acting on behalf of the investor (indirect holding systems). In other CSDs, the investor is listed in the records of the depository system (direct holding systems).

In the UK, for example, firms that wish to settle their securities transactions and hold their stock in CREST (operated by Euroclear UK and Ireland) typically have two options – to become either:

- a user (ie, a direct member), or
- a sponsored member, operating via another CREST user (sponsor).

3.2 Certificated, Immobilised and Dematerialised Securities

Securities can be held in a range of formats:

- **Certificated securities holdings** – a certificate may be registered or bearer. For registered securities, the register will represent a full list of holders of the securities concerned. The registrar is responsible for recording change of ownership following sale or transfer. For bearer securities, there is no share register. The issuer prints certificates (hence a certificated security) and these are sent to the investor in accordance with their holding. The holder's name does not appear on the security. Similar to holding banknotes, the owner 'bears' all risk associated with the loss of theft of securities in this form. Securities may also be held as a global or **jumbo certificate**, where a single consolidated certificate representing the entire issue of the security is held with an independent agency (known as a common depository). Jumbo certificates are often held in bearer form (see chapter 3, section 3.3). In some instances, smaller-denomination securities certificates may be consolidated into a single, jumbo certificate that is registered.

- **Dematerialised (or uncertificated) securities holdings** – registered holders in many CSDs hold securities electronically via a method known as book entry. The progressive transition in the securities industry from physical (ie, certificated) holdings to book-entry format has been important in reducing the costs and risks associated with clearing, settlement and asset servicing across the industry. It also speeds up settlement and improves settlement performance and efficiency.

When a depository accepts certificated securities, these may be immobilised such that the depository holds the underlying certificate in secure storage and transfer of ownership takes place via book-entry movement between participants' accounts at the CSD. Note that Euroclear UK & Ireland provides depository services for dematerialised UK and Irish securities (see section 3.3) and, thus, certificated securities are never immobilised within this CSD.

In the EU, the CSD Regulation will require all securities which are traded on regulated markets or MTFs to be dematerialised. When this requirement comes into force, it will no longer be possible for shareholders of traded companies to hold their shares in certificated form. This regulation will apply to all new securities issued from 1 January 2023 and to all securities traded on EU-regulated markets or MTFs from 1 January 2025.

3.3 Depository Arrangements in the Selected Markets

Learning Objective

2.2.1 Understand the roles of ICSDs and CSDs generally for the selected markets: depositories available; participation requirements

Depository arrangements in the selected markets are summarised below:

UK and Ireland

Euroclear UK & Ireland provides depository services for dematerialised UK and Irish securities and some foreign securities, facilitated by the CREST system. This CSD was previously operated by CRESTCo, which was merged with Euroclear Group in September 2002. CRESTCo was renamed Euroclear UK & Ireland in early 2007.

- All CREST-eligible securities are registered, including all equities and bonds.
- The majority of UK and Irish securities are available to settle in Euroclear UK & Ireland, or can be rematerialised.
- Transfer of title is by **book-entry transfer** in CREST, since the CREST system is fully dematerialised. Physical certificates do exist, but have to be dematerialised in order to be settled through CREST.

The CREST electronic settlement system provides real-time settlement (on trade date if required) and provides real-time direct access to live data in the CREST system. Members contract with one of the CREST payment banks that provide credit and liquidity to facilitate the settlement of transactions on a DVP basis. CREST maintains a cash memorandum account for each member, which shows the net balance of payments made and received at any time during the course of a settlement day. However, US dollar settlements are excluded from **real-time gross settlement (RTGS)** in CREST.

As mentioned earlier, firms that wish to settle their securities transactions and hold their stock in CREST have two main options: to become a user (ie, direct member) or to become a sponsored member operating through another CREST user (a sponsor). Users are firms that have the hardware and software to connect directly to CREST. A user can be a direct member of CREST and/or can act as a sponsor for other members that do not have a direct connection to CREST. A member (whether direct or sponsored) has securities and cash functionality in CREST and is the legal owner of the securities held in its account in CREST.

In the UK, CREST records its members' securities balances and these represent the legal record of title throughout the day. CREST confirms the electronic transfer of title (ETT) for all uncertificated stock at the point of settlement. The legal register is made up of two parts: the issuer register (the certificated holdings held with the issuer or its registrar) and the operator register (the electronic holdings in CREST). The issuer has real-time access to all movements on the operator register and, in order to make up the issuer's record, adds a copy of the operator register to the issuer register. The issuer's record is used to calculate shareholder entitlements for corporate actions, dividends, voting and other ownership benefit rights.

United States

The **Depository Trust Company (DTC)** provides depository services for corporate stocks and bonds, municipal bonds, money market instruments (eg, commercial paper), ADRs and some mutual funds.

The Federal Reserve Bank (FRB) provides depository services for most US government bonds and securities issued by federal agents and mortgage-backed securities. Transfer of securities held by DTC is by book entry. However, DTC will safekeep some physical securities on customers' behalf through its DTC custody service.

Settlement at DTC offers net end-of-day transfer of funds via the Federal Reserve Funds Transfer system. In the case of some physical certificates, there needs to be a reregistration at a transfer agent. US government debt securities cleared by the Fixed-Income Clearing Corporation (FICC) are settled by J.P. Morgan Chase and the Bank of New York Mellon. Mortgage-backed securities (MBS) trades are cleared and settled through the FICC MBS Division.

Europe

Euroclear France acts as the CSD and primary settlement system for trading on NYSE Euronext Paris, supporting securities settlement on the **Euroclear Settlement of Euronext-zone Securities (ESES)** platform (see below). All securities are dematerialised at Euroclear France.

The NYSE Euronext-zone CSDs (namely Euroclear Belgium, Euroclear France and Euroclear Nederland) are supported by an integrated settlement solution and harmonised custody service for stock exchange and OTC activities. This system, known as ESES, was introduced via a phased roll-out during 2007 and 2008, and replaces the legacy systems previously operated independently by these three CSDs.

Interbolsa, a wholly owned subsidiary of NYSE Euronext Lisbon, is the CSD for the Portuguese market and primary settlement system for trading at NYSE Euronext Lisbon.

LCH.Clearnet SA provides central counterparty (CCP) services for all the NYSE Euronext European markets.

Germany

Clearstream Banking Frankfurt (CBF) acts as the CSD. Shares exist in both registered and bearer form. The majority of securities are immobilised at CBF.

Transfer is by book entry via one of two settlement processes:

- The CASCADE system (Central Application for Settlement, Clearing And Depository Expansion) operates within Deutsche Börse for German domestic business. It runs via a combination of batch and real-time processing.
- Clearstream Banking's CREATION settlement communication platform operates for international users through the Clearstream Banking ICSD. It uses both overnight batch and several daytime batches.

Physical transfer of shares is possible, but this must be done outside of CBF and shares cannot be sold while being reregistered.

CBF and the Clearstream ICSD are owned by Deutsche Börse AG.

Spain

Iberclear is the Spanish CSD, bearing responsibility for registration of securities held in book-entry form, and clearing and settlement of all trades on the Spanish stock exchanges, the public debt market, the AIAF fixed-income market, and Latibex – the Latin American stock exchange denominated in euros.

Iberclear is a member of the Bolsas y Mercados Españoles (BME) group that embraces the Spanish equity market, AIAF fixed-income market and derivatives markets and their clearing and settlement systems. The BME Group is formed by the Barcelona, Bilbao, Madrid and Valencia stock exchanges, MF Mercados Financieros and IBERCLEAR.

Spain engaged in a major reform of its post-trade infrastructure, designed to align its market practice with other EU securities markets and to ready the market for release of TARGET2-Securities, the ECB's centralised platform for securities settlement in Europe. Key components of this reform package included:

1. **Change to procedures for securities transfer.** Previously, when a securities transaction has resulted in change of ownership, Iberclear has issued a 'register reference (RR)' for the transaction. This will result in cancellation of original ownership and transfer of the CSD register to the new legal owner. However, this RR system has been abolished as a result of Spain's ongoing post-trade reforms, thus bringing Spanish market practice into line with that in other major securities markets around the world. With this change, settlement finality is established on settlement date, rather than on trade date as was the case under the RR system.

2. **Iberclear has established a single CSD platform for securities processing that will link with T2S.** Previously, Iberclear has managed two technical platforms for the registration, clearing and settlement of securities, notably: (i) the SCLV platform for securities traded on the Spanish equities exchanges and Latibex; (ii) the CADE platform for securities traded on the AIAF fixed-income and public debt markets. The reform programme has consolidated these activities onto a single CSD platform, while providing the technical capability that Iberclear requires to fulfil its key infrastructure functions in a T2S Europe. Equities settlement moved onto this new platform in 2016, with fixed-income securities having moved in 2017.

3. **Creation of a CCP for securities settlement in the Spanish market.** For a number of years, Iberclear has offered a settlement guarantee for trades executed on BME. However, Iberclear has not previously offered **novation** as part of this service, mitigating credit risk by becoming direct counterparty to buyer and seller. As part of this major reform package in the Spanish market, from 2015 BME Clearing now provides CCP clearing services for fixed-income securities and equities.

Australia

All securities traded on the ASX are cleared and settled through the ASX's **Clearing House Electronic Subregister System (CHESS)**. CHESS is owned and operated by the ASX Settlement Corporation, a wholly owned subsidiary of the ASX Group.

Share certificates are dematerialised in CHESS. Investors can choose to have their holdings registered electronically in one of two ways:

- on an issuer-sponsored subregister, or
- on the CHESS subregister.

Final settlement of payments system obligations occurs through transactions on accounts at the Reserve Bank of Australia (RBA). The RBA's Reserve Bank Information and Transfer System (RITS) is Australia's real-time gross settlement (RTGS) system and lies at the heart of the Australian payments clearing and settlement system. RITS also provides cash settlement facilities for other interbank obligations (ie, low-value transactions and those arising from Australian equity transactions in CHESS) on a netted basis.

Between 1991 and February 2002, RITS provided depository and settlement services for government securities (known as Commonwealth Government Securities, or CGS). These services are now provided by the Austraclear system, which is operated by the ASX Settlement Corporation. Austraclear also provides settlement and depository services for corporate debt, semi-government debt (debt issued by state governments) and a range of other instruments.

ASX Group was established in July 2006 out of the merger of the Australian Stock Exchange (ASX) Ltd and the Sydney Futures Exchange Corporation (SFE).

Japan

Japan Securities Depository Centre (JASDEC) acts as the CSD for equities, along with corporate and municipal bonds. Settlement within JASDEC is by book-entry transfer. Dematerialisation of stock certificates in JASDEC became mandatory in January 2009. JASDEC's book-entry transfer system for corporate bonds was launched in January 2006.

Bank of Japan (BOJ) provides the central clearing system and depository for Japanese government bonds (JGBs) and Treasury bills.

Hong Kong

The Hong Kong Securities Clearing Company (HKSCC) is the central depository for equities, and share certificates are immobilised at the Hong Kong and Shanghai Banking Corporation Ltd. All shares, and most warrants, must be registered. Depository shares are registered to the CCASS nominee, HKSCC Nominees Ltd.

The depository for corporate and government debt securities is the Central Moneymarkets Unit (CMU) operated by the Hong Kong Monetary Authority (HKMA).

Singapore

The CDP (Central Depository), a wholly owned subsidiary of the Singapore Exchange (SGX), provides integrated clearing, settlement and depository services in the Singaporean market. With CDP acting as CCP to all CDP clearing members, trades are novated to CDP, providing guarantee of settlement.

As the CSD in Singapore, CDP acts as a central nominee for its account holders. The depository has two categories of participants, namely direct account holders and depository agents (DAs). Investors can opt to hold their securities in custody via a direct account with CDP, or in sub-accounts with the DAs.

DAs are given access to CDP's sub-accounting system, enabling them to maintain securities accounts on behalf of their private or institutional clients. The identities of these sub-account holders are known only to the respective DAs, ensuring the confidentiality and anonymity of their clients.

India

India has two depositories, the National Securities Depository Limited (NSDL) and the Central Depository Services (India) Limited (CDSL). These hold and transfer securities electronically and support electronic transfer of securities between the two depositories.

Dematerialised settlement accounts for over 99% of turnover settled by delivery. To prevent physical certificates from sneaking into circulation, it has become mandatory that all new securities must be issued and traded in dematerialised form. Transfer of ownership of securities takes place electronically by book entry at NSDL and CDSL.

South Korea

The Korea Securities Depository (KSD) acts as the central depository, clearing and settlement agent for equities and fixed-income securities. More than 80% of shares and 95% of bonds are dematerialised within the KSD.

Settlement within KSD is by book-entry transfer on a **multilateral netting** basis. Transfer of ownership in KSD is immediate upon settlement. Partial settlement is not allowed.

Brazil

The CBLC (Companhia Brasileira de Liquidação e Custódia) is the clearing house and central securities depository for trades in equities and corporate bonds listed and traded through BOVESPA and SOMA. Shares are dematerialised and issued in book-entry form. Similarly, fixed-income instruments are held dematerialised at SELIC and CETIP (see overleaf).

SELIC (Sistema Especial de Liquidação e Custódia) is the depository and clearing system for government debt issued by BACEN (Banco Central do Brasil – the central bank) and the Brazilian National Treasury. SELIC is operated by BACEN.

CETIP (Central de Custódia e Liquidação Financeira de Títulos Privados) is the depository and clearing house for corporate debt and OTC derivatives.

3.4 International Central Securities Depositories (ICSDs)

Learning Objective

2.2.5   Know the range of custody and settlement services offered by the ICSDs

2.2.3   Understand the roles played by Euroclear Bank and Clearstream Banking, including the Bridge

2.3.4   Know the communication methods used with Euroclear Bank and Clearstream Banking

---

The development of the eurobond market in the 1960s created a deregulated international market for issuers and investors, considerably increasing the amount of cross-border bond trading.

ICSDs came into being initially to meet the need for integrated clearing, settlement and custody services for eurobonds, a market that was certificate-based and, thus, paper-intensive. The ICSDs have now expanded the range of services that they offer and overlap and compete in many areas with the custodian community.

This has created competition among service providers in some instances, with custodians using the services of ICSDs as providers of depository facilities, but also competing with ICSDs in the provision of value-added services (including custody, asset servicing, cash and collateral management, FX, proxy voting and securities lending and borrowing).

The facilities provided by Euroclear Bank and Clearstream Banking are summarised below. You will note that there is significant overlap between the services provided by these two ICSDs.

3.4.1   Euroclear Bank

The Euroclear System was founded in December 1968 by Morgan Guaranty Trust Company of New York, and is headquartered in Brussels.

Sold to the market in 1972, Euroclear is now owned by Euroclear's clients through Euroclear plc. Morgan Guaranty relinquished its banking and operating roles to Euroclear Bank, which was created in 2000 for this purpose. Euroclear Bank has become the world's largest ICSD.

The Euroclear Group currently services thousands of institutional clients across 80 markets worldwide and retail investors in some domestic markets. This client base is composed principally of banks, broker-dealers and investing institutions. Euroclear currently holds securities valued at approximately 27.5 trillion euros in custody on behalf of its clients.

Methods of Holding Stock and Cash at Euroclear Bank

Each Euroclear Bank client has a set of accounts which represent a consolidated logical view of the assets, and the currencies in which they are held, regardless of where they are physically deposited.

Euroclear Bank aims to offer clients a single access point to post-trade services, covering domestic securities from over 40 markets held in dematerialised form. Eligible securities include equities, eurobonds, funds and various other forms of debt instrument, including government bonds, corporate bonds and money market instruments.

Also, securities may be held in immobilised form via one of Euroclear Bank's network of depository banks. Participants hold a depot account with Euroclear Bank which records the securities that they hold. Settlement is by book-entry transfer across these accounts.

Each of the instruments that are eligible for processing in Euroclear Bank has a specialised depository in which they are ultimately held. This is particularly significant for bearer securities, as the specialised depository has to verify the authenticity of any certificates deposited. Cash is held in a cash account with Euroclear Bank in one of the multiple currencies in which Euroclear Bank is active.

Settlement Services

Euroclear Bank provides DVP settlement with simultaneous and irrevocable transfer of securities and cash proceeds. This can be achieved via batch or real-time settlement functionality:

- **Batch process** – runs overnight, and is completed early in the morning of the business day for which settlement is intended.
- **Real-time process** – runs between 01:30 and 19:30 Central European Time (CET) on each business day, for settlement that same day.

Settlement instructions are received via SWIFT, EasyWay (a web-based tool providing access to Euroclear Bank's services) or **EUCLID** (Euroclear Bank's proprietary communication network).

There are three ways that settlement can take place within Euroclear Bank:

- **Internal settlement** is the simplest, as it only involves a debit and credit within participants' accounts.
- **Bridge settlement** involves an exchange of messages with Clearstream Banking across an electronic **bridge**. The first phase of an automated daytime bridge was introduced in June 2004, with the second phase completed successfully in November 2004. The automated daytime bridge is a reflection of growing acceptance in the market that Europe needs to be more integrated, representing an important step towards interoperability of markets in Europe. This facility has enhanced settlement efficiency and gives clients more opportunity to settle bridge transactions that failed during the overnight settlement process.

   Euroclear Bank and Clearstream Banking have undertaken an important and long-awaited programme of enhancements to the bridge settlement. This has resulted in extended deadlines for settlement via the bridge and faster settlement turnaround times. Phase 1 of the release was in September 2015, and introduced an average 25-minute turnaround time; phase 2 was implemented in June 2017 with bridge matching now close to real time.

- **External settlement** involves the exchange of messages with CSDs that are not part of the Euroclear group. Receipt of bearer bonds for settlement is also possible, but the bonds may be frozen until they are authenticated by the specialised depository.

Custody Services

Euroclear Bank provides a range of asset servicing facilities, which include:

- safekeeping
- administration of interest, dividend and redemption payments
- assistance with recovery of tax withheld
- exercise of warrants and other options
- assistance with corporate actions
- treasury and FX services
- proxy voting services
- securities lending and borrowing services, and
- triparty collateral management.

Euroclear Bank also provides a comprehensive suite of order management, settlement and asset-servicing for investment funds via its FundSettle platform.

3.4.2 Clearstream Banking

Clearstream International was formed in 1999 by the merger of Cedel International and Deutsche Börse Clearing. It has banking status and operates from offices in Luxembourg, Frankfurt, London, New York, Hong Kong and Dubai. Cedel Group was created in September 1970, its shareholders consisting of more than 90 of the world's major financial institutions, principally banks. There was a holding company, Cedel International, with subsidiary companies, including Cedel Bank, which contained the core clearing and settlement business. Cedel Bank was based in Luxembourg, an operating centre that Clearstream Banking Luxembourg retains today.

Clearstream Banking operates settlement and custodian services on behalf of approximately 2,500 customers across 50 markets and in 110 global locations. It settles over 250,000 transactions per day across 150,000 securities. The businesses at Clearstream's chief operational centres are known as Clearstream Banking Luxembourg (CBL) and Clearstream Banking Frankfurt (CBF).

Customers can access Clearstream Banking's clearing, settlement and custody services through a range of avenues:

- CreationConnect which provides a real-time suite of connectivity channels for users to link to Clearstream Banking. The transition to CreationConnect was completed in July 2005, and CEDCOM, Clearstream Banking's legacy proprietary communication system, was decommissioned at that time,
- Creation via SWIFT, offering a message-based solution using ISO 15022,
- Standalone access via CreationOnline.

Via these communication gateways, clients can access a range of transaction processing and custody services offered through the CreationOnline package, including the following:

Settlement

Fully automated overnight and daytime DVP settlement processing is via Clearstream Banking's CreationOnline settlement engine. This single system offers a central point of entry for settlement on a range of markets. Bridge settlement supports the exchange of settlement messages with Euroclear Bank across the electronic bridge.

In March 2008, Clearstream Banking launched a new-generation post-trade infrastructure processing environment for its ICSD activities, extending real-time processing across the full instruction life-cycle throughout the daytime settlement period. With this development, Clearstream Banking handles all steps for the transaction life-cycle that impact market efficiency within this processing environment on a real-time basis. This includes instruction validation, matching, domestic market instruction handling and confirmations, instruction sequencing, collateral management and customer reporting.

This creates a framework through which users can optimise movement of securities and collateral across a daytime processing window extending from 21:30 on the business day preceding settlement (SD-1) to 20:00 CET. Clearstream Banking's programme of settlement extension has seen its ICSD settlement deadline extend to 21:30 CET and also now provides full coverage of the North American business day, improving cash and securities settlement deadlines for its North American and Latin American links.

Custody Services

Clearstream Banking provides a range of asset-servicing facilities, which include:

- safekeeping,
- administration of interest, dividend and redemption payments,
- assistance with recovery of tax withheld,
- exercise of warrants and other options,
- assistance with corporate actions,
- proxy voting services,
- securities lending and borrowing services,
- triparty collateral management,
- treasury and FX services, and
- issues handling.

Clearstream Banking also provides a comprehensive suite of order management and settlement services to investment funds via its Vestima+ and Central Facility for Funds (CFF).

3.5   TARGET2-Securities (T2S)

Learning Objective

2.2.6   Know the purpose and functions of Target2-Securities (T2S)

In 2006, the ECB announced a plan to launch a centralised settlement platform, known as TARGET2-Securities (T2S), for the settlement of euro-denominated securities transactions (equities, fixed income, investment funds) and some non-euro-denominated securities transactions, in central bank money. In March 2009, 27 CSDs signed a memorandum of understanding confirming that – subject to appropriate contractual arrangements being arranged with the Eurosystem (the ECB and national central banks of countries that have adopted the euro) as owner and operator of the platform – they would outsource securities settlement to the T2S platform. CSDs outside the eurozone will also have freedom to outsource settlement of securities transactions to the T2S operator, providing that their central bank agrees to make its currency available to settle securities transactions via the platform. The objective of the T2S project is to integrate and harmonise the diverse settlement structures that exist in Europe. The industry's infrastructure is highly fragmented and T2S aims to reduce the costs of cross-border securities settlement and to increase competition and choice among the providers of settlement and clearing services in Europe. It is seen as yet another vital step in the objective of the EC in the creation of a single market for financial services in the EU.

An important landmark for the project was set for June 2012, by which time CSDs were required to confirm whether they would make a legally binding commitment to the T2S project according to terms laid down in the T2S framework agreement. This framework agreement details the project governance and the legal conditions under which CSDs will outsource settlement of securities transactions to T2S. In a public announcement on 8 May 2012, the ECB confirmed that nine CSDs had signed the framework agreement – collectively accounting for approximately two-thirds of the securities transactions settled in euros. These were:

* Bank of Greece Securities Settlement System (Greece)
* Clearstream Banking (Germany)
* Depozitarul Central (Romania)
* Iberclear (Spain)
* LuxCSD (Luxembourg)
* Monte Titoli (Italy)
* National Bank of Belgium Securities Settlement System (Belgium)
* VP LUX Sárl (Luxembourg), and
* VP Securities A/S (Denmark).

A further 15 CSDs signed the framework agreement prior to the 30 June deadline. The additional signatories were:

* Eesti Väärtpaberikeskus (Estonia)
* Central Depository (Bulgaria)
* Centrálny Depozitár Cenných Papierov (Slovakia)
* Cyprus Stock Exchange

- Euroclear Belgium
- Euroclear Finland
- Euroclear France
- Euroclear Nederland
- Interbolsa – Sociedade Gestora de Sistemas de Liquidação e de Sistemas Centralizados de Valores Mobiliários (Portugal)
- KDD – Centralna Klirinško Depotna Družba, d.d. (Slovenia)
- KELER – Központi Elszámolóház és Értéktár Zrt. (Hungary)
- Lietuvos Centrinis Vertybinių Popierių Depozitoriumas (Lithuania)
- Malta Stock Exchange
- Oesterreichische Kontrollbank Aktiengesellschaft (Austria), and
- SIX SIS (Switzerland).

The 24 CSDs that signed up before the 30 June deadline have had their joining fees waived, equivalent to 25% of the total fee paid by the CSD in its first year after joining. The nine that signed up before 30 April also had their first three months of fees waived.

Also, central banks outside the euro area were asked – under the terms of the currency participation agreement – to confirm whether they will make their currency available to support settlement of securities transactions in T2S. To date, just one central bank outside of the euro area, namely the Danish Central Bank, has signed the T2S currency participation agreement. Danmarks Nationalbank will make the Danish krone available in T2S in 2018. In the UK, the Bank of England's position not to commit to the T2S project has been apparent for some time.

The ECB governing council has assigned the development and operation of T2S to four European central banks, namely Deutsche Bundesbank, Banco de España, Banque de France and Banca d'Italia, commonly known collectively as 4CB.

The Eurosystem central banks participating in the T2S project conducted extensive testing on the T2S platform during mid-2014. CSDs began a detailed testing programme in October 2014, including testing communications with the T2S platform, and commenced user testing with CSD participants in Q1 2015.

In a meeting of CSDs in December 2015, agreement was reached to follow a migration plan that would allow a migration wave in September 2016, which included the Euroclear ESES CSDs. The next phase, which includes Clearstream Banking, will migrate on 6 February 2017. Clearstream Banking migrated on 6 February 2017 and the final wave was Iberclear (Spain) and the Baltic CSDs in September 2017.

3.5.1 The CSD Regulation (CSDR) in the EU

Learning Objective

2.2.7   Know the impact of CSDR on European markets

On 15 April 2014, the Regulation on Settlement and Central Securities Depositories (known as the CSD Regulation, CSDR) was adopted by the European Parliament. This new Regulation entered into force on 17 September 2014 and is designed, alongside the Regulation on OTC derivatives, CCPs and trade repositories (European Market Infrastructure Regulation – EMIR) that entered into force on 16 August 2012, and the Markets in Financial Instruments Directive (MiFID II), to provide a framework in which systemically important securities infrastructures (trading venues, CCPs and CSDs) are subject to common rules on a European level (see also chapter 3, section 3.6).

Since the global financial crisis, the EU has conducted an evaluation of each stage of the securities transaction life-cycle to identify points of weakness and to ensure that financial structures are in place that will minimise the chance of future disorder. With experience gained during the crisis, financial authorities in the EU have deepened their interest in post-trade infrastructure, recognising the importance of a market infrastructure that minimises post-trade risk, that is robust under stressful conditions and that serves the needs of the end investor.

The EC notes that, while typically safe and efficient within national borders, CSDs commonly operate less safely and efficiently across borders, dictating that investors face higher risks and costs for cross-border investments. In the absence of an efficient single market for settlement, important barriers to efficient post-trade operations continue to exist, including inconsistencies in CSD operating rules and licensing requirements, constraints on the access that issuers have to CSDs in other jurisdictions, and limitations on CSDs' ability to compete effectively for the delivery of services. The result, notes the Commission, is a very fragmented market.

The CSDR was introduced to increase safety in the system and to open the market for CSD services. Among a range of objectives, it aims to harmonise settlement periods and settlement discipline regimes across the EU. It proposes that all transferable securities should be recorded in book-entry form at a CSD prior to being traded on a regulated market or MTF. And it proposes a common set of rules governing CSDs' operations and services across the EU – thereby ensuring that CSDs will benefit from uniform licensing requirements and an EU-wide passport for provision of services, thus helping to eliminate barriers to access.

Thus, a noteworthy feature of the CSD Regulation is that it contains a number of provisions that do not relate explicitly to CSD activities, but instead deal more broadly with long-standing points of inefficiency in securities trading and post-trade activities. These include, among others, harmonisation of settlement periods, the introduction of fails coverage mechanisms and measures relating to dematerialisation of securities traded on a regulated market. In doing so, CSDR builds on the groundwork laid down by other important industry initiatives, including the work of the European Commission's Clearing and Settlement Advisory and Monitoring Expert Group (CESAME), the Giovannini Group (which identified 15 barriers to efficient cross-border clearing and settlement in the EU – see chapter 3, section 3.6), and the provisions of the 2006 EU Code of Conduct on Clearing and Settlement. Importantly, CSDR recognises the need for a consistent regulatory approach to settlement systems and settlement processes in preparation for the launch of the Eurosystem's T2S project, a centralised platform for the settlement of securities transactions in the EU.

Under CSDR Article 5, the settlement period for securities transactions has been harmonised and set at a maximum of two business days after the trading day for securities traded on stock exchanges or other regulated markets (previously two to three days were necessary for most securities transactions in Europe). Twenty-seven markets migrated to T+2 settlement on 6 October 2014. Spain is yet to adopt a T+2 cycle for fixed-income settlement, but equities settlement moved to a T+2 cycle in September 2016. Germany already operated a T+2 settlement cycle prior to this date for trades executed and settled between two German counterparties and it has now extended this to T+2 settlement for all securities transactions on regulated markets.

Steps to promote a harmonised T+2 trade-to-settlement framework for listed securities across EU member states have been driven strongly by the ECB in line with its T2S settlement project. To make the T2S platform work efficiently, this requires a common settlement period for traded securities and a harmonised settlement discipline framework.

3.5.2   Settlement Discipline

As well as proposing a harmonised T+2 trade-to-settlement framework for listed securities, CSDR aims to harmonise settlement discipline measures across the EU. These include *ex ante* measures to prevent settlement fails and *ex post* measures to address settlement fails. The key objective, notes the European Commission, is to reduce settlement fails and to discourage any competition that may lower standards of settlement discipline, for example between markets that may have different penalty regimes in place.

In practice, CSDs will typically be required to apply a system of settlement fines to counterparties responsible for late settlement (many CSDs in Europe already operate such a system of penalties). Also, the CSDR imposes a mandatory buy-in process for any security which has not been delivered within four business days of the intended settlement date. This period may be increased to seven days for certain illiquid securities and, in certain circumstances, to 15 days for transactions on small and medium enterprise (SME) growth markets.

3.5.3   Issuer Services

CSDR aims to extend greater choice to securities issuers regarding the CSD that they utilise when issuing securities (the 'issuer CSD'). Previously, securities issuers in some EU member states were required by law to issue certain types of securities, most notably equities, in the national CSD. Article 47 of CSDR introduces the right for issuers to record their securities in any CSD in the EU, along with a right for CSDs to provide services for securities that have been issued under the law of another Member State. This is an important step in order to unlock the full benefits of T2S proposed by the ECB.

However, while CSDR extends new freedoms in this area, we should not assume that all issuers will immediately take advantage of this additional flexibility. In many cases the choice of issuer CSD will not be the primary factor that will determine where an issuer decides to issue securities. Rather, issuers will typically identify an investor base (ie, a community of investors that they will target to buy these securities) and they will then select the most appropriate jurisdiction, listing and trading venue in order to reach out to that investor base.

3.5.4 Provision of Commercial Banking Activities by CSDs

CSDR outlines restrictions on the range of commercial banking activities that a CSD can undertake and provides guidelines on how CSDs should be structured if they wish to provide commercial banking functions.

With the implementation of the Eurosystem's T2S platform, these provisions are likely to become particularly important. When T2S goes live, CSDs are likely to experience a reduction in the revenue that they generate from processing transaction settlements and they will need to generate revenue from other sources. When it announced the T2S project in 2006, the ECB extended an invitation to CSDs to *step up the value chain*' and to compete more actively with the subcustodian community in the delivery of asset servicing functions. To do so, it is important that guidelines are in place through which CSDs can deliver commercial banking services while ensuring that, as key infrastructure entities, CSDs remain robust and secure in their operation.

The guidelines in this area are slightly complex. However, in essence, the CSDR indicates that CSDs should have the ability to offer 'limited-purpose' banking functions, subject to strict regulatory conditions, from the same legal entity that delivers the core CSD functions. Alternatively, a CSD should be able to draw on the services of a limited purpose bank that is not owned or controlled by the CSD. We may picture these two options as follows: (i) an integrated '1+2' model, where a single legal entity provides both core CSD services and commercial (ie, 'value-added') banking services; (ii) a '2+2' model based on two separate legal entities, one providing core CSD services and a separate legal entity providing 'limited purpose' banking services. By ensuring legal separation between core CSD functions and commercial banking services within a CSD group, the aim is to minimise systemic risk and to ensure that, in an emergency situation, asset owners will have prompt access to their securities without these being frozen for an extended period by insolvency procedures.

4. Straight-Through Processing (STP)

Learning Objective

2.3.1   Understand the advantages of straight-through processing (STP)

Straight-through processing (STP) is the automated passage of a financial transaction from execution to settlement without manual intervention.

This process involves the seamless passage of information from the first placement and capture of a trade order through to final settlement. Information should pass electronically to all parties involved in the transaction process (including investment managers, broker-dealers, custodians, exchanges, depositories, registrars and third-party information vendors), employing standard information flows, and technology and processes that are compatible with each other.

4.1   Why is STP Necessary?

There is clear recognition that human intervention in trade processing and asset-servicing procedures is one of the principal sources of error, and therefore of risk and cost, in the financial services industry.

Key concerns include the following:

• In the current financial services environment, some participants still conduct their trade reporting by telephone and fax. This type of reporting requires participants to rekey information, resulting in processing errors, reporting and confirmation delays, and increased potential for settlement failure when compared with automated systems.
• In some companies, front-office trading systems and back-office operations have evolved independently, with weak connectivity between these systems. This limits potential to establish automated end-to-end communication from front to back office without manual intervention.
• Some companies retain their own proprietary systems and procedures for holding data and communicating messages between process areas. Lack of standardisation impedes interconnectivity between participants and ultimately impairs the timely and accurate free flow of information.
• This concern is exacerbated because consolidations in the industry have brought multiple legacy systems under one roof. Often there is poor connectivity between these disparate systems.

In summary, the full benefits of developments in technology and communications cannot be realised without a shift to STP.

4.2   Barriers to Promoting STP

Different jurisdictions maintain their own procedures and legal requirements. Tax regulations, for example, differ significantly across European jurisdictions. Similarly, some types of corporate actions follow markedly different procedures in different markets. This lack of standardisation presents a barrier to handling tax reclaims and corporate actions in a seamless, automated manner.

In a challenging economic climate, participants in the transaction cycle often demand a quick return on investment if they are to commit development resources to automating their systems and promoting an STP culture.

When development money is limited, a small investment manager, for example, may feel that its firm may profit more from updating its front office stock selection technology rather than in automating process flows through its operations department. Unless STP is seen to deliver immediate cost benefits, it may remain low in the list of development priorities for some investment companies.

New standards (eg, ISO 15022 and ISO 20022, FIX protocol, see section 4.4) have been introduced that facilitate the automation of trade processing and asset servicing procedures. However, these will only deliver STP if used in the correct way.

For example, some companies have failed to make the best use of the structured message types available under ISO 15022, with appropriate fields in the structured message not completed in the correct way. It is still possible to send typed instructions using free-format message types (eg, MT 599) available in ISO 15022, effectively sending instructions as an electronic fax. This demands that the instruction is read manually by the recipient and that information is rekeyed into its own system.

4.3 The STP/T+1 Initiative

One of the key drivers that has given momentum to efforts to promote STP has been the STP/T+1 initiative, a project conceived by the Securities Industry Association (SIA) and the Canadian Capital Markets Association (CCMA) to address rising trading volumes in the US and Canadian securities markets. The original goal of the STP/T+1 programme was to move from T+3 to T+1 settlement in the US and Canada by 2005. In practice, the challenge of moving to a next-day settlement cycle (ie, T+1) was abandoned in October 2002, but the SIA and CCMA have continued with their efforts to promote STP in their respective markets.

Why was the T+1 goal put on hold? Because, ultimately, the SIA and CCMA felt that the 2005 deadline, which had initially been important in galvanising market participants, had gradually become an obstacle to the real job in hand, namely to improve levels of STP within the industry.

A T+3 settlement cycle offers counterparties time to ensure that their settlement instructions are correct and sent on time, that instructions are matched, and that cash and securities are in position to ensure effective settlement on settlement date. However, in a T+1 settlement cycle, the time window that exists for ensuring that these prerequisites are in place is much narrower. Fund managers and broker-dealers must agree terms of settlement and dispatch settlement instructions to custodians on trade date. Moreover, efforts to shorten the T+3 settlement cycle may be impractical in markets where certificates need to be dematerialised to support electronic settlement (see chapter 3).

A reduced settlement cycle has the advantage that it reduces counterparty risk, since credit exposure to the counterparty is shorter in a T+1 cycle. However, on the negative side, this may increase the likelihood that trades may fail because the timely dispatch of instructions, affirmation/matching of instructions and positioning of cash and securities may not be completed effectively in the shorter cycle. In short, you may reduce risk and cost on the one hand (through lower counterparty/credit risk) and increase risk and cost (through higher fail rates and repair costs) on the other.

As noted in section 3.5.1, EU markets moved to a T+2 settlement cycle in October 2014 for securities transactions conducted on a regulated market or MTF. This represents one of a number of important provisions contained in the EU CSD Regulation (CSDR).

In line with many participants within the securities industry, the SIA adjudged that, while T+1 settlement may be a realistic goal for the industry in the future, it is not currently an appropriate time to be trying to put next-day settlement into practice. Rather, the industry must make further progress in its transition towards universal STP before a T+1 business case can be considered to be a realistic objective.

4.4 Financial Information Exchange (FIX) Protocol Messaging

Learning Objective

2.3.3 Know the features and benefits of Financial Information Exchange (FIX) protocol messaging

The Financial Information Exchange (FIX) protocol provides a standardised format for the electronic communication of pre-trade and trade execution messages. Established originally in 1992 as a bilateral communications framework between Fidelity Investments and Salomon Brothers for equities trading, the FIX protocol has been developed at the industry level through collaboration between investment managers, broker-dealers, exchanges, IT vendors and other key participants to provide a standard for communication of trade information between buy-side investment companies and sell-side broker-dealer firms.

Although the use of FIX is not universal across the industry, FIX is integral to many order management and trading systems, and efforts continue to encourage firms to use FIX to communicate their trade information.

Since its inception as a protocol designed to promote standardised communication and STP for equities trading, FIX protocol is gathering momentum as it continues to expand across the FX, fixed-income and derivative markets.

5. Society for Worldwide Interbank Financial Telecommunication (SWIFT)

Learning Objective

2.3.2 Know the features and benefits of SWIFT and SWIFT messaging

SWIFT has played a central role in promoting the use of standardised and secure messaging services and interface software within the financial services industry since its inception in 1973.

The 1960s saw rapid growth in international banking business, brought about by the expansion of international trade. Until that time, administration and control systems were paper-based and the growth in business volumes put increasing pressure on these systems. To improve business efficiency, banks started to install computer systems. Each bank had its own system, which improved internal efficiency, but a lack of common standards meant that one bank's system could not communicate seamlessly with the proprietary system developed by another bank. Therefore, interbank payments and transfers commonly relied on telex, mail or physical delivery.

To address these inefficiencies, 239 banks from 15 countries formed a co-operative to, as they termed it, automate the telex. This cooperative was named the Society for Worldwide Interbank Financial Telecommunication, or SWIFT. It was registered in Brussels and became operational in May 1977. The goal was to develop a series of standardised financial messages that could be employed to transmit transaction instructions and data between participants securely and efficiently.

In the early days, SWIFT hoped that, ultimately, business use might grow to 300,000 messages per day. In reality, daily messages sometimes now hit 20 million, with SWIFT serving 10,000 members and participants in more than 200 countries. SWIFT's business objectives include:

- to work in partnership with its members to provide low-cost, competitive financial processing and communications services of the highest security and reliability,
- to contribute to the commercial success of its members through greater automation of the end-to-end financial transaction process, based on its expertise in message processing and setting financial standards,
- to capitalise on its position as an international open forum for the world's financial institutions to address industry-level threats, issues and opportunities.

SWIFT's worldwide community includes banks, broker/dealers and investment managers, as well as their market infrastructures in payments, securities, treasury and trade. SWIFT operates around the clock, 24 hours a day, seven days a week. Its main areas of activity are:

- **Payments** – the systems to support bank instructions, customer instructions, advice, statements, clearing and settlement. SWIFT provides the network infrastructure for systems in several countries and interlinks the participating banks in TARGET2 (see chapter 3, section 3.2.5). Almost 60% of message volume in its core FIN message type relates to payments. SWIFT is in the process of developing SWIFT global payments innovation (SWIFT gpi) which is due to improve the speed, transparency and end-to-end tracking of cross-border payments. At the time of writing, over 150 banks from Europe, Asia-Pacific, Africa and the Americas have already signed up and more are expected to join.
- **Securities** – providing messaging communication to support trade confirmation, clearing and settlement, and custodial operations. SWIFT provides network services to CREST. Just over 30% of FIN message volume relates to securities.
- **FX, money markets, treasury services** – providing the systems to support confirmation messaging, matching, bilateral or multilateral netting and reporting of treasury and FX trades.

SWIFT, along with BT, employs standardised message formats suitable for automated data-handling that are designed to minimise language and interpretation problems. SWIFT messages present data in a structured manner, facilitating STP.

SWIFT has been heavily involved in the implementation of the ISO 15022 messaging standards, introduced in November 2002, which established a common format for securities-related messages. It has also been active in promoting the adoption of the newer and more flexible ISO 20022 standard messaging over its network, which ultimately is likely to be the successor to ISO 15022 standard financial services messaging.

SWIFT supports ten categories of message types grouped by business use. These are listed below for informational purposes. (*You are not required to learn these for your examination.*)

Category	Message Group
0	General Information
1	Customer Payments and Cheques
2	Financial Institution Transfers
3	Foreign Exchange, Money Markets and Derivatives
4	Collection and Cash Letters
5	Securities Markets
6	Commodities and Reference Data
7	Documentary Credits and Guarantees
8	Travellers Cheques
9	Cash Management and Customer Status

Category 5 – Securities Messages

Securities messages can be classified into eight categories, as follows:

1. Trade instructions and confirmations.
2. Settlement instructions and confirmations.
3. Corporate actions and event notices.
4. Capital and income advice.
5. Statements.
6. Securities lending and borrowing.
7. Inter-depository clearing systems.
8. General.

End of Chapter Questions

Think of an answer for each question and refer to the appropriate section for confirmation.

1. What is:
    a. an investment manager?
    b. an institutional investor?
    c. an individual investor?
    Answer Reference: Section 1.1

2. What is a custodian? Why does an investor appoint a custodian to administer and safekeep its assets?
    Answer Reference: Section 2

3. What is a global custodian? Summarise the range of services offered by a global custodian to an investor client.
    Answer Reference: Section 2.1.1

4. What is a subcustodian? In what circumstances will a subcustodian be employed and what services does it provide?
    Answer Reference: Section 2.1.2

5. Summarise the relative advantages and disadvantages of appointing a local or a regional custody provider.
    Answer Reference: Sections 2.1.2

6. What is the purpose of a custody agreement signed between a custodian and an investor client? Summarise the main elements that a custody agreement is likely to address.
    Answer Reference: Section 2.2.1

7. What is the purpose of an SLA between a global custodian and a subcustodian? What are the key service elements addressed by the SLA?
    Answer Reference: Section 2.2.3

8. What is the purpose of an RFP in the selection of a global custodian by an investor? What are the key elements addressed in an RFP?
    Answer Reference: Section 2.3

9. What is:
    a. an immobilised security, and
    b. a dematerialised security?
    Answer Reference: Section 3.2

10. List the CSDs and settlement systems employed in each of the core markets addressed in this course.
    Answer Reference: Section 3.3

11. List three mechanisms through which settlement can take place within Euroclear Bank.
Answer Reference: Section 3.4.1

12. What function is served by the electronic bridge between Clearstream Banking and Euroclear Bank?
Answer Reference: Section 3.4.1

13. List three communication gateways through which customers may access Clearstream Banking's CREATION system.
Answer Reference: Section 3.4.2

14. Why is STP a requirement for improving efficiency, and reducing risk and cost, in the securities industry?
Answer Reference: Section 4.1

15. What is SWIFT and what are its main areas of activity?
Answer Reference: Section 5

Chapter Three
Settlement Characteristics

This syllabus area will provide approximately 11 of the 50 examination questions

If an investor decides to invest in securities, they will take a decision about how they wish to allocate their investment money across different types of security. This is known as asset allocation. They must decide, for example, how they wish to divide their investment pool across equities (domestic and international), government bonds, corporate bonds, and other categories of security. They may also invest in asset classes such as property, commodities, hedge funds and private equity.

Having decided how they wish to allocate their money, the investor must decide whether they wish to:

1. manage these investments themselves, or
2. appoint investment managers who specialise in investing in asset types and investment styles required by the investor.

It is common for both institutional investors and private investors to employ specialist fund managers to manage investments on their behalf. However, some large pensions and life insurance firms do manage investments in-house, and some own fund management companies.

Having outlined the process through which an investor allocates their pool of investment money across different asset classes, we will now examine the mechanisms through which assets are bought and sold and held in safekeeping, and how legal title to the security is registered and transferred between owners.

1.   The Trade Cycle

The process of investing money in securities (eg, equities, government bonds, corporate bonds) will involve a number of steps:

- **Trading** mechanisms were described in chapter 1. The process of buying or selling an instrument is generally termed execution, representing the procedure through which counterparties agree to conduct a financial transaction on specified terms.
- **Pre-settlement and clearing**. As soon as a trade has been executed, a number of procedures and checks must be conducted before settlement can be completed. These include matching the trade instructions supplied by each counterparty to ensure that the details they have supplied for the trade correspond. It also involves conducting checks to ensure that the seller has sufficient securities to deliver and that the buyer has sufficient funds to cover the purchase cost.
- **Settlement** is the process through which legal title (ie, ownership) of a security is transferred from seller to buyer in exchange for the equivalent value in cash. Usually, these two transfers should occur simultaneously.
- **Post-settlement** entails the management of failed transactions and the subsequent accounting of trades.

2. Pre-Settlement

2.1 Matching Settlement Instructions

Learning Objective

3.1.1 Understand the data required for matching of settlement instructions

When a trade has been executed, a key step in the management of risk in the post-execution, pre-settlement stage is for the two sides to the trade to compare trade details and to eliminate any mismatches, prior to the exchange of cash and securities.

The matching of the buyer's and seller's trade data is typically conducted at two levels:

1. Trading counterparties compare trade details. This may take place bilaterally, via matching facilities extended by the securities settlement system (at the central securities depository [CSD] for example), or via a third-party central matching facility that will compare trade details electronically and issue a report on matching status (ie, whether matched or unmatched). Trades conducted via an electronic order book will effectively be auto-matched – matching engine software is integrated into the electronic order management technology that will provide automated matching of buyers' and sellers' orders in the order book. For centrally cleared transactions, matched instructions may be forwarded to the central counterparty (CCP) for clearing (see below).
2. Custodians acting on behalf of buyer and seller will compare settlement instructions in order to identify potential mismatches prior to settlement date.

Generally, the following data is required for the matching of settlement instructions:

- Title of security.
- Security identification code.
- Counterparty details and account numbers (ie, custodian depot/**nostro account** details, business identifier code (BIC).
- Trade date.
- Trade price.
- Whether a purchase or sale of securities.
- Quantity of security.
- Settlement currency.
- Net settlement value (the cash value to be paid or received).
- Trading conditions (eg, ex-dividend, ex-rights).
- The number of days and the amount of accrued interest, if a fixed-income security.
- Settlement date.
- Settlement method (ie, DvP, FOP).

2.2   Clearing

Learning Objective

3.1.2   Understand the process of clearing (matching and the assumption of risk – trade for trade versus central counterparty [CCP])

Clearing (or clearance) is the process through which the obligations held by buyer and seller to a trade are defined and legally formalised. In simple terms, this procedure establishes what each of the counterparties expects to receive when the trade is settled. It also defines the obligations each must fulfil, in terms of delivering securities or funds, for the trade to settle successfully.

Specifically, the clearing process includes:

- Recording key trade information so that counterparties can agree on its terms.
- Formalising the legal obligation between counterparties.
- Matching and confirming trade details.
- Agreeing procedures for settling the transaction.
- Calculating settlement obligations and sending out settlement instructions to the brokers, custodians and CSD.
- Managing **margin** and making margin calls. This relates to collateral paid to the clearing agent by counterparties to guarantee their positions against default up to settlement.

Trades may be cleared bilaterally between the trading counterparties or via a CCP that interposes itself between buyer and seller. When trades are cleared bilaterally, each trading party bears a direct credit risk against each counterparty that it trades with. Hence, it will typically bear direct liability for any losses incurred through counterparty default (see below and chapter 6).

CCP services are available in a range of markets in order to mitigate this risk. For example, LCH.Clearnet provides CCP services in the UK and NYSE Euronext European markets for trading in equity, derivatives and energy products, for platforms trading the majority of euro-denominated and sterling bond and **repo** products, along with commodity and energy derivatives and the bilaterally traded interbank interest rate swaps market.

In the US, clearing of broker-to-broker trades in equities, corporate bonds, municipal bonds, unit investment trusts (UITs) and exchange-traded funds (ETFs) takes place through the **National Securities Clearing Corporation (NSCC)**, a subsidiary of the **Depository Trust and Clearing Corporation (DTCC)**. Eurex Clearing AG, which is part of Deutsche Börse Group, provides a CCP service for exchange-traded equities executed on Xetra that are denominated in euros and listed on Xetra. Also, ISE Xetra is the electronic trading system for the Irish Stock Exchange, and Eurex Clearing provides clearing services for trades conducted via this system. In its role as clearing house, Eurex Clearing additionally assures the fulfilment and clearing of trades on the Eurex derivatives exchange, Eurex Bonds and Eurex Repo.

Since the Markets in Financial Instruments Directive (MiFID) implementation, a number of new CCP facilities have been established in Europe, predominantly to clear trade flow from **multilateral trading facility (MTF)** platforms. These CCPs include the European Multilateral Clearing Facility and EuroCCP, which merged in December 2013 to form EuroCCP N.V.

2.3   Clearing via a Central Counterparty (CCP)

A CCP interposes itself between the counterparties to a trade, becoming the buyer to every seller and the seller to every buyer. As a result, buyer and seller interact with the CCP and remain anonymous to each other. This process is known as novation.

The introduction of a CCP can offer a number of benefits for its members:

1. The credit risk that market participants previously held against each counterparty that they trade with is substituted by a single credit risk held against the CCP.
2. Hence, clearing relationships are streamlined and counterparty risk is significantly reduced. Each market participant communicates only with the CCP in managing risk mitigation measures (eg, requesting collateral or margin payments), rather than managing a series of bilateral relationships with each counterparty that it deals with.
3. The risk of default by the CCP is, typically, significantly lower than that of individual counterparties. A CCP is expected by regulatory authorities to maintain effective risk management controls that are sufficient to withstand severe shocks, including defaults by one or more of its participants.
4. Since the CCP assumes the obligations and acquires the rights of settlement, it is obliged to finalise settlement between participants, even if a participant fails to meet its settlement obligations. In these situations, CCPs will typically provide a settlement guarantee scheme through which: (a) the loss is compensated with the defaulting participant's property, such as its clearing fund deposited with the CCP; and (b) if this amount is insufficient, the loss may be met through mutual guarantee by the other participants.

All trades cleared at the CCP must be cleared via a registered clearing member. An individual clearing member (ICM) is a firm that is eligible to clear only its own trade obligations. A general clearing member (GCM) is eligible to clear its own obligations and/or to clear trades on behalf of other trading firms. By appointing a GCM to clear trades on its behalf, a trading firm can focus on its core trading activities – and this eliminates the need to meet the capital requirements and technical investment necessary to clear its own trades at the CCP. In these circumstances, the trading firm will assume non-clearing member (NCM) status, allowing it to trade in its own name while employing the services of a GCM to clear its trades at the CCP.

With systemic risk uppermost in the minds of the financial authorities, regulators are increasingly keen to promote the use of CCPs across a wide range of financial products. While this does not eliminate the risk of institutions going into default, it does spread this risk across all participants, and makes these risks progressively easier to monitor and regulate. The risk controls extended by a CCP effectively provide an early warning system to financial regulators of impending risks and are an important tool in efforts to contain these risks within manageable limits.

The European Market Infrastructure Regulation (EMIR) establishes a set of common organisational, conduct of business and prudential standards for CCPs with activities in European Union (EU) member states.

2.4   Netting

Learning Objective

3.1.4   Understand netting in pre-settlement

Netting occurs when trading partners agree to offset their positions or obligations. By doing so, they reduce a large number of individual positions to a smaller number of positions (or even a single position), and it is on this netted position that the two trading partners settle their outstanding obligations to transfer cash or securities.

Besides reducing transaction costs and communication expenses, netting is important because it reduces credit and liquidity risks (refer to chapter 6 for further explanation of different types of risk).

By netting the settlement obligations held by its members, a CCP may improve the efficiency of securities and funds transfer, and may boost liquidity within the system. This may also reduce the credit risk exposure and collateralisation requirements borne by its members. Rather than market participants having to settle securities and cash on a trade-by-trade (gross) basis with each of the counterparties that it conducts business with during the trading day, the CCP will net off each participant's respective sales and purchases to a single transfer of securities and a single transfer of cash (see below). A CSD may also offer settlement-netting functions in some markets.

From a liquidity risk standpoint, netting reduces requirements for a particular stock. Imagine a similar scenario where US$1 million and US$900,000 worth of shares in a company were to be exchanged. Under trade-by-trade arrangements, each counterparty would need to have access to this gross quantity of stock, when in practice only US$100,000 of stock would actually be exchanged between the counterparties. Netting allows counterparties to offset their mutual obligations, and this is particularly advantageous when the stock is illiquid and may be difficult and expensive to secure.

While we have outlined the benefits extended by CCPs in this section, the introduction of a CCP may not always be welcomed by all market participants. The costs of developing a CCP can be substantial and will typically need to be borne, at least in part, by clearing members. Trading parties will need to bear the cost of CCP fees and the associated cost of putting up collateral at the CCP. Furthermore, netting of trades reduces volumes passing through to settlement, thereby reducing the transaction-based income that accrues to settlement agents, unless they raise their settlement fees to adjust for this drop. CCPs typically bring added surety and efficiency, but the benefits that ensue need to be carefully weighed up against the costs involved.

2.5 Automating the Functions Between Execution and Settlement

Learning Objective

3.1.3 Understand the role of third-party service providers in the pre-settlement process: Omgeo; TRAX; Traiana; SWIFT Accord

While some firms do continue to match trades locally, the use of central **trade-matching** facilities has become increasingly widespread.

Several firms have introduced facilities designed to centralise and automate trade processing in the post-execution, pre-settlement arena.

Omgeo, a subsidiary of the DTCC, introduced its Omgeo **Central Trade Manager (CTM)** and Omgeo Oasys-Tradematch facilities in 2001 in order to support centralised matching and communication between buy-side and sell-side customers and their respective settlement agents.

The Omgeo solution consists of:

- a central matching system (eg, the Omgeo CTM) that notifies each entity of settlement from the same source,
- a central static database of settlement instructions (Alert) which are applied automatically to transactions.

Standard settlement instructions (SSIs) should now appear on the electronic trade confirmation (ETC) as they are attached with Alert.

Settlement instructions will only pass to a subcustodian/agent bank if the Omgeo participant has a direct custody relationship with that party. Otherwise, settlement instructions will go via the global custodian who will, in turn, instruct the subcustodian/agent bank. This arrangement will ensure that the global custodian's records remain aligned with those of the sub-custodian.

With the launch of the Omgeo Connect facility, buy-side customers can monitor trades from point of execution through to settlement in Omgeo, and in third-party systems, providing a single point of entry for equity and fixed-income trades matched via Omgeo CTM and Omgeo Oasys-Tradematch.

TRAX, a matching system developed by the International Capital Market Association (ICMA), was launched in 1989 to provide a one-stop trade matching and regulatory reporting system. It was designed to eliminate the costs and risks associated with paper-based trade confirmation. TRAX provides electronic real-time post-trade matching for a range of OTC-traded instruments, including bonds, equities, derivatives and repo trades. TRAX was acquired by MarketAxess in 2013, and was previously owned and operated by Euroclear Bank – between 2009 and 2012.

Automation improves processing times by eliminating the requirement to send information back and forth manually between parties and by reducing the errors inherent in manual processing. At its most sophisticated, automation allows manual intervention to be eliminated from post-trade processing, enabling trade data to be entered only once, and for this data to be employed at each stage that it is required in the straight-through processing (STP) process flow from execution through to trade settlement.

Efforts to promote automation in the post-execution, pre-settlement space have been supported by key advances in messaging and communication.

The Financial Information Exchange (FIX) protocol provides a standardised format for the electronic communication of pre-trade and trade execution messages (see chapter 2, section 4.4).

SWIFT offers a suite of standardised electronic trade confirmation messages, extending ETC to an expanding number of investment management companies, global broker-dealers and banks. This allows firms that have already invested in connecting to SWIFT, typically for cash and securities settlement and **reconciliation**, for example, to build on the SWIFT-compatible infrastructure that they have in place, in order to extend STP in the trade confirmation area (see chapter 2, section 5). For example, **SWIFT Accord** is a central electronic trade data matching service for equity and fixed-income trades. This solution can be used between custodians and executing brokers to match trades originating from investment managers, as well as between executing brokers to confirm and match OTC trades that are not automatically cleared by an exchange.

Traiana, a subsidiary of inter-dealer broker ICAP, provides a comprehensive electronic network to support automation of trade matching and confirmation and to facilitate STP of clearing, settlement and other post-trade activities for a range of exchange-traded and OTC transactions (including equities, fixed income, FX, derivatives and contract for difference [CFD] trades).

A number of technology vendors, including SmartStream, SunGard, Trace Financial and Broadridge City Networks, have developed ETC technology designed to support and interface with ETC initiatives outlined above.

3.   Settlement

Settlement is the process through which legal title (ie, ownership) of a security is transferred from seller to buyer in exchange for the equivalent value in cash. Ideally, these two transfers should occur simultaneously.

3.1   Financial Institutions in the Settlement Process

Learning Objective

3.2.1   Know the role of the following types of financial institutions in the settlement process: brokers; investment banks; investment managers; custodians; sub-custodians; central counterparty (CCP) clearing houses and clearing members; international central securities depositories (ICSDs) and central securities depositories (CSDs)

To understand the roles played by key financial institutions in the settlement process, it may be useful to break the settlement life-cycle down into its component parts. For a cross-border trade, the key elements commonly are:

Order Placement

1.   The investment manager places an order with its broker.

Trade Execution

2.   The broker executes the client's order, either via a stock exchange or MTF, via a systematic internaliser, or OTC with another counterparty. If it is a cross-border trade, this global market maker may use a local market maker to execute the trade.
3.   The broker notifies the investment manager of the trade using ETC or manual communication such as fax or telephone.
4.   An execution can take place via the counterparty's own bespoke electronic trading systems.

Confirmation/Affirmation

5.   If the trade is a block trade, the investment manager notifies the broker of how the purchased securities are to be allocated across different accounts. On receipt of this information, the broker will issue a trade confirmation.
6.   The investment manager will check the trade details and, if these are correct, it will send an affirmation message to the broker.

Settlement Instructions

7.   The investment manager sends a settlement instruction to the global custodian, notifying the custodian of the settlement details.
8.   The global custodian will instruct its subcustodian to settle the trade, or it may settle the trade itself if it acts as its own settlement agent in that market. The trade will settle at a local CSD, or, rarely, physically, depending on the form in which the instrument is held.

Positioning of Cash and Securities

9. For CSD-eligible trades, the settlement agent sends settlement instructions to the CSD. These are generally matched at the CSD against settlement instructions submitted by the counterparty.

10. The CSD will send notification of those that match, and any trades that fail to match. Any mismatches must be investigated and resolved.

11. If a successful match is found, the trade will be queued and will go forward for settlement. For trade settlement to be completed successfully, the necessary cash and securities must be in position on the settlement date to discharge the settlement obligations of the respective counterparties. This process is known as **positioning**.

12. The settlement agent will receive notification from the CSD of whether successful settlement has taken place. This settlement notification is communicated by the subcustodian to the global custodian and then back to the investment manager.

Investigation and Repair of Trade Fails

13. Failed trades are investigated and resolved.

Given that trade confirmation, affirmation and settlement instructions pass through a large number of hands before final settlement, there is a need to exercise considerable vigilance to ensure that settlement details are correct and sent to the appropriate parties.

Indeed, the settlement instructions have to be correct between a large number of parties. The investor must instruct its global custodian correctly. For a cross-border trade, the global custodian will send settlement instructions to its subcustodian, which will, in turn, send settlement instructions to the CSD (or ICSD, if settling at Clearstream Banking or Euroclear Bank).

On the broker side, the broker must correctly instruct its settlement agent, which must in turn correctly instruct the CSD or ICSD, as appropriate. The large number of links in the chain dictates that great care must be taken to ensure that instructions are accurate and aligned across each of these participants. This situation is complicated further by the fact that settlement instruction formats can differ across markets, brokerage entities and types of investment instrument (eg, equities, bonds). This lack of harmonisation can generate mismatches if market participants employ non-standard settlement instruction formats.

The requirement to submit settlement instructions is designed to ensure that CSD (or ICSD) members have control over delivery of securities held in their accounts at the CSD (or ICSD) and over delivery of cash payments. This arrangement is designed to ensure that securities are not delivered from settlement members' securities accounts, and cash payments are not raised, without instructions being actively issued by the member concerned and delivered to the CSD (or ICSD) via an approved means of communication.

We noted in chapter 2 that many investment managers opt to focus on their core competency, namely, the task of fund management, and outsource their investment administration to a third party. For example, some investment managers have chosen to outsource their back-office responsibilities to a global custodian.

Many hedge funds employ an investment bank (such as Goldman Sachs, Morgan Stanley) to manage their execution, clearing and settlement functions globally, as well as to provide them with access to credit lines, extend securities lending and borrowing facilities, and provide collateral management, cash management, market information and reporting, and a range of other services.

This bundled function extended to hedge funds is generically known as prime brokerage, and has represented a major growth area for a number of leading investment banks in recent times.

By employing a third-party clearing agent in this way, the investor eliminates the need to become a member of the clearing house itself. In Europe, for example, the clearing agent is typically a clearing member (either directly or via a local agent acting on its behalf) of each of the major clearing houses and is able to provide a pan-European clearing function via a single point of entry, managing the client's collateral, extending credit lines, and covering the requirement (via its agent network) to settle trades.

A number of leading international investment banks provide this style of service package on a global or regional basis.

3.2   Payment Systems

Learning Objective

3.2.2   Know the characteristics of the following cash systems: clearing house interbank payments system (CHIPS); clearing house automated payment system (CHAPS); trans-european automated real-time gross settlement express transfer (TARGET2); Fedwire; continuous linked settlement (CLS)

A range of domestic and international payments systems offer finality of payment in central bank money. In the UK, the C**learing House Automated Payment System (CHAPS)** extends real-time gross settlement (RTGS) payments functionality for sterling interbank payments. In the US, the bulk of large dollar transfers are conducted through the **Clearing House Interbank Payments System (CHIPS)** (a private sector funds transfer network specialising in international payments) and through the Federal Reserve Bank's Fedwire funds transfer service.

3.2.1   The Clearing House Interbank Payments System (CHIPS)

CHIPS is a computerised network for the transfer of US dollar payments. It was originally launched in 1970 by the New York Clearing House Association, a group of the largest New York City commercial banks, for eight of its members that held Federal Reserve system membership. CHIPS operates on a multilateral netting basis and enables banks to settle dollar payments by electronic transfer. Messages are transmitted by SWIFT.

CHIPS now provides intra-day payment finality through a real-time system. CHIPS settles small payments, which can be met by the banks' available balances, on an RTGS basis. Other payments are netted bilaterally or multilaterally.

Each participant in the intra-day netting system is required to pre-fund its CHIPS account by depositing a quantity of funds sufficient to cover its intra-day exposures. The level of pre-funding that each participant must advance is assessed by CHIPS on the basis of the number and size of its recent CHIPS transactions. At the end of the day, CHIPS uses these deposits to settle any still unsettled transactions.

Banks that have positive closing positions at the end of the day are credited with the cash balance through the Fedwire payments system (see below). The vast majority of CHIPS members are Fedwire participants.

3.2.2 Fedwire

Fedwire is the Federal Reserve's electronic funds transfer system. It is an RTGS system in which more than 11,000 depository institutions initiate funds transfers that are immediate, final, and irrevocable when processed. It allows member banks to transfer funds on their own behalf, or on behalf of their customers. Participants that maintain a reserve or clearing account with a Federal Reserve Bank may use Fedwire to send payments to, or receive payments from, other account holders directly. Participants use Fedwire to handle large-value, time-critical payments, such as payments for the settlement of interbank purchases and sales of federal funds, the purchase, sale, and financing of securities transactions, the disbursement or repayment of loans and the settlement of real estate transactions.

All Fedwire transfers are completed on the day they are initiated, generally in a matter of minutes. They are guaranteed to be final by the Fed as soon as the receiving institution is notified of the credit to its account.

For online transfers, the Fedwire funds transfer service operates from 21:00 New York time on the preceding calendar day (thus it overlaps with the European and Asia-Pacific time zones) through to 18:30 New York time, with a cut-off for foreign payment orders of 17:00 New York time.

For offline funds transfers, the Fedwire funds service operates from 09:00 until 18:00 New York time, with a cut-off of 16:30 for foreign payment orders.

The Fedwire securities service operates from 08:30 until 19:00 New York time for online instructions and from 09:00 until 16:00 for offline instructions.

3.2.3 The Clearing House Automated Payments System (CHAPS)

CHAPS is the UK's high-value payments system, providing RTGS for credit transfers. This provides RTGS settlement for sterling payments via CHAPS Sterling. CHAPS Euro, the settlement service for euro payments that utilised the same settlement systems as CHAPS Sterling, was decommissioned in May 2008 after nine years of service.

The CHAPS RTGS payments infrastructure is extended to CHAPS members by the Bank of England and the CHAPS Clearing Company.

3.2.4 Faster Payments

Faster Payments Service was launched in May 2008 to handle the processing of internet, telephone and standing order payments in the UK market. This service runs alongside existing UK payment schemes BACS, which stands for bankers automated clearing services (for direct debits and direct credits) and CHAPS, and represents the first new payments service to be introduced to the UK market for more than 20 years.

Although it was initially operated by CHAPS Co, responsibility for operation of the Faster Payments system was transferred to Faster Payments Scheme Ltd when the latter company was formed in November 2011.

Faster Payments Service membership is open to credit institutions with a settlement account at the Bank of England that can connect to the central payments infrastructure. Since the beginning of 2012, all internet and telephone payments in the UK have been processed via Faster Payments. All payments must reach the recipient's account by the next working day after the customer has initiated the transaction. In practice, telephone or internet payments sent using Faster Payments will typically be available for withdrawal from the beneficiary's account on the same day that the payment is sent.

3.2.5 Trans-European Automated Real-time Gross Settlement Express Transfer System (TARGET)

Trans-European Automated Real-time Gross Settlement Express Transfer system (TARGET) is the RTGS system for the euro and ensures same-day payment finality in central bank money. This went live in January 1999 to support the creation of a unified money market in the eurozone and the delivery of a single monetary policy.

TARGET2, the more recent European RTGS system, went live in November 2007, replacing the decentralised TARGET system with a single technical platform, developed by Banca d'Italia, Banque de France, and Deutsche Bundesbank. These three banks operate the TARGET2 system on behalf of the Eurosystem (ie, the ECB and the central banks of EU states that have adopted the euro currency), thereby providing users with a homogenous payment service throughout the eurozone.

Migration from TARGET to the TARGET2 platform took place via a phased migration between November 2007 and May 2008.

TARGET2 is open from 07:00 to 18:00 CET, with a deadline of 17:00 for customer payments.

3.2.6 Continuous Linked Settlement (CLS) Bank

The **Continuous Linked Settlement (CLS)** Bank is a private initiative that began in 1996, supported by the largest FX banks – the Group of 20 (G20) – to eliminate settlement risk and to reduce the systemic liquidity risk in the FX market. CLS was launched commercially in 2002.

The system initially supported seven eligible currencies: the Australian, Canadian and US dollars, the euro, the Japanese yen, the Swiss franc and the UK pound sterling. Four additional currencies were added in September 2003: the Danish krone, the Norwegian krone, the Swedish krona, and the Singaporean dollar. A further four currencies were added to the CLS community in late 2004: the South African rand, the Korean won, the Hong Kong dollar and the New Zealand dollar. The Israeli shekel and Mexican peso were added in May 2008, and the Hungarian forint joined in November 2015. CLS now has 18 central banks that have currencies eligible for settlement in CLS.

With the average daily turnover in global FX transactions at more than US$5 trillion, the FX market has long needed an effective cross-currency settlement process. While transaction volumes have increased, the methods by which they are settled have stayed virtually the same for 300 years. Before CLS, each side of a trade was paid separately. Taking time-zone differences into account, this heightened the risk of one party defaulting. CLS was implemented to combat **Herstatt risk** (see section 3.3.7) by providing real-time payment versus payment (PVP) settlement between participating currencies.

CLS Bank is owned by more than 70 of the world's largest financial groups throughout the US, Europe and Asia Pacific. Banks wishing to make use of CLS to settle FX transactions either take out direct membership at CLS Bank, or go via a settlement member or user member, which can introduce CLS trades on their behalf.

A settlement member must be a CLS shareholder and must demonstrate that it has the necessary financial and operational capability, and sufficient liquidity, to support its financial commitments to CLS. Each settlement member has a multi-currency account with CLS Bank. Settlement members have direct access and, consequently, can send settlement instructions direct to CLS on their own behalf and on behalf of their customers. They can also provide a branded CLS service to their third-party customers as part of their agreement with CLS Bank.

User members can submit settlement instructions for themselves and their customers. However, user members do not have an account with CLS Bank. Instead they are sponsored by a settlement member, acting on their behalf. Each instruction submitted by a user member must be authorised by a designated settlement member. The instruction is then eligible for settlement through the sponsoring settlement member's account.

3.3   Key Concepts in the Settlement Process

Learning Objective

3.2.3   Understand the following settlement concepts: trade for trade; netting – bilateral and multilateral; trade date netting, continuous net settlement; fixed date settlement; rolling settlement; free of payment transactions; delivery versus payment (DvP); book entry settlement; physical settlement; foreign exchange (FX) settlement

Settlement of a securities transaction refers to the process of exchanging securities and cash between the buyer and seller in order to discharge their respective obligations. Delivery of securities commonly takes place at a CSD (or ICSD). Funds transfer (ie, delivery of cash) commonly takes place through a banking or payments system.

A trade cannot be deemed to be settled until both the securities transfer and cash transfer are final and irrevocable (ie, neither of the transfers can be rescinded). Traditionally, trade settlement would have been completed by physical delivery of certificates from seller to buyer in return for cash. However, we have noted that many securities markets are now dematerialised or immobilised and transfer takes place electronically by book entry rather than physical movement of certificates.

To minimise the principal risk incurred in the case of default by either counterparty, a working group of the world's leading securities regulators and central banks recommended that settlement providers should reduce to a minimum the credit risk created if securities or cash are delivered without receipt of assets of corresponding value by the counterparty.

3.3.1   Free of Payment (FOP) Settlement

FOP settlement typically refers to the separate, non-simultaneous exchange of cash and securities between counterparties (see DvP arrangements below). In FOP settlement, one or both parties to the trade will be forced to deliver securities or pay cash before they have taken delivery of the corresponding asset from the other counterparty. Owing to the higher risks of FOP settlement when compared with DvP, regulatory authorities are encouraging companies to employ DvP whenever possible.

3.3.2   Delivery versus Payment (DvP)

DvP is a procedure whereby appropriate technical, legal and contractual arrangements are in place to ensure that a transfer of securities is final if, and only if, the corresponding transfer of funds is final. More simply, DvP involves simultaneous exchange of securities and cash between buyer and seller (in practice, this commonly takes place via their respective custodians on the books of the CSD and central payments system). Hence, both parties are protected against risk of counterparty default.

DvP can be achieved in several ways:

*   Via an RTGS system that provides simultaneous and immediate transfer of securities and cash throughout the working day. RTGS is the continuous settlement of funds and securities transfers individually on an order-by-order basis.
*   Via netting systems that offer finality of cash and securities transfer by the end of the working day. Hence, necessary procedures must be in place to ensure that intra-day transfers are final and that end-of-day net settlements of cash payments will be realised, even if one or more participants fail to meet their obligations.
*   On the books of a CSD that operates a combined clearing and depository service and is linked to a final payments system (eg, settlement takes place in central bank money).
*   When securities are delivered against a guaranteed cheque that provides the party concerned with cleared funds.

In the UK, for example, Euroclear UK & Ireland (EUI) provides DvP in central bank money, with simultaneous and irrevocable transfer of cash and securities (this arrangement is known as DvP model 1) for all sterling and euro payments. Full legal title in CREST is also transferred at the point of settlement for all UK-registered shares and government bonds.

At the point of settlement in CREST, the CREST payment, which discharges the buyer's obligation to the seller, is accompanied by a simultaneous payment from the buyer's settlement bank to the seller's settlement bank across the books of the central bank (the Bank of England for sterling settlement, the Central Bank of Ireland for euros). This substantially reduces the risk to an investor arising from the failure of its counterparty's settlement bank.

3.3.3 Netted Settlement

Netting can be bilateral (between two counterparties only) or multilateral (involving many counterparties, as in a CCP).

Bilateral

- Trades between the same two counterparties in the same security are offset (ie, netted off) so that there is only one transfer.
- This can be in respect of cash and securities.
- In respect of cash only, there is only one cash transfer, but each securities transfer is carried out separately.
- Separate netting agreements must be in place with each counterparty.

Multilateral

- Extends **bilateral netting** to cover all trades in the same security by any number of counterparties.
- For each security traded, this will result in each counterparty making only one transfer of cash or securities, either to another counterparty or to the central clearing system.
- Requires the use of a central clearing system to establish the cash and securities obligations of each counterparty and to instruct respective settlement obligations to settlement agents and CSD.

Example – Multilateral Netting

Consider, for example, that trading company BCD conducts trades in a specified share with three counterparties, DEF, LMN and TUV.

1. BCD buys 7,000 shares from DEF for £28,000 cash.
2. BCD sells 4,200 shares to TUV for £17,220 cash.
3. BCD sells 2,000 shares to LMN for £7,600 cash.

Settled on a trade-for-trade basis, BCD would need to settle each trade individually with these three respective counterparties. By netting multilaterally via the CCP, each trading company settles just a single cash balance and a single securities balance with the CCP.

This can be represented diagrammatically:

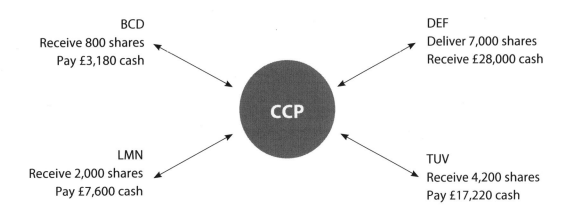

BCD
Receive 800 shares
Pay £3,180 cash

DEF
Deliver 7,000 shares
Receive £28,000 cash

CCP

LMN
Receive 2,000 shares
Pay £7,600 cash

TUV
Receive 4,200 shares
Pay £17,220 cash

In **trade date netting**, each trading company will settle a single netted cash balance and a single netted securities balance calculated at close of business on trade date. This settlement of cash and securities relates only to trades flagged for netting on the trading day, and will not include failed trades from previous days that have been brought forward.

In the above example, when these three individual trades are netted at the CCP, BCD will be required to pay £3,180 to the CCP to settle its net outstanding cash balance and its net securities balance will be +800 shares (ie, it will receive 800 shares). In **continuous net settlement (CNS)**, failed trades from previous days may be re-presented for netting in a later multilateral netting cycle.

The following rules and steps are applied by the CNS process:

- For **securities** – the CNS algorithm will attempt to net positions against other positions with opposite-signed quantities, with the oldest positions being netted first. So it will try to net POS1 against POS2. If POS1 cannot net to zero against POS2, it will try against POS3, POS4 … POSN (see example below). The netted security quantity is always kept on the position having the bigger security quantity, irrespective of the Intended Settlement Date (ISD).
- For **cash** – the CNS algorithm will attempt to net opposite-signed cash amounts, with the oldest positions netted first. The net cash amount is always kept on the position having the bigger cash amount in absolute value, irrespective of the intended settlement date.

Example – CNS

At close of business on trade date, D, we have: three failed trade positions in a specified security (POS1 to POS3) linked to the same customer account, along with a new position (POS4) traded on the current business day D:

ISD for these securities is, respectively, D–3 for POS1, D–2 for POS2, D–1 for POS3 and D+1 for POS4. The oldest position will be forwarded for netting first.

Positions	ISD	Quantity	Value (eur)
POS1 fail	D–3	–40	+300
POS2 fail	D–2	–5	+10
POS3 fail	D–1	–100	+1,000
POS4 new	D+1	+90	–1,200

Securities Quantity Pre-netting		
Positions	ISD	Quantity
POS1	D–3	0
POS2	D–2	–5
POS3	D–1	–100
POS4	D+1	+50
Positions	ISD	Quantity
POS1	D–3	0
POS2	D–2	0
POS3	D–1	–100
POS4	D+1	+45
Positions	ISD	Quantity
POS1	D–3	0
POS2	D–2	0
POS3	D–1	–55
POS4	D+1	0

Cash Amount Pre-netting		
Positions	ISD	Value (eur)
POS1	D–3	0
POS2	D–2	+10
POS3	D–1	+1,000
POS4	D+1	–900
Positions	ISD	Value (eur)
POS1	D–3	0
POS2	D–2	0
POS3	D–1	+1,000
POS4	D+1	–890
Positions	ISD	Value (eur)
POS1	D–3	0
POS2	D–2	0
POS3	D–1	+110
POS4	D+1	0

Final result at end of CNS process:

Positions	ISD	Quantity	Value (eur)
POS3	D+1	–55	+110

Source: LCH.Clearnet

3.3.4   Finality of Transfer

Whichever settlement model is employed, the settlement system must specify the moment of finality of transfer in its rules, through binding contracts on the parties involved. Once finality of transfer has been assured, these rules must allow the buyer to use the securities, and the seller to use the cash without further delay, in the safe knowledge that the transaction will not at that stage fail and the trade have to be unwound.

We have noted previously that RTGS systems have an important role to play in ensuring real-time settlement finality and in limiting systemic risk. **Gross settlement** systems have been widely employed to mitigate the risks in large-value funds transfer systems where the main participants have access to intra-day liquidity extended by the central bank.

However, trade-for-trade settlement can place substantial demands on liquidity, requiring that cash and securities obligations are met in full for each trade (ie, without being netted against other positions). This can create gridlock within the system, when delivery of funds or securities does not move sufficiently quickly to release the liquidity needed to allow subsequent trades to settle.

We saw in section 3.3.3 that netting systems can ease these liquidity pressures, since positions are offset and settled at the end of the settlement batch. By reducing the overall value of money that market participants must transfer to deliver their obligations at the end of a settlement batch, the efficiency of cash payments and securities transfer mechanisms can be improved.

On the downside, a participant's true exposure may only be revealed at the end of the settlement batch. If a market participant defaults on its settlement obligations at this point, this could impact on a series of counterparties with which it has conducted transactions during the settlement batch. If adequate cover is not in place (eg, requiring participants to put up collateral in advance to cover their intra-day credit exposure), then default by a counterparty may dictate that this whole series of trades may need to be unwound.

3.3.5   From Physical Settlement to Book-Entry Transfer

Many trading and settlement systems have advanced from the days when securities were held and traded in physical form, with paper certificates exchanged between counterparties against transfer of funds in order to conduct a trade – a process known as physical settlement.

When a depository does accept certificated securities, these will typically be immobilised, such that they no longer need to be delivered physically from one counterparty to another. In practice, the certificated security remains in the vaults of the CSD throughout the transaction (hence it is immobilised), with the security being debited from the account of the seller and credited to the account of the buyer.

Many markets now employ computer-based mechanisms for transferring ownership, with records of ownership being held in electronic book-entry format. The security ceases to exist in paper form, with the certificate being replaced by computer records. This transition from physical to electronic format is known as dematerialisation. Euroclear Settlement of Euronext-zone Securities (ESES), for example, holds securities in dematerialised form.

The shift to a dematerialised securities environment has:

- improved processing efficiency by allowing trading, clearance, settlement and asset servicing procedures to be increasingly automated
- enabled shorter settlement timing
- improved security by reducing the possibility that a physical security may be lost, stolen or fraudulently copied.

The transition to book-entry settlement and dematerialised trading commonly demands a corresponding change in the market's legal framework in order to ensure that ownership rights are fully protected through electronic records. Necessary business continuity procedures must also be put in place to ensure effective back-up of electronic records and systems in the instance of any systemic shock or crisis.

In the EU, the CSD Regulation will require all securities which are traded on regulated markets or MTFs to be dematerialised (see chapter 2, section 3.5.1).

3.3.6 Fixed Date Settlement and Rolling Settlement

In **rolling settlement**, settlement occurs on a specific number of business days after the trade date. In the UK, for example, settlement for equities and fixed-income securities occurs two days after trade date, which is commonly denoted as T+2. Rolling settlement is now the norm in securities markets around the world, including each of the core markets highlighted in chapter 1, section 14.

At an earlier stage in their development, some securities markets may have operated a **fixed settlement** period (sometimes known as account settlement), whereby trades executed within a specified period (known as an account period) settled on a specified date. For example, all trades executed during the week beginning Monday 9 May settled on Monday 16 May; all trades conducted during the week beginning Monday 16 May settled on Monday 23 May, and so on.

Fixed-date settlement has the following disadvantages:

- There can be a lengthy delay between trade execution and trade settlement, dictating that sellers may not receive prompt payment for their securities and resulting in extended credit exposure to the counterparty.
- Failed trades cannot be re-presented for settlement until settlement date at the end of the next account period. Hence, failed trades may remain unsettled for an extended period.
- The market value of the security may move significantly during this period, creating a sizeable replacement risk (the risk that non-defaulting parties will incur a loss when replacing unsettled contracts) in instances of trade failure.
- Fixed-date settlement creates peaks and troughs of settlement activity, with trades being queued to settle on a specified date at the end of the account period. This puts a strain on operations at these peak times.

The longer the period from trade execution to settlement, the greater the risk that one of the parties may become insolvent or default on the trade, the larger the number of trades that will be awaiting settlement, and the greater the opportunity for the prices of the securities to move away from the contract prices. These factors collectively accentuate the risk that non-defaulting parties will incur a loss when replacing the unsettled contracts.

In contrast, under a rolling settlement cycle, trades settle a specified number of business days after the trade date, rather than at the end of an account period, thereby limiting the number of outstanding trades and reducing aggregate market exposure.

3.3.7　Foreign Exchange (FX) Settlement

FX transactions are used for three main purposes:

- to obtain currency to settle immediate payment commitments,
- to hedge against future exchange rate movements, and
- to speculate, or trade, in currencies in order to make profits from changes in exchange rates.

When a price is quoted on a trading screen or a website it will look something like this:

GBP/USD 1.7426–30

- The three-letter acronyms denote the currencies. The first currency is the base currency and the second is the quoted currency. Many currencies are quoted against the US dollar as the base currency (ie, the reverse of the rate shown above). Sterling and the euro are exceptions to this generalisation. Both AUD and NZD are also quoted as the base against the US dollar.
- One unit of the base currency will buy the amount shown in the quoted currency. In the example quoted, one pound sterling will purchase US$1.7426.
- The first price is the bid price, which is what an investor would obtain if buying the second currency with the first.
- The second price is the offer price, which is the amount of the second currency that one will need to pay to buy one unit of the first, in this case US$1.7430 will buy £1.00. Note that the second price is not quoted in full, only the last two digits; this is because the spread is normally less than 1% and the whole amount does not need to be quoted.
- The spread is the difference between the bid and offer prices and is the trader's profit margin on the transaction.
- The mid-price is the average of the bid and offer prices. It is normally not quoted for trading, but it is reported in the financial press, for example, to illustrate how currencies are moving relative to one other.

FX is not traded on-exchange. Instead, FX traders deal directly with each other, informed by screen-based pricing systems and transacting by phone or electronically. Banks are the main players. Settlement of FX transactions (the actual movement of cash) may take place immediately (spot, ie, on a T+2 basis, see below) or in the future (forward), either as outright forwards or as FX swaps. In addition, currency **futures contracts** can be traded on many derivatives exchanges.

Average daily turnover on the global FX market is roughly US$5.1 trillion per day according to data from the Bank of International Settlements' Triennial Central Bank Survey in 2016. Approximately 33% of this daily turnover is in spot forex transactions, with currency swap transactions accounting for 47%, and outright forwards a further 14%. Options on interbank FX transactions represent a further 5% of average daily turnover.

- **Spot transactions** – a spot transaction is a single outright transaction involving the exchange of two currencies at a rate agreed at the time of the contract. Settlement takes place within two business days.

- **Outright forwards** – a forward transaction is one for settlement more than two days in the future. There are no standard settlement dates as there are with futures contracts: a forward outright can be for a few days, months or years. The exchange rate is fixed at the time that the transaction is agreed, but there is no exchange of money until settlement date.
- **Foreign exchange swaps** – a foreign exchange swap is the simultaneous purchase and sale of a specified amount of foreign currency for two different settlement dates.
  - A single transaction combines two deals, one spot and one forward.
  - For example, Bank X may sell £20 million for spot dollars to Bank Y and simultaneously buy £20 million forward for dollars for, say, seven-day settlement.
  - The spot deal takes place at the **spot rate** and the forward deal at the **forward rate**. A foreign currency swap allows each party to use a currency for a period in exchange for another currency that is not needed during that time.
  - The FX swap is arranged as a single transaction with a single counterparty. The majority of forward transactions are undertaken as swaps. When a forward transaction is mentioned, it usually means a swap.
- **Non-deliverable forwards** – the exchange rate is set for some date in the future, but at that date the quoted currency is not exchanged. Instead, the rate is compared against the prevailing spot rate. The profit or loss is calculated as if a reverse transaction had been completed. This is the amount that is settled. An investor will enter into a non-deliverable forward if:
  - they wish to speculate in the currency, but do not wish to execute the reverse transaction,
  - there are liquidity or dealing restrictions that will prevent (or make it difficult for) the investor from executing the reverse transaction. For example, in Brazil, FX transactions above BRL10,000 must be registered and, if considered to be an international transfer (to a foreign bank), they are subject to a 2% finance tax.
- **FX options** – these provide a right, but not an obligation, for the option holder to enter into a FX transaction, usually at some date in the future, at a predetermined exchange rate with the issuer of the option. This option will be exercised (or closed out at a profit) if the rate at which the deal can be struck is preferential to the prevailing market rate. For example, an option written in June that allows the holder to exchange JPY100 million for USD at a rate of JPY100 per US$1 in December will be exercised if the USD market rate is greater than JPY100 per US$1. The purchaser of an option pays a premium to the seller (or writer) of the option.

The next sections will examine factors which cause the spot FX rate to move up or down and will describe how cross rates and forward rates are calculated.

Note: the following text is for information only and will not be examined.

Spot Rate Determination

Spot FX rates are driven up and down by forces of supply and demand and are likely to be influenced by a range of economic and political considerations that shape the positions that FX traders will take on particular currency pairs (eg, how the US dollar will move against the Japanese yen). These include:

- Economic factors, for example:
  - balance of payments
  - government budget surplus or deficit
  - inflation
  - economic growth,
  - interest rates, and
  - purchasing power parity (see below).

- Political factors, for example:
  - government policies
  - political stability
  - central bank intervention, and
  - regulation and control by the government and central bank.
- Market sentiment.

Purchasing Power Parity

Purchasing power parity (PPP) is a theory that states that identical goods should cost the same in two countries. For example, if a basket of goods costs £100 in London, and the same basket of goods costs US$150 in New York, then the exchange rate should be £1 = US$1.50.

If, after a number of years, the same basket of goods costs £125 in London and yet it remains at US$150 in New York, then one might expect the exchange rate to be £1.00 = US$1.20; this would demonstrate a decline in the value of sterling.

This Law of One Price describes the principle of absolute PPP.

The principle of relative PPP tells us that the rate of appreciation of a currency (ie, currency A relative to currency B) is equal to the difference in inflation rates between the two countries. For example, if the UK has an inflation rate of 2.0% and the US has an inflation rate of 3.5%, the US dollar will depreciate against UK sterling by 1.5% annually.

PPP is not a perfect guide to how currencies will behave, but it provides a basis for understanding the long-term relationship between currencies.

Cross Rate Calculation

Increasingly, rates between most currencies are calculated and are publicly available to investors wishing to conduct an FX transaction. However, in some instances, an investor wishing to exchange between two less-quoted currencies may need to go through the dollar. The cross rate can be calculated from the two dollar exchange rates.

Forward Rate Determination

The determination of the forward rate does not involve any guess or estimate of what exchange rates will be in the future. The forward rate reflects the interest rate differentials between the currencies at the time the deal is done. In theory, the forward rate could be the same as the spot rate, but this will only occur if interest rates in the two countries are the same. In practice, the forward price is normally higher or lower than the spot rate.

For example, if UK interest rates are 5% and US rates are 4%, an investor may be tempted to:

- borrow dollars and pay interest at 4% on the loan,
- convert the dollars into sterling at the spot rate, put the pounds on deposit and earn interest at 5%,
- agree a forward rate of exchange for converting the pounds back into dollars to repay the loan.

The forward rate will be calculated such that the investor will not profit from this arrangement. In this example, it means that forward dollars will have to be more expensive than spot dollars (ie, forward dollars will be at a premium to the spot rate). If US interest rates were higher than UK rates, forward dollars would be cheaper than spot (thus, forward dollars would be quoted at a discount to the spot rate).

The principle that allows us to calculate forward rates from spot rates and interest rates is called interest rate parity and is explained below.

Forward rates are not quoted outright but at a premium, or discount, to the spot rate. For example, if the spot rate is £1.00 = US$1.60 and the three-month forward is 0.25 cents discount, the three-month forward rate is thus US$1.6000 – US$0.0025 = US$1.5975. Note that the discount is deducted from the spot rate, thus making dollars more expensive for three-month delivery.

The reason for quoting the premium is that swaps are based on the interest rate differential. A second benefit is that premiums and discounts are subject to much less fluctuation than spot rates, so quoting differentials requires fewer amendments to published prices.

Forward Rate Calculation

Taking the previous scenario, imagine that an investment company were to borrow US$1 million in the US at 4%, and agrees to repay the loan in a year. It enters into a forward transaction at the spot price.

Firstly, it would convert it to sterling using the spot rate. It would receive:

$$\frac{US\$1,000,000}{1.60} = £625,000$$

It then places this on deposit at 5% for one year and receives:

$$£625,000 \times 1.05 = £656,250 \text{ (principal plus interest)}$$

It converts this back to dollars:

$$£656,250 \times 1.60 = US\$1,050,000 \quad (1)$$

The original loan has to be paid off, plus the 4% interest:

$$US\$1,000,000 \times 1.04 = US\$1,040,000 \quad (2)$$

Leaving it with a profit of US$10,000.

To calculate the forward rate, we set (1) and (2) to be equal, so no profit is generated.

To generate a general formula for this:

R^{GBP}	=	UK interest rates	=	5% (in the example)
$R^{\$}$	=	US interest rates	=	4%
X^{spot}	=	the spot rate	=	1.6
X^{for}	=	the forward rate	=	1.6 (same as spot in the example)

To make equations (1) and (2) the same, the forward rate in equation (1) must be less than the spot rate. The left hand side of (1) must amount to the US$1,040,000 in (2):

$$£656,250 \times X^{for} = US\$1,040,000$$

$$X^{for} = \frac{US\$1,040,000}{£656,250}$$

$$= 1.5848 US\$/£$$

The example will be worked again, but substituting symbols for amounts. The investor would convert its loan to sterling using the spot rate, X^{spot}, giving:

$$\frac{US\$1m}{X^{spot}}$$

The investor then places this on deposit at R^{GBP} for one year and receives:

$$\frac{US\$1m}{X^{spot}} \times (1 + R^{GBP})$$

The investor converts this back to dollars at the forward rate:

$$\frac{US\$1m}{X^{spot}} \times (1 + R^{GBP}) \times X^{for}$$

This will be equal to the original loan, plus the $R^{\$}$ interest:

$$\$1m \times (1 + R^{GBP}) \times X^{for} = \$1m \times (1 + R^{\$})$$

Rearranging gives:

$$\frac{X^{for}}{X^{spot}} = \frac{(1 + R^{\$})}{(1 + R^{GBP})}$$

Or:

$$\text{Forward rate} = \frac{1 + R^{\$}}{(1 + R^{GBP})} \times \text{spot rate}$$

This is known as interest rate parity.

Note: *this is the end of the non-examinable text.*

Settlement Risk in FX Transactions

Given that there is no central dealing exchange for FX transactions in the same way as exists for securities, settlement has traditionally involved payments between both counterparties' banks. When conducting FX transactions under these arrangements, there is a finite risk that one party to the trade may default before both counterparties have met their settlement obligations. This may result in a situation where one leg is paid, but the counterparty goes into liquidation before the second leg is paid out.

This is known as Herstatt risk, named after Bankhaus Herstatt, a German bank active in the FX market. In June 1974, the bank had its banking licence withdrawn after the interbank payment system in Germany had closed. It had received Deutschmark payments from its counterparties. However, its correspondent bank in New York, which had just opened when the news broke, would not make the USD payments that Herstatt was due to pay.

We noted earlier that CLS (see section 3.2.6) was implemented to eliminate Herstatt risk by providing real-time PVP settlement between participating currencies. It intermediates between the two sides of an FX transaction, requiring both counterparties to pay the funds due for delivery to the other directly into accounts with CLS Bank.

Only after these funds have been fully paid into CLS will the latter pay out the funds owed to each party. Hence, if either counterparty fails to meet its obligations to pay in funds, it will not receive its pay-out; rather, the funds will be returned to the party that originally remitted them.

3.4   Transfer of Title

Learning Objective

3.2.4   Understand the transfer of legal title: bearer; registered

When securities are sold or transferred to a new owner, the method for transferring legal title will depend on whether the security is in bearer, certificated or dematerialised form and whether there is a requirement to reregister the security. See the table below.

	Bearer	**Registered (certificated)**	**Registered (dematerialised)**
Typical method of holding securities	Certificate and book entry	Register and certificate	Register and book entry
Typical method for securities transfer	Book-entry transfer	Transfer and reregistration	Book entry and reregistration
Holder's name appears on register	No	Yes	Yes

3.4.1   Bearer Securities

Investors typically hold bearer securities in secure storage at the local CSD, or sometimes with their custodian. The CSD or custodian will maintain records of the total quantity of a specific security that it holds, and the quantity held by each investor. However, the CSD or custodian will not usually record the identification numbers of the individual certificates deposited by each investor.

Like bank notes, bearer securities are said to be fungible, meaning that the certificate deposited by the investor may not be the exact certificate that it receives on return, should it opt to withdraw the security from safe storage. Like bank notes, holders of bearer securities bear the risk of theft or loss of the certificate.

If both buyer and seller have securities accounts at the CSD (or with the same custodian), transfer of legal title can take place electronically by book-entry transfer, without the immobilised certificates leaving the vaults of the CSD (or the vaults of the custodian concerned).

3.4.2   Registered Securities in Certificated Form

If an investor sells or transfers registered securities that are in certificated (ie, physical) form, the seller is typically required to complete a securities transfer form, confirming that the seller authorises transfer of legal title to the buying counterparty. Transfer of title will be effected on the securities register.

Subsequently, the registrar will cancel the seller's certificate, as it is now void. The registrar will then issue a new certificate in the buyer's or transferee's name. This method of transferring legal title is called transfer and reregistration, after accounting for any transfer tax liability.

3.4.3   Registered Securities in Dematerialised Form

Transfer of title takes place via book entry with reregistration in instances when the **registered security** is held in dematerialised form, or the buyer wishes to hold in dematerialised form (when available) a registered security that was previously held as a physical certificate.

Under this method, the CSD will send an electronic notification to the registrar confirming details of the change in holding from seller to buyer. The register will then be updated electronically, confirming transfer of legal title by book entry transfer. This arrangement offers the advantage that the security can be traded as soon as the stock settles. With certificated securities, there may be a longer time delay while transfer of title is processed by the registrar and a new certificate is sent to the buying investor or transferee.

3.5   Contractual Settlement

Learning Objective

3.2.5   Understand Contractual Settlement Date Accounting (CSDA) and Actual Settlement Date Accounting (ASDA)

Actual settlement date accounting (ASDA) refers to accounting procedures by which the proceeds of a securities sale are credited to the seller's account, and the costs of a securities purchase are debited from the buyer's account, on the date that a trade actually settles.

If trade settlement is delayed, this dictates that the seller will not receive due funds until after the proposed settlement date. For example, if a trade is scheduled to settle on T+2, but does not actually settle until T+5, the seller will not receive funds until three days after the proposed settlement date. As a result, the seller is disadvantaged by losing the opportunity to utilise these funds, or earn interest on this money, for three days.

Conversely, ASDA works to the advantage of the buyer, who will not need to pay cash to settle the transaction until three days after the originally scheduled T+2 settlement date.

To provide clients with greater certainty over their cash flows, some custodians have introduced contractual settlement date accounting (CSDA) arrangements, whereby, subject to certain conditions, funds will be credited or debited on settlement date (or an otherwise pre-agreed value date), even if trade settlement is not yet final and irrevocable on that date. Contractual settlement will typically only be offered in well structured and liquid markets, and custodians will specify in their service level agreement (SLA) where this applies.

Contractual settlement arrangements imply a risk to the custodian, since it is absorbing liquidity pressures from the client, by extending provisional credit to the client's account.

In some circumstances, CSDA arrangements may not apply, or may be withdrawn – eg, if the seller's stock was not available to complete settlement successfully.

To control the risk that it takes on through these arrangements, the custodian should have procedures in place to monitor late settlements and, if appropriate, to reverse any provisional credits made to the client's account.

The terms under which provisional credits are extended to the client under CSDA arrangements must be clearly established between custodian and client. If the client is unaware that credits are provisional in certain circumstances, it may, for example, underestimate its overall credit exposure, or be faced with an account overdraft in circumstances where a provisional credit is reversed.

3.6 The Giovannini Barriers to the Creation of a Harmonised Securities Market for Europe

Learning Objective

3.2.6 Know the main Giovannini Barriers to the creation of a harmonised market for Europe

The Giovannini Group (a consultative group of market participants formed in 1996 to advise the European Commission (EC) on issues relating to EU financial integration and the efficiency of euro-denominated financial markets) produced two reports that analyse barriers to efficient and secure clearing and settlement in the EU, the first in November 2001 and the second in April 2003. The 2001 Giovannini Report highlighted 15 factors preventing the efficient provision of cross-border clearing and settlement services within the EU.

These barriers are classified as technical or market-practice barriers, legal barriers, and barriers related to tax procedures:

Barrier 1	There is a need to eliminate connectivity problems resulting from national differences in information technology and interfaces used by clearing and settlement providers. This includes encouraging the use of standardised communication based on ISO standard electronic messaging.
Barrier 2	National restrictions on the location of clearing and settlement should be removed as an essential pre-condition for a market-led integration of EU clearing and settlement arrangements. Barrier 2 is to be treated jointly with Barrier 9, as they both address location restrictions. Unlike Barrier 9, however, Barrier 2 is more of a market structure issue, since it refers to the linkage between exchange and settlement systems.
Barrier 3	National rules relating to corporate actions processing should be harmonised, as well as the timing of transfer of ownership.
Barrier 4	Intra-day settlement finality in all links between settlement systems within the EU should be guaranteed.
Barrier 5	National governments should draw up a set of conditions that will enable remote access to national clearing and settlement mechanisms to be guaranteed across the EU. The Giovannini report stresses the need to tackle Barrier 5 with action from public authorities, so as to ensure remote access on a strictly non-discriminatory basis.
Barrier 6	Settlement periods for all equity markets within the EU should be harmonised. Barrier 6 is linked to Barrier 1, as both aim to render the settlement process more efficient by standardising operational procedures across EU states.
Barrier 7	Operating hours for national clearing and systems should be standardised across the EU.
Barrier 8	Securities issuance practices across European markets should be harmonised.
Barrier 9	National restrictions on the location of securities must be removed.
Barrier 10	Restrictions on the activity of primary dealers and market makers should be removed.
Barrier 11	All financial intermediaries established within the EU should be allowed to offer withholding agent services in each of the EU member states.
Barrier 12	Any provisions requiring that taxes on securities transactions be collected via local systems should be removed.
Barrier 13	There is a need to establish an EU-wide framework for the treatment of ownership of securities.
Barrier 14	There is a need to address inconsistencies across EU states in the legal treatment of netting procedures.
Barrier 15	There is a need to address inconsistencies in conflict of law rules applicable across EU states. The current framework addressing conflicts of laws (the Settlement Finality Directive and Financial Collateral Directive) is incomplete, and could potentially be improved through the approval of the Hague Securities Convention.

In response to these barriers, the EC outlined a set of proposals designed to promote a safe and efficient European clearing environment and a level playing field across providers of clearing and settlement services. This includes steps to:

- liberalise and integrate existing securities clearing and settlement systems, particularly by providing access rights at all levels and removing barriers to cross-border clearing and settlement,
- remove restrictive market practices and to monitor industry consolidation in accordance with the requirements of competition policy,
- adopt a common regulatory and supervisory framework that ensures financial stability and investor protection, leading to the mutual recognition of systems,
- implement appropriate governance arrangements so as to address national authorities' concerns regarding the way in which clearing and settlement infrastructures operate (see further in chapter 2, section 3.5.1).

4. Failed Settlement

Learning Objective

3.3.2 Understand the risks associated with: buy-ins/sell-outs; counterparty risk; interest claims; settlement fines; matching fines; suspension of trading; short sale fines

---

If a trade fails to settle, then a firm has several options. This section will cover why trades fail, **buying in** or **selling out**, and interest claims.

4.1 Failure Reasons and Penalties

Learning Objective

3.3.1 Understand the main reasons for failed settlement: failure to match; insufficient stock; insufficient cash; counterparty default; corporate event

---

Settlement failure may be caused by a number of factors:

- **Non-matching settlement instructions** – trade instructions are unmatched because, for example, one of the counterparties has entered incorrect or incomplete trade details, or the counterparties may be in dispute, or no instruction has been submitted.
- **Insufficient securities** – the seller has insufficient securities to deliver and has been unable or unwilling to borrow securities to meet its shortfall. The shortfall may result, for example, because the seller is awaiting delivery of a purchase of securities, or because securities are out on loan and the seller has been unable to recall them to meet its settlement obligations.
- **Insufficient funds** – the purchaser may have insufficient cash to settle the cash leg of the trade because, for example, it is awaiting the proceeds of a sale or is experiencing a **cash funding** problem.

- **Corporate actions** – securities are not available for delivery because the clearing organisation has blocked delivery in respect of some corporate action or event. For example, if shareholders (or proxies acting on their behalf) are invited to vote on a motion at a company meeting, then shares may be blocked for a number of days in the lead-up to the meeting.
- **Counterparty default** – a counterparty may have gone into default (liquidation) and been unable to honour its trading commitments.

If a buyer of securities fails to provide sufficient funds to meet its settlement obligations, they are likely to be charged penalty interest for the period that the trade is unsettled. The exchange (or the other counterparty) may initiate a buy-in of securities (see below).

Other penalties for failure vary from market to market, but may include:

- interest claims,
- various fines,
- suspension of trading,
- fines for short selling,
- damage to a broker's image and reputation.

4.2   Buy-Ins and Sell-Outs

If the seller fails to deliver securities by the value date, the buyer (or potentially the CCP or exchange) may initiate a buy-in of securities to allow trade settlement to be completed. Commonly, the buyer (or potentially the CCP or exchange) will issue notification to the seller indicating that unless delivery of the requisite securities takes place by a specified deadline, then a buy-in will be initiated. Depending on market regulations, this communication may be copied to the exchange and/or market authorities.

If the seller has failed to deliver securities by the specified deadline, the buyer will purchase the securities from a third party at the current market price. Any additional costs (the difference between the price paid on the buy-in and the price agreed with the original seller) are passed on to the offending seller.

If the selling counterparty is in a position to deliver securities, but the buying counterparty is unable to deliver cash payment to enable the trade to settle, the seller may opt to sell-out the securities involved. The procedure involved broadly mirrors that described above for buy-ins: the seller will notify the buyer that, unless necessary funds are delivered by a specified deadline, the selling party will initiate a sell-out procedure. The sale proceeds raised by the sell-out are used to cover the cash leg of the trade settlement. Additional costs of raising these funds at market rates through the sell-out procedure are passed on to the original buyer. It should be noted, however, that selling out has never been widely used.

- **Buying in** – the purchaser buys in from an alternative source and any additional costs (the difference between the price paid on the buy-in and the price agreed with the original seller) are passed on to the offending seller, along with associated fees.
- **Selling out** – the seller sells out to an alternative purchaser, with any additional costs being passed on to the offending purchaser.

Both procedures may be instigated by the firm and/or the market authorities in accordance with local market conventions and rules. In some markets, buying-in and selling-out are triggered automatically if a trade fails. For example, in Singapore, trades not settled on SD+1 are posted on a buy-in board.

4.3 Fines

A firm may be fined by the exchange or CSD if it fails to match or settle trades within a defined period. With the transition to T+2 settlement in the UK, Euroclear UK & Ireland introduced new matching requirements on 1 September 2014. These require firms to match all trades by close of business on T+1 in order to avoid potential matching fines. A fine of £4.00 will be charged for each transaction that remains unmatched at close of business on T+1. An additional fine of £2.00 will be charged for each subsequent day a transaction remains unmatched in Euroclear UK & Ireland. Unmatched transactions will be subject to fines for a maximum of 30 local business days. Any unmatched instruction is automatically cancelled in the CREST system after this period.

For trade settlement, EUI will impose a fine if a firm fails to meet the following targets for trade settlement during a two-month period:

- 85% must settle on SD,
- 90% must settle by SD+1,
- 95% must settle by each of SD+2 to SD+9,
- 98% must settle by each of SD+10 to SD+15,
- 99% must settle by each of SD+16 to SD+20.

In line with local market practice, settlement fines for failed deliveries will only be calculated up to 20 local business days after the contractual settlement date.

A trading firm will often use stock borrowing arrangements as a means to cover a shortfall of securities in a securities transaction, in order to prevent the exchange initiating a buy-in or to prevent a fine. In the US, the Federal Reserve Bank of New York's Treasury Market Practice Group (TMPG) advises that financial penalties be imposed on parties failing to meet their obligation to deliver securities required to settle a trade in US Treasury securities, agency debt securities (ie, debentures issued by the **Federal National Mortgage Association** (Fannie Mae), the **Federal Home Loan Mortgage Corporation** (Freddie Mac) or the Federal Home Loan Bank) and agency mortgage-backed securities. For inter-dealer trades in US Treasury securities and agency debt securities, the Fixed Income Clearing Corporation (FICC) will calculate any outstanding fines automatically and these will be applied to FICC members' monthly bills.

When the trade involves one or more parties that are not FICC members, the TMPG advises that the non-failing party should submit a claim for fails penalty charges to the failing party. This is also the case for trades in agency mortgage-backed securities (MBSs) that do not settle within two business days following the contractual settlement date. The recommended threshold for claims is US$500; claims below this amount will not be raised or honoured.

4.4 Interest Claims

Learning Objective

3.3.3   Understand interest claims (ICMA rules on fixed-income and ISITC for equities)

3.3.4   Be able to calculate interest claims based on the ICMA rules

If a buyer or its clearing agent has caused a trade settlement to fail, the seller will normally make an interest claim for the loss of interest on the net amount that they would have received had settlement happened on time.

The International Capital Market Association (ICMA) has rules and recommendations relating to these claims for fixed-income products. If both counterparties are members of ICMA, then they are bound by these rules. For equities, the International Securities Association for Institutional Trade Communication (ISITC) has advanced a comparable set of guidelines relating to claims for interest. The worked example is for a fixed-income product and the differences under ISITC are noted at the end. The amount is calculated according to the following formula:

$$\text{Claim amount} = \text{net amount} \times \frac{\text{overdraft rate}}{100} \times \frac{\text{number of calendar days}}{360 \text{ or } 365/366}$$

The overdraft rate is the one applicable to the seller at its agent bank.

The number of days in the third term (360 or 365/366) is that used for cash overdrafts in the cash market of the settlement currency. For example, for GBP it is 365/366, but many other currencies use 360.

Example

A buyer was due to pay £219,000 for a number of bonds.

Settlement was delayed by five days because the buyer instructed its agent bank incorrectly and then took several days to recognise and correct the error. The seller pays 4% on its overdraft:

$$\text{Claim amount} = £219,000 \times \frac{4}{100} \times \frac{5}{365} = £120$$

The buyer has 15 days to dispute the claim or 30 days to pay it. A buyer will dispute the claim if, for example, it disagrees about the number of days that a transaction remained unsettled, or it believes that the overdraft rate used in the calculation was significantly above the published borrowing rate. To ensure that the claims process is not excessively onerous, there are two recommendations:

1. That any claim under US$500 (or the equivalent in another currency) is written off. This is to prevent more money being spent on the administration (checking and payment) of a claim than the claim is worth.

2. That a claim is not paid if 30 calendar days have lapsed since the actual settlement date. For claims beyond this period, it may be difficult or exceptionally time-consuming to investigate.

This takes into account that the investment manager who transacted the trade may not be the third party who is responsible for the failed or delayed settlement. The guidelines indicate that the actual overdraft rate incurred should be used for the calculation. They also prohibit claiming any additional administration costs for the time and effort of calculating and chasing the claims.

4.4.1 International Securities Association For Institutional Trade Communication (ISITC) Differences

The claims threshold is US$500. Netting of interest claims is discouraged, with certain exceptions. The timetable for response by each entity involved is shown below.

Action	Time (Days)	Cumulative Time
Initial claim issuance (to investment manager)	60	60
Initial claim acknowledgement issuance (by investment manager)	07	
Onward claim transmission to third party	10	70
Claim acknowledgement by third party	07	
Claim investigation/rejection	20	90
Claim settlement/rejection acceptance	30	120

Source: ISITC, International Interest Claims – Best Practices & Market Guidelines

End of Chapter Questions

Think of an answer for each question and refer to the appropriate section for confirmation.

1. Define the following processes involved when an investor decides to buy securities:
   a. trading,
   b. pre-settlement,
   c. settlement.
   Answer Reference: Section 1

2. What data is required for the matching of a settlement instruction?
   Answer Reference: Section 2.1

3. What is clearing and what purpose does it serve?
   Answer Reference: Section 2.2

4. What is novation?
   Answer Reference: Section 2.3

5. What functions are performed by a CCP? How can use of a CCP reduce credit risk for its members?
   Answer Reference: Sections 2.2, 2.3, 2.4

6. What is the purpose of a settlement instruction?
   Answer Reference: Section 3.1

7. What is positioning?
   Answer Reference: Section 3.1

8. Give four examples of secure payment systems and summarise their main features.
   Answer Reference: Section 3.2

9. What is TARGET2 and what function does it serve?
   Answer Reference: Section 3.2.5

10. What is FOP settlement?
    Answer Reference: Section 3.3.1

11. What is DvP? List four mechanisms through which DvP may be achieved.
    Answer Reference: Section 3.3.2

12. What benefits are offered by:
    a. bilateral netting,
    b. multilateral netting?
    Answer Reference: Section 3.3.3

13. What advantages does book-entry transfer offer over physical transfer of securities?
    Answer Reference: Section 3.3.5

14. What is rolling settlement?
    Answer Reference: Section 3.3.6

15. Describe the bid price, the offer price and the spread. Why are these different prices quoted for FX transactions?
    Answer Reference: Section 3.3.7

16. What is:
    a. a spot transaction,
    b. an FX swap,
    c. an outright forward transaction, and
    d. an FX option?
    Answer Reference: Section 3.3.7

17. How does CLS reduce Herstatt risk?
    Answer Reference: Section 3.3.7

18. What is registered ownership?
    Answer Reference: Section 3.4

19. What are the principal differences between ASDA and CSDA?
    Answer Reference: Section 3.5

20. List four reasons why a trade may fail.
    Answer Reference: Section 4.1

21. List two reasons why a counterparty may have insufficient securities to meet its settlement obligations.
    Answer Reference: Section 4.1

22. What is buying-in and selling-out?
    Answer Reference: Section 4.2

23. What system of fines does EUI have in place to penalise firms that fail to meet its targets for matching and trade settlement?
    Answer Reference: Section 4.3

24. What is the formula used to calculate interest claims?
    Answer Reference: Section 4.4

25. What are the ISITC interest claim thresholds?
    Answer Reference: Section 4.4.1

Chapter Four
Other Investor Services

This syllabus area will provide approximately 11 of the 50 examination questions

1.   Safekeeping

Learning Objective

4.1.1   Understand the principles of safekeeping client assets: to safeguard assets; to segregate safe custody investments; to reconcile safe custody investments; to maintain records and controls in respect of the use of mandates

Regulatory authorities in each of the selected markets lay down guidelines and requirements for firms holding client assets and **client money**. These regulations typically uphold the following general principles.

1.1   Requirements for Safeguarding Assets

Firms must ensure that they have effective arrangements in place to protect client assets held in their care. These must prevent the co-mingling of assets owned by the client and the firm to minimise the risk that the client's safe custody investments might be:

- used by the firm without the client's agreement or knowledge, or
- treated as the firm's assets in the event of its insolvency.

1.2   Segregation of Safe Custody Assets

In keeping with the above, a clear distinction must be maintained between safe custody investments held on behalf of clients and the firm's own designated investments.

In practice, this implies that:

1.   As provider of custody services, a firm must ensure that, if it holds client assets, the title of the account must make it clear that the safe custody investment belongs to the client, and is segregated from the firm's own designated investments. This requirement is necessary to ensure the client's assets are fully protected in instances of the liquidation or insolvency of either the custodian or third parties it relies on for custody services.
2.   When employing the services of a custodian, a firm must ensure that it is made clear in the title of the account that it holds assets belonging to a client of the firm. Before a firm holds a custody asset with a custodian that is in the same group as the firm, it must typically inform the client in writing that it intends to do so.
3.   When using nominee arrangements, a firm must ensure that the same standards of care are delivered to the client by any nominee company (see section 3) that is controlled by the firm.

A firm must ensure that arrangements for holding any document of title to a safe custody investment are appropriate to the value and risk of loss of the safe custody investments concerned. It must also ensure that adequate controls are in place to safeguard these documents from damage, misappropriation or other loss.

1.3   Reconciliation of Safe Custody Investments

Firms are required, at periodic intervals (in the UK this is at least every 25 business days), to perform a reconciliation of the record of safe custody investments for which they are accountable, but which they do not physically hold themselves.

This reconciliation process must be supported by appropriate statements obtained from custodians detailing client assets held in their safekeeping. Similarly, for any dematerialised investments that are not held through a custodian (eg, assets held at a central securities depository [CSD]), appropriate statements must be obtained from the body that maintains the record of legal entitlement.

A firm must periodically (in the UK at least once every six months, or twice in a period of 12 months but at least five months apart) conduct a **count** of all safe custody investments it physically holds on behalf of clients, and reconcile this with its records of assets held in safe custody.

- **Nominee and other safe custody holdings** – this reconciliation process must include all safe custody investments recorded in the firm's books and records, and those of any nominee company controlled by the firm that it uses for providing safe custody services.
- **Correcting discrepancies** – a firm must promptly correct any discrepancies that are revealed through the reconciliation process, and compensate for any unreconciled shortfall for which there are reasonable grounds for concluding that the firm is responsible.
- **Record-keeping** – a firm must ensure that proper records of the custody assets that it holds on behalf of clients are kept and retained for a period of three years after they are made.
- **Stock lending and borrowing** – a firm that uses a safe custody investment in stock lending activity must ensure that its records identify clearly which safe custody investments are available to be lent, and which are currently out on loan.
- **Non-compliance** – a firm must inform the regulator in writing without delay if it is unable to comply with any element of the reconciliation requirements specified by **Client Asset Safekeeping (CASS) rules**.

Note that a designated investment need not typically be treated as a safe custody investment in respect of a delivery versus payment (DVP) transaction through a commercial settlement system if it is intended that the designated investment is to be:

- due to the client within one business day (though a different time window may apply in some jurisdictions) following the client's fulfilment of a payment obligation, or
- in respect of a client's sale, due to the firm within one business day following the fulfilment of a payment obligation.

1.4   Custodian Appraisal

A firm that holds safe custody investments with a custodian, or recommends custodians to private customers, must have an effective and transparent process in place for evaluating the performance of its custodians. The frequency of these risk reviews should be dependent on the nature of the market and the types of services that the custodian delivers to the client. The firm should maintain clear records detailing the criteria and rationale employed to appoint and reappoint custodians.

In conducting a risk assessment of the custodian, a firm should give due consideration to the following criteria:

- the expertise and market reputation of the custodian

- the arrangements for holding and safeguarding an investment
- an appropriate legal opinion regarding the level of protection afforded to custody assets in the event of the liquidation or insolvency of the custodian or a subcustodian it employs
- procedures for disaster recovery and to ensure technology resilience
- current industry standard reports (eg, an Auditing and Assurance Facility [AAF] 01/06 report [see chapter 6, section 4.1] or its equivalent)
- whether the custodian is regulated, and by whom
- the capital or financial resources of the custodian, and
- any other activities undertaken by the custodian and, where relevant, any affiliated company.

1.5   Records and Controls Relating to the Use of Mandates

The mandate rules apply to a firm that has been granted written authority by a client to control the client's assets and/or to create liabilities in the client's name. These rules require that the firm maintain appropriate records and internal controls to prevent the misuse of this authority granted by the client. This must include:

- an up-to-date list of these written authorities and any conditions placed by the client, or the firm's management, on how these may be used
- a record of all transactions conducted using this mandated authority, and details of internal controls that are in place to ensure that these transactions are within the scope of the authority
- details of the procedures covering how instructions should be sent to and from the custodian under this authority
- where the firm holds a passbook or similar documents belonging to the client, details of the internal controls that are in place to safeguard (against loss, unauthorised destruction, theft, fraud or misuse) any passbook or similar document belonging to the client.

2.   Substantial Shareholder Reporting

Learning Objective

4.1.2   Understand the requirements of substantial shareholding reporting

Substantial shareholder reporting regulations require shareholders to inform a company when their ownership moves above, or below, a specified percentage of the overall issued capital in that company. The initial disclosure threshold in the UK is 3% of the **listed company's** voting shares. Elsewhere in the world it might be 5% (as in Hong Kong and the US) or 10% (as in Taiwan or Sri Lanka). Shareholders may then be required to disclose further increases or reductions in their holding relative to this threshold (ie, for each 1% increase or decrease in its holding, as in Hong Kong, or when their holding crosses other specified thresholds).

Typically, substantial shareholder reporting rules also empower companies to enquire into the ownership of their shares. To do so, a company must send a written notice to any investor or company that it has reasonable cause to believe has owned or had rights over its share capital (under Section 793 of the UK Companies Act 2006, for example, this is any investor that has owned, controlled or had rights over its shares during the last three years).

The recipient of the notice is required to inform the company (typically, within three or five business days, although this will vary from market to market) of its interest in the company. If it fails to do so, the company may approach the court to apply restrictions on the rights attached to the shares in question. In practice, this may involve disenfranchising the shares by, for example, prohibiting their sale or transfer, and by suspending dividend payments, voting rights and other corporate ownership benefits attached to the shares.

3. The Nominee Concept

Learning Objective

4.1.3   Understand the functions of nominee companies and the following concepts: legal title; beneficial ownership; pooled nominee holdings; designated nominee holdings; nominee as bare trustee; omnibus accounts; segregated accounts

When institutional investors or investment managers hold significant volumes of overseas assets in multiple locations, it is sometimes logistically impractical or impossible for them to hold these assets in their own name (known as name on register) and much more convenient to register them in the name of the custodian or nominee that is providing safekeeping and investment administration services for these cross-border assets. This is known as the nominee concept.

Nominee companies have long been established as the mechanism by which custodians (or another intermediary authorised by the investor) can process transactions on behalf of their clients. Given that many investment management firms outsource some or all of their investment administration activities to a specialist custodian, the vast majority of institutional shareholdings, and those of wealthy private investors, now reside in nominee accounts overseen by specialist custodians.

Under UK company law, the nominee name appearing on its share register holds legal title to the share and is thus the legal owner of the shares for the purposes of benefits and for voting. However, **beneficial ownership** continues to reside with the underlying client.

Because the nominee's name appears on the share register, all shareholder communication will be addressed to the nominee and can be processed promptly by the nominee according to instructions that it receives from the beneficial owner.

Nominees can be classified into three types:

- **Pooled nominee holdings**, whereby individual clients' assets are grouped together in a single nominee registration (also called an omnibus account).
- **Designated nominee holdings** can also provide anonymity, where each client's asset holding is registered separately next to the nominee company's name. Hence, the nominee name includes a unique account identifier for each individual client, eg, XYZ Nominees Account 1, XYZ Nominees Account 2, XYZ Nominees Account 3.
- **Sole nominee holdings**, where a single, dedicated nominee name is used for each specific client, eg, LMN Pension Fund Nominees Ltd.

Appropriate regulations need to be in place to ensure that the firm properly accounts for such nominee holdings and to safeguard the investor's position. Regulations governing firms holding client assets (see section 1) typically require that the custodian has a separate nominee company to hold clients' investments, thus ensuring that a client's investments are segregated from those owned by the firm itself. The money that is attributable to clients must also be held in a designated client money account that is beyond the reach of creditors, should the firm go into liquidation.

For a large custodian providing safekeeping services for a large number of cross-border clients, using an omnibus account structure can reduce the complexity and costs involved in servicing clients' assets in a number of ways:

- Entitlements due to the custodian's investor clients will be paid directly by the issuing company into the custodian's nominee account as an aggregated payment, rather than as many individualised payments for each beneficial owner.
- The custodian has only to reconcile one holding on receipt of each issue, rather than multiple beneficiary-level accounts.
- Only the nominee's name appears on the records of the registrar, providing anonymity to beneficial shareholders.
- Transfers of securities between clients of the custodian do not need to be reregistered. Legal title to the securities remains in the name of the custodian, as nominee, before and after the transaction. Hence, the transaction is recorded purely as a transfer of securities against cash from Client A to Client B on the books of the custodian. However, custodians will typically be required to report the transaction to the relevant authorities and to account for any transfer taxes or other obligations that may be due.

When deciding whether to allow an intermediary (eg, its custodian) to use a nominee account structure to administer its assets, an investor should take into account how it will affect the following:

- receipt of annual report and accounts
- voting rights on shares
- timing of dividend receipts
- impact on other corporate ownership privileges and benefits
- cost structure applied by the nominee
- legal status of the nominee concept in the jurisdiction concerned
- security and segregation of assets
- corporate action instructions.

Indeed, the type of registration structure employed has an important bearing on the rights held by beneficial owners when it comes to voting shares. Clients pooled together with others in an omnibus account structure are typically not visible to the company: the nominee is recognised by the company as legal owner of the client's assets. Thus, from a voting perspective, it is only the nominee that is entitled to vote. No separate entitlement is extended by the registrar to each individual client making up the total omnibus holding. In practice, the nominee may canvass the voting preferences of the underlying clients, but it may not hold a formal obligation to do so unless this is spelt out in the custody agreement.

Given the growing importance attached to corporate governance, some investors may wish to maintain their visibility on the share register and to ensure that their voting rights are protected and exercised directly. In these instances, they may require that their custodian registers their holding via a designated nominee structure, or as a segregated (ie, sole) nominee holding. This will protect their voting rights before the company registrar.

From the nominee's perspective, there may be advantages, in certain circumstances, in registering the client via a designated nominee structure. This approach will ensure that the custodian receives a separate set of company reports and documentation for each beneficial owner. This can then be forwarded to the client as required. Of greater importance, however, is the fact that a unique nominee registration or designation will generate an individual, identifiable voting entitlement for each company meeting, thereby enabling voting instructions to be carried out cleanly and with a clear audit trail.

Summary: Characteristics of Pooled Nominee and Designated Nominee Holdings

Pooled	Designated
<ul><li>The company registrar maintains just one registration for any particular company.</li><li>The nominee retains records of each client's holdings.</li></ul>	<ul><li>Each beneficial owner's holding is registered separately.</li><li>Still in the nominee company's name.</li><li>With an additional identifying code.</li></ul>

If the nominee is asked by the client to serve as bare trustee, then the custodian carries no discretionary powers and will be required to act only on the basis of instructions from the beneficial owner. As bare trustee, the custodian must only act when it is instructed to act, and must act only as instructed.

4.   Custodian Fee Schedules

Learning Objective

4.1.4   Understand how a custodian charges for the services it provides to its clients

4.1.5   Be able to calculate the cost of custody for a given portfolio given a value of assets held and the basis point price

The methods employed by global custodians to charge for their services are arranged on a case-by-case basis and are dependent on the volume of business that the client puts through the custodian, the length and strength of the relationship, the reputational benefits that the custodian may experience by having that client on board, and a range of broader factors.

Prestigious clients can sometimes negotiate preferential terms, given the size of their business and the valuable endorsement that their custom may bring to the custodian's reputation in the marketplace.

In general terms, investor clients will pay their custodian on the basis of:

- a basis point fee charged against the value of assets that the investor holds with the custodian (known as an *ad valorem* fee) – this is sometimes set with a minimum fee, or
- a transaction fee, which will be charged according to the number of settlement transactions that the custodian processes on the client's behalf.

The *ad valorem* fee represents a payment for the asset-servicing duties that the custodian performs on the investor's behalf. The transaction fee represents a charge for clearing and settlement services.

In both areas, the precise fee paid by the investor client will vary according to volume, and according to where its assets are held and/or its transactions settled. *Ad valorem* and transaction fees in complex and high-risk emerging markets will, typically, be higher than in mature and efficient markets in which market practices comply closely with global standards.

Within this package of core services, investor clients will commonly expect to receive the following suite of services:

- safe custody
- income collection
- tax services
- processing of corporate actions
- cash management, and
- supply of market information.

For additional services (often referred to as value-added services) such as securities lending, performance and risk analysis and proxy voting services, supplementary charges are likely to be added by the custodian. The custodian will also expect to generate significant revenue by handling clients' FX and treasury requirements.

The custodian may typically offer reduced custody tariffs to customers that buy a bundled package of services. As a general rule of thumb, the more services the client buys from the custodian, the greater the number of markets in which it buys them and the larger the volume of business that it brings to the custodian, the greater the client is likely to benefit from fee discounts as a result of economies of scale.

Pricing schedules can become a point of dispute when a custodian charges separately for a service that the client feels should be covered by the core custody fee. Consequently, when drawing up their custody contract, both parties must be specific about exactly which suite of services is included in the core custody package, which services the custodian will charge separately for, and how much the client will be required to pay for these value-added services.

Example

An investment manager has a portfolio of assets with market value US$500 million held in a major market such as the US, UK, France or Germany. The custodian charges the investor – a long-established client with a medium-sized portfolio – a 1 basis point (ie, 0.01%) *ad valorem* fee to provide core custody services for this portfolio. The annual fee paid by the investment manager will be:

$$500,000,000 \times \frac{0.01}{100} = 50,000$$

The client will pay the custodian US$50,000 per annum to provide custody for this portfolio.

Example

An investment manager has invested assets with a market value of US$2 million held in an emerging market such as Brazil. The custodian charges a 20 basis point fee (ie, 0.20%) to provide custody for this portfolio.

The annual fee paid by the investment manager will be:

$$2,000,000 \times \frac{0.20}{100} = 4,000$$

The client will pay the custodian US$4,000 to provide custody for this portfolio of assets for the year.

The extra basis point fee charged by the custodian in an emerging market reflects:

1. the additional risks that the custodian will bear in providing custody for assets held in this location (when compared with holding assets in a more mature market as in the previous example),
2. a lower scale discount offered on the transaction fee (since the client's trade volumes in emerging markets will often be lower than in larger, more mature markets), and
3. the higher costs borne by the custodian in servicing assets in a less developed market.

A further reason why the fee may be larger in an emerging market is that there may be less competition, ie, not as many viable providers as there are in a developed market.

While most custodians will offer clients the option of paying for their clearing, settlement and custody services as part of a bundled package, some providers may choose to price their services on an unbundled pay-as-you-use basis.

This option is designed to provide freedom of choice to the user, allowing them, if they so wish, to purchase clearing services from one clearing agent, to settle their trades with a different settlement agent, and to buy their custody/asset servicing from somebody else.

5. Corporate Actions

The term corporate action refers to events that arise when an issuer opts to change the structure of its company's securities, or to issue benefits to shareholders, commonly in the form of cash dividends, shares, or the right to buy newly issued shares.

Corporate actions may be initiated by a company, for example, when it makes a dividend or interest payment, or when it puts a motion to a shareholder vote at a company meeting. Corporate actions may also result from action on the part of the shareholder, for example when a shareholder opts to exercise a warrant, to take up a rights issue, or to convert a convertible bond.

Any benefit arising from a corporate action is due to the beneficial owner. However, the benefit will actually accrue to the registered holder (this may be a nominee acting on behalf of the beneficial owner) on ex-date (see section 5.5). Given that shares may have been bought or sold in the lead-up to this event, this may give rise to claims in the market if the buyer is not registered in time for the corporate action.

5.1   Risks for the Custodian

Learning Objective

4.2.3   Understand the importance of receiving timely and accurate corporate action data and the risks involved

Corporate actions involve a high level of risk for the custodian. If the custodian fails to inform its investor client of an upcoming corporate event, or fails to process the client's instructions accurately or in a timely fashion, then the custodian will typically be required to compensate for any financial loss that results.

When an error is made in processing a corporate action, there is a high possibility that this will result in a capital loss for the investor. The size of this loss can be difficult to quantify until the custodian has closed that exposure down – for example, by buying shares for the client to which it was entitled, or by selling unsolicited shares issued through a corporate action that the client did not want. Until this point, the custodian is at the mercy of the market, and the more the market moves against the custodian, the larger the financial loss it is likely to incur.

Given these considerations, receipt of timely and accurate corporate actions data is crucial to effective risk management.

The principal challenge in processing corporate actions is to ensure that the entitlements owing to the beneficial owner of the securities are collected in full and at the earliest possible point. Custodians bear a primary responsibility for alerting their investor clients to forthcoming corporate events, ensuring that they have comprehensive information on the structure of the corporate event and, in the case of voluntary corporate actions, that clients' instructions are conveyed to the company registrar before the deadline in order for its entitlement to be upheld. The custodian will also need to be aware of the regulations in different jurisdictions, as there may be local rules that stipulate that residents should not be sent the documentation (eg, in Japan, Canada and South Africa).

To ensure that client instructions can be processed efficiently before this deadline, the custodian will typically specify a cut-off point, which is the latest time that instructions may be received from the client to guarantee that they are filed before the event deadline.

If instructions are sent by the client before this cut-off point, and the custodian fails to communicate these instructions before the event deadline, the custodian is likely be required to cover any resulting losses. Client instructions received after this cut-off point will typically be processed on a **best efforts** basis only, and the custodian will typically not cover resulting losses that may occur if the event deadline is missed.

Global custodians, and the subcustodians that they employ across their global agent bank networks, will draw on a range of data sources that provide information on forthcoming corporate events. This will include information which is:

* supplied directly by the company or its registrar
* supplied through data feeds purchased from data vendors, such as FT Interactive Data, Bloomberg and Reuters

- supplied via stock exchanges or CSDs
- published in the local and international press
- collected through the subcustodian's network of contacts in the local market.

To ensure the validity of this information, it is important that:

- it can be cross-checked against a number of independent sources
- data from these multiple sources is consolidated into a single, accurate source of validated information (any inconsistencies must be followed up and clarified)
- this consolidated and verified information is sent to the investor in good time, enabling a timely response from the investor before the instruction deadline.

5.2 Mandatory Corporate Events

Learning Objective

4.2.1 Know the characteristics of the following mandatory events: dividends (cash and scrip); interest and coupon payments; capitalisation issues; splits and consolidations; capital repayments/redemptions

4.2.5 Be able to calculate corporate actions-related data on capitalisations, scrip and rights issues and the effect on the underlying share price

Corporate actions can be mandatory or voluntary.

Mandatory corporate events involve entitlements that accrue to a shareholder without the shareholder needing to take a decision about whether to participate. Cash dividend payments, bonus issues, splits and **consolidations**, for example, result from decisions taken by the company's directors and are applied to all shares for all shareholders. The distribution of **nil paid rights** is also a mandatory event.

5.2.1 Dividends

A dividend payment reflects a decision by a company's board of directors, subject to shareholder approval, to distribute a percentage of its profits to shareholders by paying a fixed dividend per share. Most commonly, a dividend is paid in cash (a cash dividend) in the issue currency. However, dividends are sometimes paid in the form of shares (a **scrip dividend**) instead of cash, or dividend reinvestment.

In some instances, the shareholder may be given the option of selecting the format in which the dividend is paid, whether cash or shares. The global custodian must ensure that the client receives timely and accurate information regarding the structure of the upcoming corporate event, and that its instructions are received and recorded in timely fashion.

- If the investor is recorded by the custodian as requesting a dividend payment in cash when it actually wanted a payment in shares, the custodian may expose itself to significant loss if the market moves in the wrong direction before the error is rectified. The global custodian will typically be required to compensate for this loss to its investor clients.

- More broadly, if a custodian fails to inform its investor clients of a corporate event, it is again likely that it will be required to compensate for any resultant loss of entitlement to the investor.

Some types of fund (eg, income funds) will have standing instructions in place with their custodian specifying that cash should always be taken rather than scrip.

5.2.2 Interest and Coupon Payments

An interest payment is a cash entitlement paid to the holders of debt securities, including government bonds, corporate bonds, eurobonds, foreign bonds and convertible bonds. Interest payments are an example of predictable benefits, in that the size of the interest payment (the coupon rate) and the timing of the payment (the coupon payment date) are announced in advance, namely at the time that the debt security was issued. An exception is floating rate bonds, where the coupon rate is not announced in advance since it will vary with the benchmark interest rate.

5.2.3 Capitalisation Issues

A capitalisation (or bonus) issue is a release of new shares to existing shareholders, given free of cost from the issuing company's capital reserves. A company may elect to issue bonus shares in this way as an alternative to returning accumulated reserves to shareholders as dividend. The company will typically transfer funds from its profit and loss account to a capital redemption reserve fund and will use this to issue bonus shares to shareholders in proportion to the size of their existing holdings.

The aggregate market value of the existing and bonus shares will remain the same before and after the bonus issue. Hence, the issue of bonus shares will prompt a change in the share price.

Example

An investor holds 3,000 ordinary shares in a stock that is priced at £1.00 per share. The company subsequently issues a 1:3 share bonus, such that each ordinary shareholder receives one new share for every three existing shares in its holding. As such, the investor receives an additional 1,000 shares through the bonus issue, resulting in a total post-issue holding of 4,000 shares.

Since the aggregate market value of the shareholder's holding will remain unchanged at 3,000 before and after the bonus issue, the price of each share will fall. £3,000/4,000 shares = to £0.75 per share. The reduced price, along with the additional shares in circulation, will make the shares more marketable and thereby improve the company's share liquidity.

Why do bonus issues occur? Rather than pay a cash dividend, a company may choose to issue new shares to existing shareholders to reflect an increase in the company's capital reserves. Since this allocation is made from the company's capital reserves, it may not be liable for taxation.

5.2.4 Splits

A **stock split** or subdivision reflects a decision by a company's directors to convert a single share in the company into a larger number of shares, without any change taking place in the aggregate market value of the shares of the company.

Example

An investor owns 1,000 shares with a nominal value of €0.20 in a company, priced at €100 per share. The company then decides to split its shares one-for-two. As a result, the investor will subsequently hold 2,000 shares with a nominal value of €0.10 after the split, and the price of each share will fall to €50.

In contrast, if the company had decided to split its share one-for-four, the same investor would subsequently hold 4,000 shares with a nominal value of €0.05, each priced at €25.

The dividend per share distributed by the company will generally fall in direct proportion to the increased number of authorised shares issued in the company.

Why do share splits occur? Generally because company directors wish to reduce the share price of the shares in the company to make them more attractive to investors, while simultaneously increasing the number of shares issued, thereby leaving the market value of the company unchanged. In the above example, the board of directors may feel that, when the share price rises above €100 per share, investors (especially retail investors) may be less eager to buy the share. Directors may also wish to increase the number of shares in circulation to increase trading volumes, and therefore liquidity (in addition to access), to make the company a more attractive investment.

To encourage more individual investors to purchase the stock, it may therefore engage in a one-for-two (1:2) split that reduces the price per share to €50.

5.2.5 Consolidations

Conversely, a stock consolidation reflects a decision by a company's directors to amalgamate multiple shares in a company into a single share.

Example

An investor owns 4,000 shares in a company, each priced at US$0.25. The company then decides to consolidate its shares four-for-one. This will reduce the number of issued ordinary shares in the company fourfold, but without affecting the overall shareholder equity (ie, the aggregate market value of authorised shares). Subsequent to the split, the shareholder will own 1,000 shares, each priced at US$1.00. ('Ordinary shares' are called 'common shares' in the US.)

Why do companies opt to consolidate their shares? This may reduce the complexity of administering shares in the company by lowering the number of issued shares in circulation. As we saw above, this may also be designed to establish a market value for shares that the board of directors feel will be more appealing to existing and potential shareholders. This may particularly be the case when the share price of the authorised shares has fallen sharply as a result of tough economic conditions and/or loss of investor confidence in the company's performance.

5.2.6 Capital Repayments

A capital repayment reflects a decision by a company's directors to repay a portion of the company's issued capital to shareholders. The number of issued shares will remain the same, but the nominal value of the shares will fall by the amount of the capital repayment reimbursed per share. A capital repayment in full is when the company repays all of the issued capital in specified categories of shares to the registered shareholders.

Capital repayments are typically arranged when company directors wish to return some or all of the issued capital in a particular class of shares to shareholders.

5.2.7 Redemptions

The issuer of a fixed-income security is required to repay the principal and any outstanding coupon payments or accrued interest at maturity (ie, on redemption date) to the legal owner of the debt security.

5.3 Voluntary Corporate Events

Learning Objective

4.2.2   Know the characteristics of the following voluntary events: rights issue subscription; conversions; takeovers; exchanges; initial public offerings (IPOs); proxy voting; exercise of warrants

4.2.5   Be able to calculate corporate actions-related data on capitalisations, scrip and rights issues and the effect on the underlying share price

Voluntary corporate events demand that the shareholder communicate a response to the company regarding whether it wishes to accept the terms of the corporate action or to reject it. A response will be required to exercise certain forms of entitlement available to the shareholder (eg, to exercise a put option or a rights issue).

5.3.1 Rights Issues and Subscriptions

Rights issues give existing shareholders the right to subscribe to an issue of new shares, usually at a discount to the market price. The issuance of rights is a mandatory corporate event. However, shareholders are entitled to elect whether they subscribe to the offer of new shares and this element is, therefore, a voluntary event. The shareholders' entitlement to purchase new shares will be in proportion to the number of shares already owned.

The main stages in a rights issue are:

- distribution of the rights entitlement by the issuer to the existing shareholders
- shareholders elect or decline to subscribe to the offer of new common shares, or may trade their entitlement with another investor

- non-subscribed rights will expire at the **subscription** deadline. Typically, the company will sell off lapsed rights (ie, rights that have not been exercised) subsequent to the issue process. Any premium (ie, positive difference between the price attained through this sale of shares and the take-up price) will then be paid to shareholders that did not sell or take up their rights. If no premium was generated during this sale, then no lapsed rights proceeds will be distributed. Lapsed rights are paid minus commission and fees.

Note from bullet point two that shareholder entitlements under many rights issues are tradeable. Shareholders have the option of selling nil paid rights (ie, rights that have not been exercised) to a counterparty up to a specified cut-off point before the call payment date (in cases where rights are not transferable, these are known as non-renounceable rights).

The aggregate market value of the existing and newly issued shares will remain the same before and after the rights issue. Hence, the rights issue will prompt a change in the share price. The calculation methodology is comparable to that described for bonus issues in the previous section.

Example

An investor holds 3,000 shares in a stock that is priced at £2.00 per share. The company subsequently makes a 2:3 rights issue at £1.50, such that each ordinary shareholder has a right, but not an obligation, to purchase two new shares at this price for every three existing shares that it holds.

The investor decides to subscribe to the rights issue. Consequently, it acquires a further 2,000 shares through the rights issue at £1.50, to supplement its existing holding of 3,000 shares each worth £2.00.

Hence, the total value of the investor's shares will be:

$$(3,000 \times £2.00) + (2,000 \times £1.50)$$

$$= £6,000 + £3,000$$

$$= £9,000$$

The investor now holds 5,000 shares in total:

$$\text{Price per share} = \frac{£9,000}{£5,000} = £1.80$$

Hence, the price per share after the rights issue will be expected to adjust to £1.80 (the adjusted ex-rights price). Note that this is a theoretical price. Stock market conditions and level of investor demand dictate that the share price will constantly fluctuate for tradeable securities, so the price may rapidly move away from this predicted level.

To estimate the capital gain that the investor may secure by selling the rights, an approximate value may be calculated as follows:

Nil paid rights = adjusted ex-rights price – rights issue price

$$= £1.80 – £1.50$$

$$= £0.30$$

So we would expect the nil paid rights to be worth £0.30 per share.

5.3.2 Conversions

Investors holding convertible bonds may elect to convert these debt securities into shares. The conditions for this conversion are outlined at the time that the convertible bonds are initially issued. Typically, these allow the investor to change the convertible bonds into shares at pre-established rates and at pre-established times fixed by the issuing company.

When the time period for a conversion expires, bondholders, who have not converted into equity according to the terms specified when the convertible bond was issued, will automatically have the bonds redeemed for cash.

5.3.3 Takeovers

A takeover is an attempt by a company to acquire all or a portion of the issued share capital of another company. A friendly takeover describes a takeover bid where the bidding company has the support of the management of the target company. A hostile takeover refers to a bid where the management of the target company opposes the takeover and may attempt to obstruct the takeover process. The bidding company is often referred to as a predator.

The objective of the bidding company is to secure a majority holding in the target company. Typically, the process will involve an offer of cash or securities or both to existing shareholders of the target company. The takeover commonly advances through the following procedure:

1. The takeover is announced by the board of directors of the bidding company.
2. Subsequently, shareholders in the target company will be given a specified period in which to vote on whether to accept the offer. In some jurisdictions, if the percentage of shareholders in the target company that accept the offer reaches a specified threshold (this may be 50.01% of shareholders for example), then the bidding company gains control of the target company.
3. The proceeds of the takeover offer, in the form of cash or securities or both, will be distributed to shareholders whose shares have been acquired.

5.3.4 Debt Tenders and Exchanges

A company can offer bondholders the right to exchange their debt securities for a specified amount of cash or shares during a specified time period. This process may happen during an acquisition deal, for example when the acquiring company offers bondholders in the target company the right to exchange these debt securities for cash or shares in the merged entity.

5.3.5 Exercise of Warrants

A warrant provides the right for the holder to subscribe to shares in a company at a specified price (the strike price) at a specified date or dates in the future. When the warrant is exercised, the company will issue the specified number of shares to the warrant holder, as described more fully in chapter 1.

A covered warrant is a synthetic product structured by an investment bank or another financial institution over a range of possible underlying assets, which may be a share in a company, a share price index, a commodity, a currency or a basket of currencies. The issuer pays a cash sum for the intrinsic value of the warrants at the expiry date, or on exercise. In other words, although the terms of warrants are usually expressed as a right to purchase the underlying share(s), a covered warrant is more accurately a right to receive a cash payment equivalent to the difference between the exercise price and the value of the underlying asset at expiry.

5.3.6 Initial Public Offerings (IPOs)

IPOs refer to the mechanism through which a company first floats its shares on the stock market. In the UK, they have traditionally been known as launches or new issues, but the US term IPO is now widely used. The issue methods involved (offers for sale, private placements, introductions) were described in more detail in chapter 1.

5.4   Voting

Shareholders are periodically given the right to vote on resolutions brought before them at company meetings (commonly an annual general meeting or an extraordinary general meeting [AGM or EGM]). This may include votes on:

- election of directors,
- directors' remuneration,
- plans to issue new equity capital,
- stock repurchase plans,
- takeover bids,
- plans to appoint a new auditor,
- specific resolutions brought before the meeting by shareholders themselves,
- approval of a dividend.

A shareholder may opt to exercise this voting right in person by attending the meeting, or by voting by post or electronically. Alternatively, the shareholder may exercise its voting rights through a legally approved third party. This process is known as proxy voting.

With institutional investors and investment managers owning large holdings in some companies, investors are taking increasing interest in the way that their votes can impact on company policy, thereby having a direct influence on the returns that these investors receive on their holdings. This interest has been reinforced by bodies such as the International Corporate Governance Network, an association represented by leading figures from global corporations and financial institutions, which campaign for improved standards of transparency and accountability to shareholders.

5.4.1 Why Does Voting Make a Difference?

The importance attached to shareholder voting has been progressively rising over the last five years. Listed companies play a significant role in the economic and financial system of the UK and it is in the public interest that company directors are accountable to shareholders, who are the owners of the company. As such, it is important that accountability is exercised through the voting rights that come with owning company shares.

In the UK, efforts to formalise these concerns have led to the commissioning of a number of influential reports on corporate governance and voting practice. Building on an important consultation paper by Sir Adrian Cadbury published in 1992, the substance of these reports is now reflected in the Combined Code on Corporate Governance (the Combined Code), published by the Financial Reporting Council, which is annexed to the FCA's listing rules. These rules require listed companies to make a statement on their level of compliance with the Combined Code. A company's directors are not legally required to apply all elements of the Code, but, if they do not do so, they should explain why not. This is known as the comply or explain principle. A similar principle operates in the Netherlands and a number of other jurisdictions.

5.4.2   How the Voting Process Works

When a general meeting is convened in the UK, the company registrar will issue voting papers and details of the agenda to the shareholders and/or custodians acting on behalf of investor clients. These could be:

- an institutional investor,
- a fund manager investing on its own account, or
- a fund manager investing on behalf of an institutional investor. In this case, the institutional investor may vote itself, or may delegate this responsibility to the fund manager.

Many global custodians now employ the services of proxy voting specialists such as Broadridge (formerly ADP Investor Services) or ISS Governance Services (formerly Institutional Shareholder Services, but now a part of RiskMetrics Group) to manage the voting process on their behalf. Under this arrangement, the custodian will pass voting papers to the proxy voting agent, along with details of all holdings in the company, broken down by client. The proxy voting agent will then pass details of the resolutions to be voted, and the relevant holding details, to each investor client.

The investor will subsequently instruct the custodian (or the proxy voting agency acting on the custodian's behalf) how the votes should be cast. The latter will communicate the vote to the company registrar. The company registrar will compare the votes received against its record of owners and will tally the votes cast. In the UK, the Combined Code recommends that issuers should publish a break down of votes cast.

In the US, the Securities and Exchange Commission (SEC) initiated a ruling in 2003 that requires US-registered mutual funds to provide details of their voting policy, and their records of voting, to the SEC. This dovetailed with broader legislation introduced under the Sarbanes-Oxley Act of 2002, designed to protect investors by enhancing the reliability and accuracy of corporate disclosure. The overarching principles are:

- Mutual funds must demonstrate that they have a clear chain of responsibility for voting shares and their voting policies must be transparent to their members and other concerned members of the public.
- Mutual funds must be clearly accountable to those on whose behalf they act and they should be required to explain periodically how they have discharged their voting obligations.

Similarly, in his high-profile report on proxy voting to the UK Shareholder Voting Working Group in February 2004, Paul Myners indicated that beneficial owners should be responsible for ensuring that there is a clear chain of responsibility for voting their shares in the companies in which they own holdings.

In this report, Myners pointed to a range of obstacles to transparency in the UK voting process:

- The voting process involves many participants and the chain of responsibilities between these parties is not always clear.
- The system is not fully automated, in that some participants still rely on faxes and paper proxy cards.
- Legal title to the shares often rests with the custodian as nominee and, with individual holdings pooled into an omnibus account, the beneficial owner is effectively disenfranchised. This can create difficulties in tracing information from and to the registrar.
- The beneficial owners that own the shares often delegate voting to their fund managers – the fund manager can only issue voting instructions indirectly, given that it is not the legal owner. Automatic confirmation of receipt of voting instructions is usually only possible when the votes are cast electronically.

5.4.3   The Problem of Lost Votes

As a result of these inefficiencies, Myners reported instances where pension funds had cast votes and these votes had not been recorded by the company registrar. This he termed the problem of lost votes.

To address these problems, Myners recommended that:

- Beneficial owners should publish, and adhere to, a clear voting policy, detailing the chain of responsibilities involved in voting shares.
- Levels of automation throughout the proxy voting chain should be extended, with more extensive use of electronic voting.
- The use of designated nominee holdings should be employed to make the voting process more transparent and to make it easier to trace votes from shareholder through to registrar.

Many of these principles are enshrined in the International Corporate Governance Network's best practice guidance, providing a foundation for global efforts to encourage active and efficient shareholder voting and to raise standards of corporate governance worldwide.

Custodians and investment managers can make it easier for their institutional clients to be confident that votes are being cast by reporting on their systems and internal controls through an AAF 01/06 or **SSAE 16** report (see chapter 6), which will normally include details of their voting process. Beneficial owners should ensure that they receive copies of such reports.

5.5 Ex-Benefit versus Cum-Benefit

Learning Objective

4.2.4 Understand the following terms: record date; ex-date; pay date; effective date; cum-benefit; ex-benefit; special-ex and special-cum

If a company's board of directors vote to pay a dividend (quarterly, semi-annually or annually), it will announce the type of dividend to be paid, the amount to be paid per share, the payable date (ie, the value date) and the record date. The ex-dividend date (ex-date) is the date that determines the eligibility of a shareholder to receive the declared benefit. The registrar will inspect the share register on record date, and will pay the declared dividend per share to all shareholders whose names appear on the register at that point. This entitlement will be paid to these shareholders on pay date (also known as payment date, or payable date).

The same principle applies to rights issues. Companies raising additional money may do so by offering their shareholders the right to subscribe to new or additional stock, usually at a discount to the prevailing market price. The buyer of a stock selling ex-rights is not entitled to the rights.

When considering claims on rights issues, note that in some markets the ex-date will precede the record date (often known as record date-driven markets). In other markets, the ex-date will be after the record date (typically labelled ex-date-driven markets).

Example

Consider a situation where Investor A purchases 1,000 shares from Investor B in a market that is record-date-driven, operating a T+3 settlement cycle for equities.

The ex-date for a rights issue event is 3 November. The record date is 5 November. Investor A purchases shares on 1 November (ie, two days before ex-date) and thus will be entitled to the rights. This transaction will settle on T+3 (ie, 4 November). The registrar will examine who is the owner of the shares at close of business on record date (5 November) and will pay the rights to Investor A, who is legal owner of the shares at this time.

Now consider a situation where Investor A purchases 1,000 shares from Investor B in a market that is ex-date-driven, operating a T+3 settlement cycle for equities.

The ex-date for a rights issue event is 4 November. The record date is 3 November. Investor A purchases shares on 2 November (ie, two days before ex-date) and thus will be entitled to the rights. The registrar will examine who is legal owner of the shares at close of business on record date and will pay the rights to Investor B (who is still legal owner since the transaction will settle on T+3, ie, 5 November).

Consequently, Investor A will need to claim these rights from Investor B.

If the security has been purchased before the ex-date, the purchaser is entitled to the dividend or rights (this is called the cum-benefit), given that they will be the beneficial owner of the security on record date.

If the security has been purchased on or after the ex-date, the seller is entitled to the dividend or rights (this is called the ex-benefit). Consequently, after the ex-date, the stock begins to trade in the market at a lower price because it assumes no dividend or rights.

5.5.1 Ex-Benefit and Cum-Benefit Periods for Dividend Payments

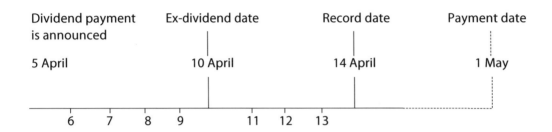

Cum-dividend period	Ex-dividend period
Entitlement paid to buyer	Entitlement not paid to buyer
Seller does not receive entitlement	Seller receives entitlement

The date on which entitlement is accredited to the legal owner of the security is commonly known as the effective date. After a stock split, for example, the owner will receive their converted shares on the effective date.

When shares are traded, you should be aware whether they are traded with the entitlement to the next dividend (cum-dividend) or without that entitlement (ex-dividend).

While we have used dividend payments as an example, the same logic will apply when considering interest payments on debt securities, and some other entitlements due to shareholders by virtue of their corporate ownership rights.

5.5.2 Special-Ex and Special-Cum

In some markets, counterparties conducting a trade during the cum-benefit period have the right to agree that the security is being sold ex-benefit. This is known as special-ex. Similarly, in some markets, counterparties conducting a trade during the ex-benefit period may agree to trade the security cum-benefit. This is known as special-cum.

When these special conditions are applied, the trade price agreed between buyer and seller will reflect whether the security is traded ex-benefit or cum-benefit.

6. Cash Management

Learning Objective

4.3.1 Understand the importance and use of cash management

4.3.2 Understand the advantages and disadvantages of operating single and multi-currency accounts

4.3.3 Know what is meant by the terms sweeping and pooling as they relate to base currency and settlement currency

4.3.4 Understand the importance of cash forecasting tools

Cash management refers to the set of strategic policies that an organisation will employ to optimise the use of its cash resources. Specifically, this includes collecting payments, controlling disbursements, covering shortfalls, forecasting cash needs, investing uninvested cash and managing liquidity.

The goal is to ensure that cash holdings are employed in the most effective way possible, either covering payments or generating income for the company concerned. Leading global custodians commonly offer a wide range of treasury and FX services to institutional investors and corporate clients. These are designed to provide integrated multi-currency banking and payments facilities through their global networks that are tailored to the needs of individual clients.

This demands:

1. A detailed knowledge of the client's business in order to understand where cash needs to be at a particular time (eg, to settle a pending transaction) in order to meet payment obligations and avoid penalties.
2. A detailed understanding of the cash flows into the client's business and when these are likely to arrive. For securities investment companies, key cash flows will be through profit and loss on their portfolio trading, and through income paid (dividends, coupons) on their investments.
3. Sophisticated cash forecasting tools to predict a client's cash flows on a short-term (covering one day to two weeks) and medium-term (covering a few weeks up to one or two years) basis. This is necessary to ensure that funding requirements are met as cheaply as possible and that cash balances are utilised efficiently to generate optimum return. The goal is to predict in advance the amount of credit balance (or overdraft) that is expected at the custodian at a forthcoming date (eg, over the next two business days) and then to act on this prediction. When a trade is settled on behalf of the client, for example, the resultant credit (or debit) should be offset by a corresponding cash movement to or from the client, so that there is a zero cash balance at the custodian and no debit or credit interest is incurred at the custodian.
4. Appropriate designated client money bank accounts to ensure that the client's cash holdings are protected, should the custodian go into liquidation.

6.1   Sweep Accounts

To avoid clients having funds sitting overnight in non-interest-bearing accounts, custodians will often offer the use of sweep accounts which allow clients to transfer (or sweep) uninvested cash into overnight investments (or an interest-bearing deposit account) at the end of the business day.

These may be used in parallel with zero-balance accounts, which allow clients to make payments from an account where the balance is held at zero without penalty. Cash is drawn from a central account whenever cash obligations arise that require payment.

6.2   Pooling

Global custodians hold single-currency or multi-currency accounts for their clients. For interest calculations, custodians may pool balances by currency into one larger balance in order to attract a higher rate of interest or reduce the penalties incurred by some accounts being overdrawn. Clear provisions must be in place to ensure clients' cash holdings remain legally separated from those of the custodian and other clients.

6.3   Single-Currency Accounts

With single-currency accounts, cash management is conducted in the investor's base currency. Credits paid to the investor in a foreign currency (eg, income generated from dividend and interest payments, proceeds realised from trading in securities) will be converted through an FX transaction back into the investor's base currency and held in a cash account maintained in the base currency. Similarly, debits paid by the investor (eg, the cost of settling the cash leg of a securities purchase) will be drawn from this single cash account maintained in the base currency and converted through an FX transaction into the required foreign currency.

The benefits of maintaining a single-currency account structure include:

*   Cash reconciliation, audit and accounting processes are conducted in a single currency, aiding simplicity and control.
*   Risk exposure to foreign currency volatility is mitigated. Transactions that yield payment in a foreign currency are converted immediately back into the base currency.
*   The client can shop for the best FX rates for each transaction, which may be more competitive than FX rates offered by its global custodian. If the client wishes to do so, it will need to maintain bank accounts in currencies other than the base currency in order to effect FX settlement (ie, bank accounts in the settlement currency).

Potential disadvantages of employing a single-currency account structure include:

*   Multiple FX transactions engender settlement risk and counterparty risk associated with each individual FX trade.
*   Single account structures may lack the sophistication and flexibility necessary to process the cash management needs of a large global corporation with high-volume cross-border business in multiple locations.
*   The potentially smaller amounts being converted may result in a wider spread on the FX rates offered, or the custodian may use a conversion rate that benefits itself.

6.4 Multi-Currency Accounts

Multi-currency accounts are commonly employed by companies that need to process regular and sizeable payments and credits in a foreign currency.

The benefits of multi-currency account structures include:

- Securities can be settled on a DVP basis in foreign currency.
- These reduce the costs and risks incurred in maintaining multiple FX transactions required by a single-currency account structure.
- A global custodian may offer integrated custody and banking services, providing a one-stop shop for investors' cross-border service needs.

Potential disadvantages of a multi-currency arrangement include:

- The use of multi-currency accounts adds to the complexity of reconciliation and control processes as a result of maintaining accounts in multiple currencies, especially because of dividends received in different currencies.
- A bundled package bought from a global custodian may not always be cheaper for a sizeable investment manager client than managing its own FX trading internally, or via a third-party FX desk.
- Not every market in which an investor client is active will require a centralised cash management function, such as that provided by a multi-currency account structure offered by a custodian.

The client must evaluate how a market-by-market approach compares to the economies of scale offered by a centralised cash management facility.

7. Securities Lending

In simple terms, securities lending is when an owner of securities lends them to a third party with an agreement to buy them back at a future date.

7.1 Legal Ownership Implications of Securities Lending and Borrowing (SLB)

Learning Objective

4.4.2 Know the definition, legal ownership implications and the advantages and disadvantages to the market

4.4.6 Understand the lenders' and borrowers' rights (including manufactured dividends and voting rights)

4.4.9 Understand the reasons why a loan might be recalled

Legal title to on-loan securities passes from the lender to the borrower for the duration of the loan. The lender's entitlements to income payments and other benefits from corporate actions will typically be protected during the loan period, with the borrower paying any benefits to the lender, either directly or via the lending agent. For dividend payments, the payment pass-through is known as a manufactured dividend, and often has taxation implications.

Since the legal ownership of the shares changes hands during this period, the lender will lose voting rights on the shares while they are out on loan. This fact has discouraged some institutional investors from allowing securities under their management to be placed on loan. However, under standard securities-lending agreements, shares can often be recalled for voting purposes. With this in mind, institutional investors are increasingly taking steps when entering into securities-lending agreements to ensure that on-loan securities can be recalled so that voting rights can be exercised.

7.2   Why is SLB Employed?

Learning Objective

4.4.3   Understand the reasons for securities lending

4.4.4   Understand the reasons why loans might be delayed or prevented

For the lender, the main benefit of lending out securities is to generate income. Lending out securities will generate cash that will boost the overall returns that the investor generates on that segment of its portfolio.

Indeed, there are sizeable returns to be made through securities lending on the expansive securities portfolios held by large institutional investors (particularly the largest pension and insurance funds).

Consequently, securities lending has become big business for global custodians and third-party securities-lending agents that have cornered the market for providing securities-lending services to this investor community.

For the borrower, it may wish or need to borrow securities because:

*   it needs to access securities to cover a settlement fail or to avoid a mandatory buy-in (ie, the borrower does not have sufficient securities to meet its settlement obligations)
*   it may be short selling the security concerned and needs to borrow securities to close its position. A market maker may be short of a security owing to strong demand for that security from its customers. Thus, the market maker may need to borrow the security in order to fulfil its obligation to promote a liquid market by buying and selling a specified list of securities at publicly quoted prices (see chapter 1, section 11).

    The rapid growth of the hedge fund industry has created a surge in demand for borrowed securities in order to cover short positions. Hedge funds have commonly satisfied this need for securities borrowing through their **prime brokers**.

The existence of liquid markets for securities lending reduces the risks of failed settlements. Market participants with an obligation to deliver securities that they have failed to receive, and do not hold in inventory, can borrow these securities to complete delivery.

Securities that are on loan cannot typically be voted by the lender in case of, for example, an AGM or EGM. Should the lender wish to exercise voting rights on the stock, they will need to recall the stock before the requisite deadline (ie, before effective date).

If a lender recalls a loaned security and the borrower fails to return it within the required time period, the lender may be forced to buy the securities in the open market (ie to initiate a 'buy in'). Delays may occur because the borrower is using the security to, for example, cover a short sale or to cover a failed settlement and has failed to free up the security in time to meet the lender's deadline for return.

Securities lending is not permitted in some markets globally – for example in many markets in Africa or the Middle East. In others, (in Bolivia, Costa Rica, Venezuela, Bulgaria, Iceland or Slovak Republic to give a few examples), securities lending is permitted but little practised. This may be because an active securities lending culture is still to be established. It may be the result of: legal or tax obstacles that impair the efficiency of securities lending markets; an inadequate legal underpinning of the concept of securities lending; ambiguities around treatment of securities lending transactions in case of a bankruptcy; or a lack of automated procedures required to achieve timely settlement of securities lending transactions.

7.3 Risks Involved and Precautionary Measures

Learning Objective

4.4.1 Understand the role of a lending agent in securities lending and the risks and rewards to those involved

4.4.7 Understand collateral and marking to market

While securities lending may be a useful tool, it presents associated risks to both the borrower and the lender. The securities on loan, or the collateral, may not be returned on the agreed date, whether because of settlement delays and liquidity problems in the market concerned, or the more intimidating prospect of counterparty default or legal challenge. Those securities will then need to be acquired in the market, potentially at high cost.

In order to mitigate the risk of such failures, lenders are advised to employ a range of precautions to ensure the safe return of the securities and to ensure that the loss is fully compensated in the event that securities are not returned. These include:

* employing detailed credit evaluations on the borrower,
* setting limits on the lender's credit exposure to any individual borrower,
* collateralising loan exposures against cash or securities (the lender will decide what quality of collateral it will accept),
* marking exposures and collateral to market (ie, ensuring that exposures and collateral are valued at current market prices) on a daily basis and making margin calls to bring collateral and exposure into line,
* employing master legal agreements that set out clear legal parameters that dictate the structure and process of the lending arrangements, and how the lender will be compensated in the event of default or systemic crisis.

When collateral is taken in securities-lending arrangements, the value of collateral taken will typically exceed the market value of the borrowed assets by an agreed percentage, known as a haircut. This protects the lender from adverse price movements of the collateral held.

7.4   Strategic Approaches to SLB

Learning Objective

4.4.8   Know the role of a stock borrowing and lending intermediary

7.4.1   Managing SLB In-House

Some large institutional investors have the scale and in-house expertise necessary to manage their securities-lending activities internally. They will employ specialist staff whose function is to identify opportunities for lending out elements of the overall portfolio, securing an optimal balance between the income generated by these securities-lending and -borrowing activities and the risks incurred.

7.4.2   Use of an SLB Intermediary

In contrast, many institutional investors prefer to outsource their securities lending and borrowing activities to a third-party securities-lending agent. Given that the investor's global custodian may already be providing safe custody and asset servicing for its securities portfolio, investors will typically find it convenient and cost-effective to draw these services from their global custodian (or sometimes an ICSD/CSD).

However, given the potential returns that securities lending can offer to a large institutional investor, some may tender for this service separately from their core custody mandate. This will allow the investor to appoint a specialised securities lending agent, alongside their main global custodian, which offers a bespoke range of services and expertise particularly well attuned to the investor's securities-lending requirements. A small number of independent securities lending bureaux (eSecLending, for example) have established themselves in this niche to meet the specialised needs of lender and borrower clients.

Some ICSDs/CSDs have established autolending programmes as a settlement fail coverage facility, designed to ensure that adequate securities are available to trading counterparties to ensure timely and efficient trade settlement. Typically, if a seller of securities has insufficient securities to meet its settlement obligation, these securities may be accessed at a cost through the auto-lending facility to ensure timely settlement. Lenders of securities to the auto-lending pool will receive income against their stock loans into the pool.

7.5 Repurchase Agreements

Learning Objective

4.4.5 Understand the use of repo agreements

4.4.7 Understand collateral and marking to market

A repurchase agreement, or repo, is a method of secured lending, whereby securities are sold to a counterparty against payment of cash, and then repurchased at a later date, with interest or a fee being paid to the cash lender. A repo may be employed, for example, to raise the funds necessary to cover the cash leg of a securities transaction. This mode of financing will typically be cheaper than seeking unsecured funding and may be particularly well suited for trading companies that hold a large inventory of stock that may otherwise be unutilised.

For the cash borrower, a key feature of repo is that a repo transaction provides a method of funding that is significantly cheaper than borrowing on an unsecured basis. The cash lender receives securities as collateral throughout the loan period and is free to utilise these securities if the cash borrower fails to repay cash plus interest (or cash plus fee) to the lender.

For the cash lender, repo provides an avenue through which it can generate income on its cash balance. Although it could potentially earn more income by lending this cash on an unsecured basis, repo affords additional security to the lender by ensuring that it holds collateral that it will inherit if the borrowing counterparty defaults on its obligations.

The collateral will be marked-to-market on a daily basis throughout the repo period to reflect current market rates. If the value of the collateral rises or falls outside of a pre-agreed band (known as the variation margin), a margin call will be made (ie, collateral is requested from, or returned to, the lender) to ensure that the value of the collateral remains aligned to the cash sum borrowed through the repo agreement.

Repo transactions can be arranged directly between counterparties on a bilateral basis. This is commonly known as direct repo. However, use of a tri-party collateral agent (known as tri-party repo) has become increasingly widespread, particularly in the wake of some high-profile defaults in bilateral repo markets that have prompted counterparties to look to the extra security afforded by using a tri-party repo agent. Use of tri-party repo also offers benefits to clients that do not have the operational capacity to take in collateral themselves, or that do not wish to dedicate staff and resources to managing their own repo operations.

The tri-party repo agent will serve as service partner to the cash borrower and cash lender, managing the transfer of cash and securities between these two parties, and ensuring that neither counterparty is uncollateralised or misses margin calls.

The types of securities that will be acceptable as collateral will usually be dependent on the risk appetite of the collateral taker (ie, the cash lender). Government debt securities (German bunds, UK gilts, US Treasuries and selected other G10 government bonds) typically represent premium-quality collateral. However, each collateral taker will apply its own collateral eligibility criteria when specifying the types of collateral that it will accept in repo transactions and other forms of secured lending. These criteria may include asset type, credit rating of issuer, currency, duration and average daily traded volume (ie, a measure of the security's liquidity).

Some collateral-takers will be willing to accept lower-quality collateral in repo arrangements. The motivation for doing so is twofold:

1. Accepting lower-quality collateral will typically yield a better return for the collateral-taker (the lender).
2. Top-grade collateral (eg, high quality government debt such as German bunds) is often in short supply – and may be expensive to borrow.

As such, some counterparties may accept asset-backed securities, high-grade corporate debt and, in some instances, equities as collateral.

Lenders can specify their eligibility criteria for collateral that they are willing to accept. Tri-party agents have become increasingly sophisticated in their ability to use their powerful collateralisation engines to provide a mix of different grades of collateral that meet the collateral taker's eligibility criteria, while making optimal use of assets in the collateral giver's portfolio that might otherwise be unutilised.

Negative Interest Rates

Since the global financial crisis, some countries' interest rates have, at times, become negative. Historically, negative *repo* rates have only occurred if a particular instrument is subject to exceptional demand and/or limited supply. When this happens, the repo rate on a particular collateral asset can fall below the prevailing interest rate and can even become negative. These are historically known as 'Specials'.

A negative repo rate means that the buyer (the cash provider) effectively pays interest to the seller (who is borrowing the cash). The buyer pays the purchase price and will receive a lower repurchase price, realising a loss. Such situations have become increasingly common in the current low interest rate environment.

End of Chapter Questions

Think of an answer for each question and refer to the appropriate section for confirmation.

1. What requirements does CASS impose regarding how safe custody investments must be held by a firm?
    Answer Reference: Section 1.1

2. Who holds legal title to securities registered in a nominee name?
    Answer Reference: Section 3

3. Name three types of nominee holding. What are the main differences between these types of nominee arrangement?
    Answer Reference: Section 3

4. List five factors that an investor should take into account when deciding whether to allow an intermediary (eg, its custodian) to use a nominee account structure.
    Answer Reference: Section 3

5. Which two types of fee arrangement are typically employed by custodians when charging an investor client for its services?
    Answer Reference: Section 4

6. What steps can custodians take to ensure that they collect timely and accurate information on corporate actions?
    Answer Reference: Section 5.1

7. Why do corporate actions typically involve a substantial level of risk for custodians?
    Answer Reference: Section 5.1

8. What is a mandatory corporate action? What is a voluntary corporate action?
    Answer Reference: Sections 5.2 and 5.3

9. Why do companies engage in:
    a. stock splits?
    b. stock consolidations?
    Answer Reference: Sections 5.2.4 and 5.2.5

10. What is proxy voting?
    Answer Reference: Section 5.4

11. Which obstacles to transparency did Paul Myners identify in the UK proxy voting system? What recommendations did he make to address the problem of lost votes?
    Answer Reference: Sections 5.4.2 and 5.4.3

12.   What is a record date?
Answer Reference: Section 5.5

13.   Define the following: ex-dividend, cum-dividend, special-ex, special-cum.
Answer Reference: Sections 5.5.1 and 5.5.2

14.   What is a sweep account?
Answer Reference: Section 6.1

15.   What are the advantages and disadvantages of:
a.   single-currency cash accounts?
b.   multi-currency accounts?
Answer Reference: Sections 6.3 and 6.4

16.   What is securities lending?
Answer Reference: Section 7

17.   What is a manufactured dividend?
Answer Reference: Section 7.1

18.   Who holds legal title to on-loan securities? Who will hold voting rights on the shares that are on loan?
Answer Reference: Section 7.1

19.   Why is SLB employed by:
a.   the lender of securities?
b.   the borrower of securities?
Answer Reference: Section 7.2

20.   What benefits can SLB bring to market efficiency?
Answer Reference: Section 7.2

21.   What is a repo? What benefits do repo arrangements offer to lender and borrower?
Answer Reference: Section 7.5

22.   What is:
a.   direct repo?
b.   tri-party repo?
Answer Reference: Section 7.5

23.   What is:
a.   marking to market?
b.   a margin call?
Answer Reference: Section 7.5

Chapter Five
Aspects of Taxation

This syllabus area will provide approximately 3 of the 50 examination questions

1. Taxation of Dividends

Learning Objective

5.1.1 Understand the tax treatment of dividends

1.1 UK Personal Tax Treatment of Dividend Income

UK-based companies sometimes pay dividends to shareholders. Dividends are paid out of profits on which the company has already paid tax. From April 2018, individuals will not pay tax on the first £2,000 of dividends received during the tax year from companies.

Tax rate on dividends over £2,000:

- Basic rate (and non-taxpayers): 7.5%
- Higher rate: 32.5%
- Additional rate: 38.1%.

The allowance is available only to those who have dividend income.

The regular tax allowances that will apply from April 2018:

- Personal Allowance: £11,850
- Basic rate limit: £46,350
- Higher rate threshold: £150,000

The £2,000 limit is in addition to any allowances (as above).

Example

A retail investor receives £6,000 from dividends and £40,000 from regular income. £2,000 of the dividend income is not subject to tax. The balance of £4,000 will be assessed for income tax as well as the £40,000, according to the allowances and thresholds.

1.2 UK Corporate Tax Treatment of Dividend Income

Generally, a UK company is not taxed on dividends received from another UK company. However, if it receives dividend income from a foreign company, it is taxed at the UK corporation tax rate applicable to the company.

The taxpayer is able to claim a credit for foreign tax deducted (see section 5 later in this chapter).

2. Tax Treatment of Bond Interest

Learning Objective

5.1.2   Understand the tax treatment of bond interest

2.1   Conventional and Index-Linked Gilts

UK individual investors are liable for income tax on interest receivable on gilts (including the interest uplift on index-linked gilts when an interest rate is revised upwards). Interest is normally paid gross, but investors may opt for net payment (ie, payment made after deduction of tax or other adjustments) on application to the gilts registrar, Computershare. However:

* individuals are not liable to capital gains tax (CGT) or income tax on the sale of gilts
* no stamp duty or stamp duty reserve tax is payable on purchases or sales of gilts
* UK individual investors may be liable for tax on accrued interest on the purchase and transfer of gilts (see chapter 1).

Example

Investor A invested £50,000 in a fixed-term bond on 1 June 2017, which lasts one year and matures on its first anniversary, 1 June 2018. On this date, interest of £1,500 is paid to the investor. The interest will be taxable in the tax year 2018–19 because this is the tax year in which the income is paid. Investor A will not need to pay tax on this income if their total income for the tax year 2018–19 is below their Personal Allowance of £11,850.

Example

Investor B invests in a fixed-term bond on 1 June 2017, which matures a year later. Under the terms of the bond's issue, no interest will be paid on the bond until maturity. On 1 June 2018, Investor B is paid interest of £12,500. This interest is taxable in the tax year 2018–19, because this is the tax year in which the income is paid. Investor B is liable to tax because the £12,500 received in interest is more than the Personal Allowance of £11,850.

2.2   Corporate Bonds

UK individual investors are liable for income tax on interest received on corporate bonds. Just as for gilts, interest payments on most corporate bonds is payable gross (ie, without tax deducted), so investors must declare this income on their income tax return unless they have made specific arrangements with the registrar to receive this income net.

Individuals are not liable to CGT on profits made on corporate bonds which are classified by HMRC to be qualifying corporate bonds (typically this applies to most UK corporate bonds that are sterling-denominated and do not offer rights of conversion into shares or other securities, or the right to subscribe for other shares or other securities).

No stamp duty or stamp duty reserve tax is payable on purchases or sales of UK corporate bonds.

2.3 Gilt Strips

Cash flows resulting from ownership of fixed-income securities may be stripped into their components (the right to receive principal on redemption, the right to receive periodic interest payments) and sold separately as zero-coupon securities. When a gilt is stripped, the principal element (or corpus) is known as a **gilt strip** and is traded independently from the coupons.

All gains and losses on gilt strips held by individuals are taxed as income on an annual basis. At the end of the tax year, individuals are deemed for tax purposes to have disposed of, and reacquired, their holdings of gilt strips at the prevailing market value. Any gain (or loss) arising during the year on the holding should be added to the gain (or loss) on any strips actually maturing in the tax year. The overall gain (or loss) is taxed as income.

2.4 Overseas Investors

Gilts held on FOTRA (free of tax to residents abroad) terms, and the interest on these bonds, are typically exempt from tax when held by persons who are not ordinarily resident in the UK. The precise tax arrangements depend on the terms under which the gilts were issued. Under current arrangements, which have been in place since 1996, income on FOTRA gilts is exempt from tax if the holder is non-resident, unless the income is received as part of a trade conducted in the UK.

3. Calculating Capital Gains and Losses

Learning Objective

5.1.3 Understand capital gains tax (CGT) as it applies to equities and bonds

Capital Gains Tax (CGT) is payable on profits generated on the sale of most assets, including equities. However, private investors in the UK are exempt from paying CGT on profits generated from the sale of gilts and qualifying corporate bonds (although gilt strips are taxable, see section 2.3). Investors are entitled to tax relief on any capital losses.

The capital gain generated on an equities transaction can be calculated as the difference between the sale price and purchase price of the quantity of shares concerned.

Example

An investor purchases 1,000 shares in a company at £1.70 per share, selling all 1,000 shares several months later for £2.00 each.

The capital gain generated on his investment is:

(1,000 x 2.00) – (1,000 x 1.70)

= 2,000 – 1,700 = 300

The investor has made a capital gain of £300 on the transaction.

The investor is permitted to offset any costs (eg, trading costs) against this profit for tax purposes. For example, if the investor incurred £25.00 cost in trading charges and other overheads, the gain potentially subject to CGT will be £275.00.

If fixed-income securities are sold before maturity, the investor may realise a capital gain or loss on the transaction. The amount of gain (or loss) will equal the difference between the amount realised from the sale and the adjusted tax basis (see example below).

Example

Purchase price:	£20.00
Sale proceeds:	£21.60 (including £0.30 in accrued income)
Adjusted tax basis:	(£20.30) (purchase price + £0.30 accrued income in sale price)
Capital gain:	£1.30
Taxable income:	£0.30 (the accrued income received on sale)

Although a gain or loss on a sale of a security is generally considered to be capital, special rules apply to securities purchased at market discount, ie, for an amount less than par value (see section 4). Subject to the exemption mentioned below, gains on the sales of equities are subject to CGT. Gains on gilts and qualifying corporate bonds (ie, those which are non-convertible debt instruments denominated in sterling) are exempt.

With the market volatility seen over the last few years, students will be aware that individuals may suffer losses, as well as make gains, from their share transactions. In the event of a net loss in a fiscal year, individuals may carry forward such losses to be offset against gains in future fiscal years. There is no limit to the number of years that such losses may be carried forward.

To calculate the amount of gain that is subject to CGT, an individual needs to ascertain the purchase price of the shares that have been sold. If the shares were bought in one tranche then that is simple, but shares may have been accumulated over a period of time or may be repurchased after the sale.

In the UK, HMRC has a set of rules that must be followed to identify which acquisitions should be allocated to a sale. These are known as the matching rules. They are applied in the following order:

- Acquisitions on the same day as the sale.
- Acquisitions during the 30 days following the sale on a first-in, first-out basis.
- Shares bought at any other time. All shares acquired prior to the day of the sale, of the same share class in the same company, are pooled together. This is called a Section 104 holding.

The cost of any given share in a Section 104 holding is calculated by dividing the total amount paid for shares in the Section 104 holding by the number of shares.

Example

An investor buys 5,000 shares in March 2008 for £4,000. In August 2009, the investor buys another 7,000 shares of the same type in the same company for £6,000.

This will create a Section 104 holding of 12,000 shares at a cost of £10,000 (ie, price per share = £0.83).

In May 2015, the investor chooses to sell 4,000 shares from this Section 104 holding. Thus, the proportion of the Section 104 holding that is being sold is 4,000/12,000.

Now multiply this by the total cost of the Section 104 holding: 10,000 x 4,000/12,000 = £3,333.33. The cost of the 4,000 shares that the investor chooses to sell from its Section 104 holding is £3,333.33.

If an investor held shares on 31 March 1982, these are included in the Section 104 holding at their value on that day, not at their original cost.

Example

An investor buys 4,000 shares in March 2007 for £5,000.

In September 2008 the investor buys another 6,000 shares of the same class in the same company for £26,000.

This would give the investor a Section 104 holding of 10,000 shares with a cost of £31,000 (Source: HMRC).

The exception to the above is shares held on 31 March 1982, which are valued at the price on that day and not at the original cost.

Tax Year 2017–18

The following CGT rates apply (the tax rate used depends on the total amount of taxable income):

- 10% and 20% tax rates for individuals (not including residential property and carried interest)
- 18% and 28% tax rates for individuals for residential property and carried interest
- 20% for trustees or for personal representatives of someone who has died (not including residential property)
- 28% for trustees or for personal representatives of someone who has died for disposals of residential property
- 10% for gains qualifying for **Entrepreneurs' Relief**
- 8% for CGT on property where the Annual Tax on Enveloped Dwellings is paid - the Annual Exempt Amount is not applicable
- 20% for companies (non-resident CGT on the disposal of a UK residential property

Individuals are entitled to an exemption of £11,700 in the fiscal year 2018–19 and therefore this amount is deducted from the individual's net gain before calculating the amount liable to CGT.

Exercise 1

An investor purchases 500 shares in a company at £1.00 per share, selling the same 500 shares several months later at £1.40 per share. The investor has incurred £30 in trading charges against this transaction. Calculate the taxable capital gain on this transaction.

The answer can be found at the end of this chapter.

4. Tax Treatment of Discount Securities

Learning Objective

5.1.4 Understand the tax treatment of discount securities

Discount securities are securities that are purchased for a price below their par value. An original issue discount (OID) exists when a bond is issued at a price below its redemption price. Market discount exists when a bond falls in value after it has been issued. An OID bond may be subject to market discount rules if purchased after original issue at a time when the price of the bond reflects a market discount, ie, if the bond is purchased at a price below its issue price.

Market discount must be declared, on an accreted basis, as ordinary taxable income in the year a bond is sold or redeemed.

In some jurisdictions, if the market discount is below a certain threshold (sometimes known as the *de minimis* amount) the market discount is considered to be zero for tax purposes and the difference between purchase price and sales/redemption price is treated as a capital gain when the bond is redeemed or sold.

Under US tax rules, for example, if a bond is purchased with a market discount to the face value of less than 0.25% for each year remaining to the bond's maturity, then the de minimis rule will apply and the market discount will be treated as zero for tax purposes.

Example

An investor purchases a 10-year bond with face value US$100 with five years remaining until maturity.

De minimis amount = 0.25 * 5 = 1.25.

So de minimis threshold = 100-1.25 = US$98.75

Thus, if the $US100 bond is purchased at a price less than US$98.75 (100–1.25), then the capital gain forthcoming to the investor when the bond matures will be subject to CGT. If the investor buys the bond for US$98.75 or more, then any resultant gain will be exempt from CGT under the de minimis rule.

5. Withholding Tax (WHT) and Double Taxation Treaties (DTTs)

Learning Objective

5.1.5 Understand the advantages, disadvantages and uses of: withholding tax (WHT); double taxation treaties (DTTs); relief at source; tax reclamation; being an authorised US-approved Qualifying Intermediary (QI); Foreign Account Tax Compliance Act (FATCA) rules; CRS rules

5.1 WHT

Tax regulations in many countries dictate that income payments accruing to non-residents are liable to be taxed at source in the jurisdiction in which the investments are incorporated. This is known as withholding tax (WHT).

Income that is paid to investors on their securities portfolio via stock dividends and coupon payments, for example, is typically subject to WHT in the country in which the issuing company is incorporated.

Investors may be eligible to reclaim WHT (in full or part) in instances where the governments of the two countries involved have signed a double taxation treaty (DTT) (see below).

WHT is typically deducted at source (ie, deducted by the issuer or paying agent and paid directly to the local tax authorities) and must be reclaimed by the investor from the local tax authorities. This is typically done on the investor's behalf by its custodian. To support this process, global custodians must maintain clear and up-to-date records of their client's tax status, with supporting documentation (including signed declarations) available to present to the local tax authorities as required.

In some jurisdictions, eg, in the US, tax relief may be applied at source, removing the need for the custodian to reclaim WHT on behalf of its investor clients.

5.2 DTTs

To address investor concerns over double taxation (ie, being taxed on income in both the country where the income is paid, and the country where the investor is resident or registered), many governments have established bilateral double taxation treaties (DTTs) with governments in other jurisdictions.

Non-resident companies or individuals may be eligible for a refund of WHT levied on income payments in instances when their country of domicile has a DTT in place with the country in which the payment is made. Tax relief at source may be possible on application to the relevant tax authorities.

There are more than 1,300 DTTs worldwide. The UK has the largest network of treaties, covering more than 100 countries. HMRC has established DTTs to:

- protect against the risk of double taxation where the same income is taxable in two states
- provide certainty of treatment for cross-border trade

- prevent tax discrimination against UK business interests abroad
- protect the UK government's taxing rights and protect against attempts to avoid or evade UK liability (DTTs typically contain provisions for the exchange of information between the taxation authorities of states).

If there is no DTT in place, a foreign investor may be able to secure unilateral relief against double taxation in their country of residency. For example, an investor resident in the UK may offset against their UK tax liability any WHT already paid on investment income overseas.

Tax administration remains a challenging area for custodians holding assets on behalf of foreign investors. The following obstacles exist in relation to efforts to automate and streamline tax processing:

- There is a distinct lack of harmonisation of tax procedures, with many jurisdictions clinging firmly to the tax frameworks that have evolved historically within their own borders.
- Different instruments may attract different WHT rates within the same jurisdiction, reinforcing the degree to which tax reclaims must be processed on a case-by-case basis.
- Lack of harmonisation obstructs efforts by custodians to standardise and automate tax processing; this adds to costs and accentuates risks that tax reclaims may be missed or processed incorrectly.
- Tax-reporting obligations can be highly demanding in some jurisdictions. A number of custodians report, for example, that meeting IRS 1441 NRA obligations in the US has placed heavy demands on them in terms of staffing costs and workflow pressures.
- The fees and resource costs may make smaller tax reclaims not worthwhile.

5.2.1   US-Approved Qualified Intermediary (QI) Status

The Internal Revenue Service (IRS), the US tax authority, established a qualified intermediary (QI) program in 2001 in an attempt to encourage foreign investment into the US and to simplify procedures for tax collection and tax reporting.

Foreign institutions granted QI status have a commitment to report to the IRS a list of their non-US clients with investment interests in US securities. There is also an obligation to report income on US securities for any US residents. This obligation also applies to sale proceeds of share sales of US assets. Subsequently, QIs will withhold taxes due on US securities held in these investors' accounts and will advance these tax obligations owed to the IRS.

5.2.2   Foreign Account Tax Compliance Act (FATCA) Rules

The US **Foreign Account Tax Compliance Act (FATCA)** was introduced in 2010 and is being enacted through a phased implementation that started on 1 July 2014. This requires US taxpayers holding foreign financial assets that exceed given thresholds to report those assets to the IRS. This information must be reported on a form (Form 8938) which is submitted with the taxpayers' annual tax return.

Additionally, FATCA requires foreign financial institutions to report to the IRS information about financial accounts held by US taxpayers or by foreign entities in which US taxpayers hold a substantial ownership interest. To comply with these reporting requirements, a foreign financial institution (FFI) is required to enter into an agreement with the IRS under which it will:

a. fulfil specified due diligence and identification procedures on its account holders,
b. provide annual reporting to the IRS on account holders that are US citizens or foreign entities with substantial US ownership.

FFIs and their account holders that do not comply with these FATCA requirements are subject to a 30% WHT on a range of income payments sourced from the US, including gross proceeds resulting from the sale of securities in the US.

A number of countries, including the UK and Ireland, have signed intergovernmental agreements (IGAs) with the US which simplify disclosure arrangements and minimise any potential conflicts with their own domestic tax law.

Common Reporting Standard (CRS)

In September 2013, G20 leaders committed to automatic exchange of tax information as the new global standard and endorsed a proposal by the Organisation for Economic Co-operation and Development (OECD).

The Common Reporting Standard (CRS) is the result of this drive and provides a benchmark for the automatic exchange of financial account information. It aims to maximise efficiency and reduce costs for financial firms and is designed to provide maximum consistency with US FATCA rules. However, there are some differences between the two regimes because of the global nature of the CRS compared to FATCA and its US-specific features.

In October 2014, 45 jurisdictions signed a multilateral competent authority agreement to start exchanging information using the CRS framework from 2017. Since then, other jurisdictions have also signed the multilateral competent authority agreement, or made a commitment to automatic exchange of information. Around 100 jurisdictions have committed to exchange information on financial accounts.

6.   Transaction Taxes

Learning Objective

5.1.6   Understand transaction-based taxes

A transaction tax is triggered by trading in specified assets (eg, trading shares, or the sale of a property) and is imposed either as a percentage of a transaction's full value, or sometimes as a flat fee. For example, in the UK stamp duty land tax (SDLT) is usually payable on purchasing or leasing land or property – and is sometimes payable on transfers of ownership of property or land. Stamp duty reserve tax (SDRT) is a tax applied to trading in securities. The SDRT rate in the UK is 0.5%.

As margins on trading costs have fallen over time, some jurisdictions have opted to remove securities transfer taxes, owing to the disincentive these may provide to trading activity. For example, Japan removed a 0.3% securities transaction tax (STT) in 1999 in the face of the Asian financial crisis, as a result of fears that transaction taxes and turnover fees might drive trading activity offshore. For similar reasons, a 2% STT was abolished in the Swedish market in 1991, when the Stockholm Exchange lost a sizeable percentage of its share trading activity to the LSE.

The French government has introduced a transaction-based tax on trading in some listed equities. This French financial transaction tax (FTT) came into force on 1 August 2012 and is designed to curb market speculation. A levy of 0.2% is applicable to transactions in French-listed equities with a market capitalisation of more than €1 billion on 1 January in the tax year concerned, irrespective of where the buyer and seller are based. The tax is payable on the first day of the month after the transaction has settled. The legal taxpayer is the broker executing the purchase order or, where no broker is involved, the bank providing custody of the buyer's account. The FTT is applicable to purchases of DRs and ADRs for the French equities concerned. A number of European Union (EU) member states have proposed that an FTT should be introduced across the EU. The European Commission (EC) has initiated public consultation relating to this proposal.

Discussions are ongoing within the EU regarding the possibility of introducing a financial transaction tax at EU level. A number of EU member states (Austria, Belgium, Estonia, France, Germany, Greece, Italy, Portugal, Slovakia, Slovenia and Spain) have agreed in principle to implement the FTT on a phased basis. The UK government has opposed this measure, arguing that imposition of an EU financial transaction tax would damage financial services in the UK and have a negative impact on economic growth, jobs and investment in the UK. The UK government has stated that any EU member states that are in favour of an FTT should design it such that it has an impact on their economies alone. The agreement and full details of the introduction of FTT still have to be agreed upon and then formally approved by the European Parliament.

Answers to Exercises

Exercise 1

The capital gain generated on the investment in these 500 shares is:

(500 x 1.40) – (500 x 1.00) = £200

The investor is permitted to offset associated costs against this capital gain for CGT calculation. Thus the capital gain subject to CGT is:

£200 – £30 = £170

End of Chapter Questions

Think of an answer for each question and refer to the appropriate section for confirmation.

1.   What is a dividend tax allowance?
       Answer Reference: Section 1.1

2.   How is tax applied to capital gains and interest on UK government and corporate bonds?
       Answer Reference: Section 2

3.   What is the tax treatment for interest earned on most corporate bonds?
       Answer Reference: Section 2.2

4.   How is the income received from gilt strips assessed for tax?
       Answer Reference: Section 2.3

5.   What type of investors can be exempted from Capital Gains Tax and on what instruments?
       Answer Reference: Section 3

6.   What is an original issue discount?
       Answer Reference: Section 4

7.   What is WHT? In which circumstances may WHT be reclaimed?
       Answer Reference: Section 5.1

8.   What is a DTT? Why do governments enter into DTTs?
       Answer Reference: Section 5.2

9.   What is the Common Reporting Standard?
       Answer Reference: Section 5.2.2

10.   Why might a country remove a securities transaction tax?
       Answer Reference: Section 6

Chapter Six
Risk

This syllabus area will provide approximately 4 of the 50 examination questions

# 1.	What is Risk?

Learning Objective

6.1.1	Know the following major categories of risk: credit; market; counterparty; issuer; settlement; operational; political; systematic

Risk in the securities industry both presents an opportunity to make sizeable profits and is a potential source of major loss. Many investment banks, for example, make a significant share of their overall profits through the successful management of market risk – namely, in the form of proprietary trading.

On the downside, a securities firm repeatedly comes into contact with events and processes that could result in huge financial losses if appropriate controls are not in place to prevent or manage these risks effectively – the bankruptcy of a major counterparty (for example, Lehman Brothers filing for Chapter 11 bankruptcy protection in September 2008), the collapse of a subcustodian or central securities depository (CSD), the danger of missing a large corporate action, a terrorist attack, or a large trading loss through unauthorised trading such as that experienced by Barings Bank in Singapore in 1995, provide just five among many possible examples.

From a financial perspective, risk may be defined as the quantifiable likelihood of loss or underperformance of invested assets.

The **Bank for International Settlements (BIS)**, a Basel-based international organisation that serves as a bank for central banks and a forum for international monetary and financial co-operation, identifies three main categories of risk in the financial services industry. These are:

- **Credit risk** – the risk of loss caused by the failure of a counterparty to settle its obligations.
- **Market risk** – the risk of loss of earnings or capital arising as a result of movements in market prices, including interest rates, exchange rates and equity values.
- **Operational risk** – the risk of loss resulting from inadequate or failed internal processes, people and systems or from external events.

The Basel Committee on Banking Supervision (BCBS) is a prime mover in identifying sources of risk in the banking industry, and in formulating strategies for protecting against risk. This was established by the central bank governors of the Group of Ten countries at the end of 1974. The Committee's members now come from Argentina, Australia, Belgium, Brazil, Canada, China, the European Central Bank (ECB), France, Germany, Hong Kong SAR, India, Indonesia, Italy, Japan, Luxembourg, Mexico, the Netherlands, Russia, Saudi Arabia, Singapore, South Africa, South Korea, Spain, Sweden, Switzerland, Turkey, the United Kingdom and the United States. The Committee meets four times a year. It has around 25 technical working groups and task forces that also meet regularly.

The BCBS sets out to formulate broad supervisory standards and best practice guidelines, which national financial authorities can refine as necessary to suit the circumstances of their own national systems. In this way, BCBS encourages convergence towards common approaches and common standards without attempting to enforce harmonisation of member countries' supervisory techniques.

In 1988, BCBS introduced a risk evaluation system, commonly known as the Basel Capital Accord. This system requires securities firms to set aside a percentage of their overall capital to protect against the risks that they face in their business. Broadly speaking, the greater a firm's exposure to risk, the higher the capital charge that it will be required to bear. Since 1988, this framework has been progressively introduced not only in member countries, but also in virtually all other countries with active international banks.

By the late 1990s, however, many in the banking world felt that the capital adequacy standards introduced in 1988 had become outdated and no longer reflected the advances in business practice and developments in risk assessment methodologies that had been introduced during the subsequent period.

Consequently, in June 1999, BCBS issued a proposal for a New Capital Adequacy Framework to replace the 1988 accord. The proposed capital framework consists of three pillars:

1. Efforts to establish new minimum capital requirements, which are more sympathetic to the actual risks that firms face and the risk controls they have put in place to mitigate these risks.
2. A supervisory review of an institution's internal assessment process and capital adequacy in order to give banks the opportunity to develop their own advanced methodologies for measuring their internal and external risks.
3. Effective use of disclosure in order to strengthen market discipline by enhancing transparency in banks' financial reporting. This complements the supervisory efforts described in 1 and 2.

Following extensive consultation with banks and industry groups, a revised framework, commonly known as Basel II, was approved by the Basel Committee on 26 June 2004. This text served as a foundation for:

- reforms at the level of individual firms, designed to enhance their own internal controls, and
- legal reforms at the national level designed to strengthen the overarching risk control framework.

Basel II came into effect in the European Union (EU) on 1 January 2007 under the Capital Requirements Directive (CRD). Lenders covered by the CRD were required to implement its provisions from the beginning of 2008.

Following the global financial crisis, banks have been required by financial regulators to raise the level of capital that they must hold against their lending, trading and operational activities. Reforms proposed under the Basel III Accord will be implemented by member countries between 2013 and 2019. Among other requirements, banks will be expected under Basel III to hold specified minimum capital levels against their risk-weighted assets (the value of an asset multiplied by a scaling factor that reflects the level of risk associated with the asset).

The three primary areas of risk identified by the BCBS are addressed in more detail below.

1.1 Credit Risk

Credit risk is most simply defined as the potential that a counterparty will fail to meet its obligations in accordance with agreed terms. The objective of credit risk management is to maximise a bank's risk-adjusted rate of return by maintaining credit risk exposure within acceptable limits.

Securities firms need to manage the credit risk inherent in their entire portfolio, as well as the risk inherent in individual credits or transactions. For most banks, loans are the largest and most obvious source of credit risk. However, other sources of credit risk extend throughout the activities of a bank, including in the banking book and trading book, and both on and off the balance sheet. Banks are increasingly facing credit risk in various business lines other than lending, including trade financing, FX transactions, financial futures and options, and settling transactions.

The term credit risk may embrace a range of risk elements:

- **Issuer risk** is the risk that an issuer may default on its obligations. In the case of a debt instrument, for example, this is the risk that the issuer fails to meet interest payments and to redeem principal on the instrument on redemption date.
- **Counterparty risk** is the risk that an institution defaults on obligations outstanding to a trade counterparty prior to trade settlement.
- **Settlement risk** is the risk that the completion or settlement of a transaction fails to take place as expected, ie, that an expected payment of an asset/security or cash is not made on time or at all. It is most likely to occur when there is a non-simultaneous exchange of value, eg, cash and securities (see chapter 3).

1.2 Market Risk

Market risk is the risk of loss of earnings or capital arising from changes in the value of financial instruments.

Financial institutions have always faced the risk of losses on- and off-balance sheet arising from undesirable market movements. However, the sharp increase of proprietary trading in many banks has heightened the need among regulators to ensure that these institutions have the management systems to control, and the capital to absorb, the risks posed by market-related exposures.

This said, the primary focus in the 1988 Basel Accord was on credit risk, and market risk only gained a high profile when the BCBS published a policy document on the supervisory treatment of market risk in April 1993. This proposed that firms should set aside capital to cover the price risks inherent in their trading activities. This document put forward a standardised measurement framework to calculate market risk for interest rates, equities and currencies.

Market risk can become an issue in securities operations in several ways:

- If the custodian misses a corporate action (eg, a rights issue), it may be required to compensate the investor for lost entitlements. If the price of the securities moves against the custodian before this exposure is closed down, this can result in major financial losses for the custodian concerned.
- If a trade confirmation remains unmatched and it is discovered, for example, that both parties have reported a sale, instead of one a sale and the other a purchase, one may have to reverse the transaction in the market and incur a loss, because the market price has changed.
- Late or failed transactions, or a missed rights issue, in illiquid markets can be difficult to rectify as additional stock may not be available to borrow or buy.

1.3   Operational Risk

Operational risk (OR) is defined by BCBS as 'the risk of loss resulting from inadequate or failed internal processes, people and systems, or from external events'.

Factors that may contribute to OR include:

*   internal and external frauds,
*   theft,
*   total or partial interruption of systems or processes,
*   unauthorised access to a company's computer systems and/or physical records,
*   lack of robust business continuity planning (BCP) to ensure continuity in response to shock events (eg, fire, earthquake, terrorist attack),
*   incorrect execution of certain processes, whether internal or external to the bank, such as a transaction that is executed in the wrong direction,
*   problems deriving from poor management supervision of administrative staff and inadequate procedures for delegating authority, and
*   problems associated with personnel employment contracts.

Events have shown that a firm can be forced into liquidation by fraud, environmental disasters, or legal action initiated by a disaffected group of clients or former employees. There is a day-to-day cost to the firm as OR is realised across its respective business lines, but there is also an overarching risk that a catastrophic event may trigger a loss from which the firm is unable to recover.

There are a large number of sub-categories of OR, including:

*   **Transaction-processing risk** – the risk that an error in the processing of a transaction will cause a direct or indirect loss to the firm.
*   **Legal risk** – the risk that a contract is unenforceable, resulting in a loss.
*   **Reputational risk** – the risk that an act conducted by a firm or one of its employees damages the reputation of the firm, resulting in a direct or indirect loss.

1.4   Other Risks

Political Risk

This is the risk of loss to an investor triggered by change in political regime or political policy. This might result through changes in regulation or through existing legal contracts being amended or rendered null and void. It may include changes in economic strategy, in tax policy, or in the legal protection afforded to private property (eg, protecting against expropriation of the assets of a foreign company or investor). It may pertain to currency convertibility and freedom to repatriate profits, and it may relate to shifts in a market's geopolitical vulnerability through threat of war, political takeover or civil unrest.

Systematic Risk

Systematic risk refers to vulnerability to events that could affect the entire market or an entire segment of the market. The characteristics of this risk are that it is very unpredictable and nearly impossible to avoid. Thus, it would be difficult to mitigate through diversifying a portfolio or using a devised **hedging strategy**.

However, investing in an asset such as bonds could, on occasions, help partially mitigate the risk of losses to portfolios that have a mix of bonds and equities. For example, a rise in interest rates can make bonds less valuable and equities more valuable, and vice versa. This could potentially limit the impact of a change in the portfolio's value from some systematic events.

Some examples of systematic risk:

- interest rate change
- oil shortage
- recession
- inflation
- war
- natural disasters, eg, earthquake.

Systematic risk underlies virtually all investment.

2. Risk Reviews of Market Infrastructure and Custodian Sub-Networks

Learning Objective

6.1.2 Understand the factors that should be taken into account when conducting risk reviews of market infrastructures, sub-custodian networks and outsourced functions

A global custodian's network management group represents the first line of risk management within the bank in terms of managing cross-border settlement and providing custody for overseas assets. In consultation with the bank's legal department, the network management team will hold primary responsibility within the bank for conducting risk assessments of:

1. market infrastructure that may process or hold clients' assets
2. the subcustodians that it employs to service these assets in the local market, and
3. any other service providers to which it may outsource functions relating to its provision of custody services.

Relating to the first of these areas, it is standard practice among global custodians that client assets should not be held in any overseas market until a thorough risk review has been conducted on clearing and settlement infrastructure, the local CSD and national payments system (these points are discussed more fully when we discuss US **SEC Regulations 17f-5 and 17f-7** in section 2.1).

Factors that must be taken into account when conducting risk reviews on subcustodian networks include the following (note that these factors apply to agents in all markets, but may assume special importance when appointing agents in low-volume, emerging markets):

- **A bank's credit rating and strength of its balance sheet** – if using a small local bank as agent in a low-volume market, does it provide an appropriate level of credit comfort? And are clients' assets fully protected in case of insolvency either of the agent or an entity (eg, depository, registrar) holding assets on its behalf?

- **Contingency planning** – are necessary business continuity provisions in place to protect against natural hazards (earthquake, hurricane, flooding), political instability and terrorist threat?
- **Track record and commitment to the business** – can the agent provide assurance of its long-term commitment to the local custody business? What provisions are in place, should client assets need to be migrated to another agent?
- **Technological capability** – are the agent's technology platforms sufficiently robust to cope with predicted daily business volumes and peaks in activity? What commitment has the agent made to support IT upgrades and technical enhancements?
- **Communication and reporting** – does the agent employ communication media (eg, SWIFT ISO 15022 or 20022 messaging) that conform to global industry standards?
- **Market information and data flows** – does the agent have the contacts and experience needed to provide timely notification of key developments within the market? In high-risk areas, such as corporate actions, does the agent have access to multiple, reliable sources of event information and the ability to provide a cleansed, consolidated notification of forthcoming events?
- **Staff expertise and succession issues** – does the agent have the required level of staff expertise and experience, and effective provision in place if key staff leave or are unable to work? Does the market have sufficient depth of talent to ensure effective replacements? What procedures does the bank have in place to address these succession issues?
- **Transparency and integrity** – does the agent, or do its employees, have any history of financial misconduct or negligence? Does the legal framework applicable in the jurisdiction concerned provide effective recourse in instance of loss, threat to business continuity or damage to reputation?

Global custodians will typically insulate investor clients from fraud, gross negligence or wilful misconduct within their own organisation, or on the part of agents (eg, subcustodians) that they employ.

Traditionally, most global custodians will not indemnify investor clients against losses sustained through systemic shocks to infrastructure, such as a CSD, clearing house or payments system. This is deemed to be part of the market risk borne by the investor. However, custodians will make every reasonable effort to ensure that investor clients are informed about prevailing risks associated with investing in a particular market.

This said, there is nothing currently to stop a global custodian providing indemnity to an investor client against this category of risk, should it choose to do so. The custodian must balance the potential for winning new business by offering this level of indemnity to the client against the sizeable additional risks that it will be taking on.

Significantly, changes introduced in the EU under the **Alternative Investment Fund Managers Directive (AIFMD)**, and under the UCITS V Directive (Undertakings for Collective Investments in Transferable Securities), are increasing the obligations borne by global custodians to provide compensation in case of any loss of assets held on behalf of fund manager clients. In the instance of failure of a sub-custodian, infrastructure entity (eg, a CSD) or other service provider to which it has outsourced custodial responsibilities, the global custodian (in this instance acting as fund depository on behalf of the fund manager client) may be required to provide full and immediate restitution to the fund client of any client assets that have been lost or frozen under the insolvency process. As a result of these increasing liabilities, global custodians are conducting a detailed re-evaluation of the risks associated with safekeeping assets on behalf of fund clients – and, in many instances, they are looking to reinforce the procedures they have in place for conducting due diligence and for monitoring performance of any service provider to which they outsource custodial responsibilities.

2.1 Securities and Exchange Commission (SEC) Rules 17f-5 and 17f-7

In the US market, the SEC has laid down strict rules governing the conditions under which a US-based investment company can hold its assets overseas. Under SEC Rule 17f-5, which was introduced in 1984 and revised extensively in 1997, US investment companies can hold securities with any custodian that meets the SEC's eligible foreign custodian criteria, dictating that rigorous due diligence is conducted on any custodian before it can be appointed.

Indeed, prior to holding assets with a foreign custodian, a US investment company must consider:

1. **Access to books and records** – whether foreign laws applying within the jurisdiction concerned will restrict the access of independent public auditors and/or the investor's accountants to books and records maintained by the eligible foreign custodian.
2. **Recovery of assets** – whether local laws will limit the client's ability to recover its assets in the event that the eligible foreign custodian goes into liquidation, or if assets are lost while under the custodian's control.
3. **Currency convertibility** – whether currency restrictions will prevent the client from repatriating cash holdings or income from the market concerned and converting these back into US dollars.
4. **Expropriation of assets** – the probability that investors' assets may be confiscated, frozen or taken under state control while in the care of the eligible foreign custodian.

Under Rule 17f-7, introduced in 2001, the SEC specified that any depository that is employed by a US investment company (or its custodian) to hold its assets must be an eligible foreign depository. This requires that it meets the following criteria:

- It must be a national or transnational centre for handling securities that is regulated by a foreign financial regulatory authority.
- It must be subject to periodic audits by the regulatory authorities or by independent accountants.
- It must provide regular and comprehensive reports to all depository participants.
- The CSD must apply equal safekeeping treatment to each depository participant.
- It must maintain a register that details the assets held on behalf of each depository participant.

Given that many global custodians have been required to collect similar information from a similar set of depositories, the Association of Global Custodians (AGC) has taken steps to reduce duplication of effort by centralising this information-gathering process. It asks depositories to submit a single annual response to a comprehensive questionnaire (over 120 questions) detailing their internal control environment and providing a broad range of data demanded under Rule 17f-7 reporting requirements. As well as simplifying the due diligence process for AGC member custodians, this has eased the reporting burden on depositories themselves, allowing each to submit one consolidated risk report to the AGC.

Within this risk report, CSDs are required to provide information on a broad body of issues:

- **Structure and Organisation of CSD**
  - Legal status and ownership structure of the depository.
  - The regulatory authority that oversees the depository's activities.
  - How frequently its activities are subject to a financial and operational audit by a regulator or external auditor.
- **CSD Participants**
  - Number of CSD participants, types of participant, criteria that must be satisfied to be a CSD participant.

- **Method of Holding Assets**
  - Controls for ensuring segregation of participants' assets, method of recording those assets.
  - Whether nominee arrangements are in place.
  - Procedure for transfer of legal ownership (ie, when is finality of transfer established?).
- **Settlement and Asset Servicing**
  - Settlement options provided by the depository (eg, availability of delivery versus payment (DVP), real-time settlement, batch settlement).
  - What broader range of services does the depository provide (eg, collection of dividends and interest, collection of corporate actions entitlements, supply of information on issues and corporate events, tax services, securities lending and borrowing, collateral handling)?
  - Links that the depository has with other CSDs or ICSDs. What protection is afforded against the collapse of an ICSD/CSD with which it maintains a link?
- **Protection against Losses**
  - The degree to which local law protects participants' assets from claims and liabilities of the depository.
  - Whether the depository imposes a lien on participants' accounts (allowing the depository to hold or sell a participant's securities in payment of a debt).
  - Whether the depository delegates any responsibilities to third party service providers. Does it accept responsibility for any losses or error resulting from the actions of these third parties? Up to what limit?
  - Whether the depository accepts liability for loss in instances of theft, fraud, **_force majeure_**.
  - Insurance policies that the CSD has in place to cover CSD default and systemic threat. Is there a guarantee fund independent of stock exchange or other market guarantees?
  - Any business continuity provisions that are in place to address such contingencies.

- **Record of Losses**
  - Any default by a depository participant that may have resulted in a significant loss over the last three years.

Although SEC 17f-5 and 17f-7 regulations apply specifically to US-based firms, the principles enshrined in these regulations have been widely adopted in other jurisdictions as a foundation for conducting risk reviews of market infrastructures and custodial networks.

3.   Global Custody Risks

Learning Objective

6.1.3   Understand the areas of global custody risk and appropriate countermeasures

Firms providing global custody services can be exposed to a wide range of risks. These may be linked to the nature of the business, the counterparties involved, credit, liquidity, market conditions, operational hazards, settlement, systemic and transfer risks.

These risks can be managed effectively, providing that appropriate controls are set in place. However, special care is required in emerging markets, where the technological infrastructure, the market systems and/or the regulatory framework are still weak.

3.1   Settlement Risk

This *Global Securities Operations* learning manual has identified a range of possible sources of trade and settlement risk. It has also identified a range of countermeasures that might be employed to mitigate these risks. A selection of key risks and countermeasures are summarised below:

Cause	Countermeasures
Late receipt of trade data and/ or trade instructions	Maintain agreed operating procedures. Employ electronic communication link between investment manager and custodian.
Inability to verify instructions from investment manager	Ensure timely pre-matching of settlement instructions, preferably through a clearing organisation or a CSD. Employ standardised, automated electronic data flow between parties involved in the trade. Use of trade matching systems.
Inaccurate or outdated pricing feeds for listed and unlisted securities	Periodically check prices against a range of information sources/ vendors supplying pricing data. Ensure regular (in many cases daily) interaction with market vendors to ensure the integrity of a firm's market data.
Acting on an unauthorised instruction	No instructions should be acted upon unless they carry valid signatures, or other authorised security procedures. Accurate and up-to-date documentation must be maintained by the custodian regarding who is authorised to give client instructions.
Transaction with a failing counterparty	Use of a central counterparty (CCP) that assumes counterparty risk through novation. Client's history of failed trades should be closely monitored, with periodic analysis of settlement failures sent to the client.
DVP settlement infrastructure unavailable	Secure DVP on books of a creditworthy settlement bank. Employ ASDA. If CSDA is to be employed, positions should be collateralised so that they can be reversed if necessary.
Late delivery of securities and/ or cash	Prompt follow-up of shortfall with counterparty. Initiate compensation claim against defaulting counterparty. Initiate a buy-in of securities.
Failure of trading parties to adhere to market standards and codes of practice (eg, use of ISO standard electronic messaging)	Industry associations and market practice groups to promote use of industry standards and global best practice. Potential use of price discounts for settlement messages communicated by ISO standard, rather than by fax or proprietary message formats.
Lack of reliable and timely dividend and corporate actions information	Use multiple information sources, including local press, to collect information on forthcoming corporate events. Subcustodians should be responsible for providing timely information of client entitlements.

Cause	Countermeasures
Delayed income collection	Dividend, interest and redeemable principal should only be credited on due date if timely payment is expected from issuer. Provision should be made in the custody contract to allow credit to be reversed if funds are not actually received from the issuer.
Inaccurate or late reporting to client	Need to implement improvements in reporting system. Need regular reconciliation of predicted with actual positions.
Clients' instructions not implemented, or implemented incorrectly	Four eyes principle involving checking of instructions by another person. Forward value payment or delivery instructions to be held in a diary system, which is to be reviewed daily.

3.2   Safekeeping Risk

This section summarises a range of possible sources of safekeeping risk and possible countermeasures through which these risks may be mitigated. These include those in the table above.

3.3   Other Operational Risks

Custodians must have effective measures in place to protect against a broader set of operational risks, which include theft and fraudulent acts by personnel, loss of securities in transportation, power cuts and system downtime, money laundering, unauthorised persons (eg, hackers) gaining access to computer systems, and effective safeguards against system faults such as a breakdown at the CSD.

3.4   Risks Associated with Contractual Relationships

In delivering custody services, global custodians may enter into legally binding contractual arrangements with institutional investors, investment managers and subcustodians. They must pay particular attention to the following set of issues:

- In managing their relationships with institutional investor clients, custodians must verify that there is a complete and unambiguous custody agreement in place.
- Custodians are required to maintain accurate and up-to-date client documentation to meet know your customer requirements.
- In dealing with an investment manager acting as principal on assets held with the custodian, a custody contract must be signed between the custodian and the investment manager.
- In dealing with an investment manager that is managing assets as an agent on behalf of an institutional investor or some other beneficial owner, the custody relationship will be between the custodian and the beneficial owner. Consequently, appropriate legal contracts must be in place between these parties. In these:
    - the beneficial owner must provide clear instructions to the custodian specifying which instructions should be accepted directly from the investment manager(s) appointed by the client,
    - credit limits for FX transactions and overdrafts must be made explicit in the custody relationship,
    - the custodian should maintain a regular, ongoing review process with investment managers and investor clients to identify whether or not agreed investment standards are being met and whether instructions are being received on a timely basis.

3.4.1　Relationship with Subcustodians

In managing its relationship with subcustodians, the global custodian must ensure that each sub-custodian is selected on the basis of effective research and due diligence. The global custodian must maintain a regular and ongoing review of subcustodian performance to ensure that required service standards are being met. This will include periodic site visits to the market concerned.

Investor clients will typically demand protection against any risk to their assets caused by default or failure by a subcustodian. This issue must be addressed by the custodian in the custody contract signed with the investor client.

4.　Reporting on Internal Control Environments

Learning Objective

6.1.4　Know the purpose of an International Standards for Assurance Engagements (ISAE) 3402 report

Investors and regulators are increasingly requiring more sophisticated reporting from custodians relating to the internal controls that they have in place to monitor and mitigate the set of risks outlined above. To facilitate this reporting process, a standardised audit methodology has been developed in the UK, entitled AAF 01/06, and in the US, entitled SSAE 16 and ISAE 3402.

4.1　Audit and Assurance Faculty (AAF) 01/06

Financial services companies must be able to demonstrate that their internal control procedures are robust and efficient. In line with this requirement, the **audit and assurance faculty** of the Institute of Chartered Accountants in England and Wales (ICAEW) issued reporting guidelines to assist directors needing to verify that their organisations have strong internal controls in place. This guidance, AAF 01/06, replaces Financial Reporting and Auditing Group (FRAG) 21, and provides an independently audited record of the internal controls employed by investment services companies, including investment custodians. Although not yet a statutory requirement, the AAF 01/06 is a widely used report, designed to make it easier for investment custodians (and other service organisations) to respond to requests for information from auditors and investor clients wishing to review the internal risk controls the organisation has in place.

The UK Pensions Act 1995 highlights the responsibilities of the management and trustees of pension funds to review the risk controls in place within their pension funds and to share this information regularly with their stakeholders. If control of assets has been outsourced to a custodian, management and trustees must ensure that the control systems employed by the custodian complement those within their own organisation, and that assets (whether in physical or dematerialised form) are protected effectively while in the custodian's care.

Importantly, the 1995 Pensions Act makes it explicit that using an external custodian does not diminish the fiduciary responsibility held by management and trustees to ensure that the overall integrity of data and safeguarding of assets is maintained.

Although primarily intended for the reporting accountants of custodians, the AAF 01/06 framework is also used selectively by investment managers, pensions administration companies and other providers of financial services to establish an independently audited review of their own internal control environment that can be presented to regulators and to their own clients.

The AAF 01/06 reporting package should include:

1. a report on the custodian's internal risk controls prepared by the custodian's board of directors (ie, an internal risk evaluation from within the company), and
2. a report on the custodian's internal controls prepared by the reporting auditors (ie, an independent external risk evaluation).

The directors' report should contain a review of the main control procedures employed by the custodian, and an analysis of how these engage with the internal control objectives employed by its customers. These main features should include:

- a general description of the custodian's activities and its dependence (if any) on fellow group members
- the overall control objectives that the directors have established
- a review of specific procedures designed to control custodial functions in accordance with the control objectives. These may include arrangements for the segregation of customer assets, reconciliation procedures, procedures for selecting and monitoring subcustodians, procedures for monitoring IT systems and communications networks, and level of compliance with investor mandates
- other relevant information that the directors may wish to provide (eg, controls that should be employed by the client when sending or receiving information to or from the custodian).

For the statement by directors to be fairly described, the directors should include in their report a description of any material weaknesses that they feel may compromise the effectiveness of the internal control procedures that the custodian has in place. Directors should also detail any corrective action that has been taken to address these areas of reported weakness.

By reporting, accountants will include an audit of the physical controls and reconciliation procedures maintained by the custodian to ensure that:

- physical securities are released only on receipt of a customer-authorised validated instruction
- all customers are contacted annually to verify the accuracy of the authorised signatory list
- six-monthly physical counts of all securities are undertaken by staff not responsible for recording and authenticating transactions
- reconciliation is conducted, on a six-monthly basis, of physical securities held against the count recorded in the custodian's books and records. This reconciliation is to be conducted by persons not responsible on a day-to-day basis for providing physical custody of these assets, or for recording and verifying customer instructions
- the securities compliance department, independent of custody operations, reviews and scrutinises the results of the securities counts and stock reconciliations. These reconciliations must be reviewed by management on a timely basis to ensure that any anomalies are promptly resolved.

Reporting accountants will also test the procedures employed by the custodian for appointing and monitoring its network of subcustodians to ensure that:

- arrangements with independent subcustodians are documented and subject to review by the compliance department
- subcustodians provide written confirmation that customer assets are held in segregated accounts in order to afford maximum protection in the event of any default
- monthly reconciliations of securities held with the subcustodian are conducted against the custodian's records. These reconciliations are to be reviewed by management on a timely basis to ensure that any differences are adequately resolved.

4.2 Statement on Standards for Attestation Engagements (SSAE) 16 and International Standard on Assurance Engagements (ISAE) 3402

SSAE 16 and ISAE 3402 are internationally recognised audit standards, developed respectively by the American Institute of Certified Public Accountants (AICPA which created SSAE) and the International Auditing and Assurance Standards Board (IAASB) of the International Federation of Accountants (IFAC), which created ISAE 3402.

Like an AAF 01/06 report in the UK, the SSAE 16 and ISAE 3402 reports in the US verify that a service organisation has had its control activities reviewed by an independent auditing firm. This audit of control processes will generally include controls over information technology and related processes.

SSAE 16 and ISAE 3402 replace SAS 70 as the authoritative guidance for auditing and reporting on service organisations.

Under SAS 70, there were two types of service auditor's reports. A Type 1 report described the service organisation's control procedures at a specific point in time and a Type 2 report not only contained the service organisation's description of controls, but also included detailed testing of these controls over at least a six-month period.

SSAE 16 and ISAE 3402 both make a distinction between Type 1 and Type 2 reports, but they add a requirement for the auditor to obtain a written assertion from the management of the service provider about the fairness of the description of their controls, the suitability of the control's design and, in respect of a Type 2 report, the operating effectiveness of these controls.

Though there are technical differences between the SSAE 16 and ISAE 3402 standards, their structure and focus is in many ways similar. It is unclear at this stage which of these two standards will become most widely used.

Without a current service auditor's report, a custodian may need to respond to multiple audit requests from its customers and their respective auditors. Multiple visits from user auditors can place a strain on the service organisation's resources. A service auditor's report, which provides evidence of effectively designed control objectives and control activities, can be valuable in helping organisations and their auditors to ensure that they have the information necessary to meet their compliance and reporting requirements.

5. Shareholder Limits and Restrictions on Foreign Investment

Learning Objective

6.1.5   Understand shareholder limits and restrictions

Share ownership may be restricted in some companies or sectors. In certain markets, investment restrictions dictate that no non-resident shareholder may own more than a specified percentage of total issued shares in any one company.

Limits may also exist on the aggregate percentage of total issued shares in any company that may be held by foreign investors. Disclosure requirements typically demand that foreign investors (or their custodian acting on their behalf) report their holdings in the company when specific disclosure thresholds are exceeded.

Prior to investment, foreign investors may be required to provide official documentation confirming the investor's nationality along with proof that it has the necessary investment licences and tax registration. Examples are provided from selected markets in the table following.

Country	Ownership Restrictions for Non-resident Investors
Australia	There are restrictions on levels of foreign ownership in some types of business activity in Australia, including banking, civil aviation and airports, shipping, media and telecommunications. Under the Foreign Acquisitions and Takeover Act, foreign shareholding of more than 15% (individual) and 20% (aggregate) in Australian business with total assets over AUD 50 million requires prior approval from, and notification to, the FIRB, Commonwealth Treasurer, and registrars.
Brazil	Foreign investment is highly regulated in Brazil. There are upper aggregate limits on the foreign ownership of investments: in air transportation 20%; cable television companies 49%; highway cargo transportation 20% and media 30%. In order to obtain a 30% share of the voting capital of a media company, a foreign investor must first create a corporation in Brazil governed by Brazilian law. Foreign ownership is prohibited with respect to some industries: cabotage (domestic transportation by water, port to port); lottery services; medical assistance or health plans; nuclear mining and production; the transportation of valuables; oil prospecting and refining. Prior government authorisation is needed for purchases of stock in the mineral exploration, mining and hydroelectric, agriculture and forestry, maritime, river and transport, and insurance sectors. Foreign investor shareholding in financial institutions is restricted to the levels they held at 5 October 1988. Additional purchase of stock must be deemed to be in the interests of the Brazilian government and, hence, requires the formal approval of the central bank. International investment in non-voting shares of Brazilian financial institutions was authorised without restriction in 1997.

Country	Ownership Restrictions for Non-resident Investors
France	Foreign investors must secure government authorisation to invest in some sectors (eg, defence, healthcare). A non-EU resident's stake in a company listed on the Premier, Second or Nouveau Marché may not exceed 20% without previous authorisation from the French finance ministry.
Germany	There are some restrictions on foreign ownership. For example, foreigners can own no more than 49.99% of Lufthansa registered shares. The Federal Cartel Office must authorise transactions if a foreign owner is gaining a dominant market position in a particular sector. Federal Savings Bonds (Bundesschatzbriefe) cannot be acquired by foreign institutional investors, and Federal Finance Bonds (Finanzierungsschätze) cannot be acquired by foreign banks. Issuing companies may also reject purchases by foreign institutional investors.
Hong Kong	There are some restrictions on foreign investment. No single investor may hold more than 5% of HKEx's shares without approval from the Securities and Futures Commission (SFC). Furthermore, no single non-resident investor may hold more than 10% of a television broadcasting company. Aggregate foreign ownership in the latter case is capped at 49% of a company's voting shares. If a foreign investor wishes to own 2% or more of the company's voting rights, it must obtain prior written approval from the Broadcasting Authority.
Japan	Limits on overseas investments are set on airline, broadcasting, energy and telecommunications companies. Specific companies within these sectors may be restricted.
South Korea	Foreign investors must obtain an investment registration card (IRC) prior to investing in South Korea. IRC holders at both individual and aggregate levels may own 100% of the outstanding shares of most listed and unlisted Korean companies, as well as short-term debt instruments. The exceptions are in a small number of companies deemed to be of national importance, or in industries such as aviation, communications and broadcasting. Korea Electric Power is deemed of national importance and has aggregate limits of 40% and individual limits of 3%. South Korea petroleum companies, airlines and mining stocks have foreign ownership limits of 50%. The aggregate limit for Korean telecommunication companies is 49%. The individual limits for banks vary, depending on whether they are large national city banks (4%) or regional banks (15%).
UK	There are some restrictions on overseas investors. Some voting shares in industries of national importance have limits on foreign ownership.
US	Overseas investors are barred from direct investments in certain industries, eg, communications, aviation, mining on federal land, energy and banking.

6

6. Mitigating Risk Through Reconciliation

Learning Objective

6.2.1 Understand the risks associated with a failure to reconcile the following: open trades; counterparty cash; corporate actions; cash accounts; custodian holdings; client assets; entitlements

Cash and securities reconciliation – the process of matching internal balances, transactions, and holdings with those held at the custodian, prime broker or other external provider – is key to the process of identifying and managing risk outlined in this chapter and throughout the workbook.

Accurate and timely reconciliation is required to ensure that a firm is fully in control of assets that it owns, or that are in its safe custody (ie, as per client asset rules, outlined in chapter 4), and any risks which may be generated through fraud or through a handling error, for example, are identified and acted upon at an early stage. For this reason, financial regulators require regular reconciliation of cash and securities holdings in a wide range of markets around the world.

A firm will reconcile on a trade-by-trade basis to ensure that trades placed, and entered in the trading book, have been entered accurately into the settlement system and comply with the records therein.

Once a trade has settled, and settlement confirmation has been received from the custodian (or from the CSD/ICSD, as appropriate), it is necessary for the firm to update internal records immediately with the details of securities and cash movements. For example, if the firm has purchased securities, it must update and reconcile records to demonstrate that:

1. the transaction is no longer shown as outstanding in internal records (ie, it is no longer recorded as an open trade) when the trade has been settled,
2. securities are recorded as having been received and added to the inventory of securities held in the relevant custodian depot account,
3. cash is recorded as having been paid and has been deducted from the relevant cash account (*nostro account*) at the custodian.

The objective of open trade reconciliation is to prove that trades recorded as open (ie, not yet settled) on the firm's internal trading book are in reality open at the relevant custodian, and vice versa, and that they correspond with the settlement instructions that the custodian is holding.

Failure to do so may leave the firm susceptible to the following risks:

1. Its contractual commitment with its trading counterparties is not represented accurately,
2. It fails to make optimal use of its operational resources: timely and effective reconciliation is vital to ensure that operations staff focus on the settlement of genuinely open trades and dedicate their time to investigating genuine errors and exceptions,
3. Its traders may trade off incorrect book positions or may open new positions when previous trading positions are not complete. Given restrictions on short selling in some markets, a firm may be subject to penalty if a trader sells a stock that it does not legally own,

4. Its stock-lending department may lend out securities that the firm does not legally own, or, alternatively, borrow securities to meet shortfalls that do not actually exist. Similarly, repo trading requires accurate and current information regarding open trades and settled securities and cash at each custodian. The firm must ensure that securities listed on internal records as being available for use as collateral are genuinely available at the custodian,

5. Its credit risk department is unable to evaluate counterparty risk accurately. In doing so, it must be able to view trades listed as open on internal records, confident that data is complete, timely and accurate. This demands an accurate record of counterparty cash payments and collateral position to monitor how exposure to the counterparty changes with time. Among other problems, failure to do so may tie up a company's capital and liquidity unnecessarily,

6. Its cash account may fall overdrawn if a securities transaction has settled but this has not been recorded accurately in the company's internal records. Alternatively, an open trade reconciliation failure may dictate that the seller fails to make available securities required to complete trade settlement.

6.1   Assets and Entitlements

In the context of the above, a firm must maintain an accurate and up-to-date record of its asset holdings and must reconcile its own internal records regularly with custodian depot accounts in order to identify:

1. unauthorised removal of securities from one of the firm's accounts at the custodian,
2. unexpected receipt of securities within one of the firm's accounts at the custodian (eg, as a result of a corporate action, or a free of payment (FOP) transfer from another account that has not been recorded correctly),
3. errors in updating ownership records subsequent to a completed transaction settlement.

This process is crucial to support efficient processing of dividends and interest payments. An accurate record of ownership and location is required to ensure that income paid on a security has been credited to the correct client cash account and that non-delivery of entitlement can be investigated. Given that entitlement is contingent on who was the legal owner of the security on record date, this demands an up-to-date picture of open trades and settled securities.

Similarly, accurate reconciliation is required to support efficient processing of mandatory and voluntary corporate actions – ensuring timely delivery of entitlements and, in the case of voluntary corporate actions, that instructions are conveyed to the company registrar before the deadline in order for the entitlement to be upheld. There is a risk of huge losses if a corporate action deadline is missed.

As we noted in chapter 4, in the UK a firm is periodically required (usually at least every 25 business days) to perform a reconciliation of its record of safe custody investments for which it is accountable, but which it does not physically hold itself. This reconciliation process must be supported by appropriate statements or electronic equivalent obtained from custodians detailing client assets held in their safekeeping. Similarly, for any dematerialised investments that are not held through a custodian (eg, assets held at a CSD), appropriate statements must be obtained from the person who maintains the record of legal entitlement.

Particular vigilance must be placed on monitoring assets held overseas, which may be held in safe custody by a subcustodian (acting on behalf of a global custodian or prime broker) or at the local CSD.

6.2   Cash Reconciliation

A firm will perform a comparable cash reconciliation process for custodian nostro accounts – the cash equivalent of the custodian depot position reconciliation. This is to ensure that cash balances (reconciled by nostro account; by currency) held on the firm's internal books and records agree with equivalent balances held at each custodian.

This process is key to ensuring efficient cash management. As we saw in chapter 4, this allows cash management staff to chase up instances of fraud or mishandling at an early stage. It is also necessary to ensure that unanticipated debits do not cause an account to fall overdrawn (thereby incurring penalty charges) or for unanticipated cash deliveries (including cash entitlements due from corporate actions, for example) to be sitting unnecessarily in accounts that do not yield interest.

This process is also important to enable the accounting department to calculate profit and loss information accurately; and, as we have noted, for the credit risk department to monitor counterparty cash payments and collateral positions in order to calculate its credit exposure to each of its counterparties.

7.   Regulation and Risk

Learning Objective

6.3.1   Know the features of regulatory risk

6.3.2   Understand the risks associated with a failure to comply with regulation

7.1   Regulatory Change

The pace of change within the financial services industry is seemingly relentless, with the financial crisis of recent times serving to exacerbate the amount of new regulation and all that it brings for firms, regulators and indeed, consumers. The financial services regulatory environment is seeing an unprecedented amount of regulatory reform across the EU and in financial centres globally. Regulated entities within financial services sectors are naturally expected to keep pace with this level of change, much of which is being imposed as EU Directives and/or Regulations.

7.2   Impact of Changing Regulation

The Markets in Financial Instruments Directive (MiFID) in 2007 was, in many ways, the first step to creating a more harmonised financial services environment within Europe. This has now been revised, with the new rules imposed by MiFID II/Markets in Financial Instruments Regulation (MiFIR) came into force in January 2018. This will likely affect all stages of the life cycle of transactions as well as many consumer and firm-related post-trade requirements.

MiFID II and MiFIR represent an overhaul of the existing rules and also expand the scope of instruments and firms. The new legislation not only focuses on trading venues for financial instruments, but also on regulating the 'operation' of these venues. It significantly applies to regulated entities' systems, processes and oversight/governance and it is likely that very few firms involved in the securities industry have escaped at least some impact on their procedures, systems, polices, operations, oversight and reporting. Like their predecessors, the new rules again focus on greater investor protection, harmonisation of regulation across the EU, enhanced competition, greater supervisory oversight and powers for regulators and an enhanced supervisory role for the **European Securities and Markets Authority (ESMA)** across all European states (see section below on Brexit).

If there is one thing that the industry can expect with little doubt, it is a continued flow of substantial regulatory change and reform that it is unlikely to significantly abate in the foreseeable future.

7.3   Regulatory Risk

The increasing cost of compliance within regulated entities is (and will no doubt continue to be) a much-debated subject. The continuous enhanced focus on regulatory compliance/risk (and its associated costs) can become difficult for some institutions, with firms being expected to demonstrate full compliance at all times in an extremely complex regulatory environment on an ongoing basis. Fines and sanctions (often public) for non-compliance, incomplete or poorly reported data and, of course, market abuse can pose a significant financial risk and often, more worryingly, a major reputational risk for firms.

The UK and the EU Referendum (Brexit)

Before the UK's General election of 2015, the then Prime Minister, David Cameron, had promised that if re-elected, his Conservative government would hold a referendum on EU membership before the end of 2017.

After the conservative election victory, the European Union Referendum Act 2015 was introduced into Parliament to allow the referendum to take place. In February 2016, the Prime Minister announced that a referendum would be held on 23 June 2016.

Referendum Result

On 24 June 2016, the day following the referendum, the result was announced that 51.9% of voters voted in favour of leaving the European Union and 48.1% voted to remain. The referendum turnout was 71.8%, with over 30 million people casting their vote.

The Term Brexit

Brexit has become a common term for the United Kingdom's departure from the European Union, being the result of amalgamating the words 'British' and 'exit'. It derives from the previously used 'Grexit', a term used for a hypothetical exit from the EU by Greece, during the recent financial crisis.

Article 50

Article 50 is part of European law and was provided for in the 2009 Lisbon treaty that made provision for any country that wishes to exit the EU. On 28 March 2017, Prime Minister Teresa May signed a letter invoking Article 50 which was submitted on 29 March 2107 to the EU. Once Article 50 is triggered, the UK has two years to negotiate its withdrawal.

As the triggering of Article 50 is unprecedented, no one really knows how the Brexit process will proceed. The terms of Britain's exit will have to be negotiated and agreed by 27 national parliaments. Until these negotiations are complete, EU law will remain in the UK right up until the point it ceases being a member. Meanwhile, the UK is obligated to conform with all EU treaties and laws.

At this stage, it is hard to predict what the likely outcome of negotiations will be and how these will lead to change in UK Financial services related regulation.

Students should follow the Brexit negotiations with interest as any future outcomes will likely affect the legislative obligations of many financial market participants.

Timeline of the EU – The Key Milestones

1945 – End of World War II.

1946 – UK Prime Minister, Winston Churchill, calls for a 'kind of United States of Europe'.

1949 – France, UK and the Benelux countries agree to establish Council of Europe.

1951 – Treaty of Paris signed by Belgium, France, Germany, Italy, Luxembourg, Netherlands, establishing the European Coal and Steel Community (ECSC).

1957 – Treaties of Rome establish the European Economic Community (EEC) and the European Atomic Energy Community (Euratom).

1958 – First session of the European Parliamentary Assembly held in Strasbourg.

1959 – Austria, Denmark, Norway, Portugal, Sweden, Switzerland and the UK decide to establish a European Free Trade Association (EFTA).

1973 – Denmark, Ireland and the UK join the European Communities.

1975 – British referendum results in 67.2% in favour of UK remaining a member of the Community.

1978 – European Council establishes the European Monetary System based on a European currency unit (the ECU) and the Exchange Rate Mechanism (ERM). The ECU has some characteristics of a real currency and is used in travellers' cheques and bank deposits. ERM gives national currencies a central exchange rate against the Ecu. All the community's members apart from the UK join the ERM.

1979 – First direct elections to the European Parliament.

1981 – Greece becomes 10th member of the European Community.

1984 – Draft Treaty on the establishment of the European Union passed by the European Parliament

1986 – Spain and Portugal join the Community.

1992 – Maastricht Treaty on the European Union is signed, leading to creation of the euro and the structure of the EU.

1993 – Single European Market enters into force.

1995 – Austria, Finland and Sweden join making the membership 15 countries. The Schengen Agreement comes into force between Belgium, France, Germany, Luxembourg, the Netherlands, Portugal and Spain, lifting border control.

1997 – Amsterdam Treaty signed, emphasising citizenship and the rights of individuals, more powers for the European Parliament, the beginnings of a common foreign and security policy (CFSP).

1998 – Establishment of the European Central Bank (ECB).

2001 – Treaty of Nice signed, allowing expansion to the east.

2002 – Euro notes and coins introduced in 12 states: Austria, Belgium, Finland, France, Germany, Greece, Ireland, Italy, Luxembourg, the Netherlands, Portugal and Spain.

2004 – Ten new countries join - Cyprus, the Czech Republic, Estonia, Hungary, Latvia, Lithuania, Malta, Poland, the Slovak Republic, and Slovenia. Treaty establishing a Constitution for Europe agreed.

2007 – Bulgaria and Romania join the EU, making the membership 27.

2009 – European Parliament elections elect 736 MEPs elected to represent 500 million Europeans.

2013 – Croatia joins the EU.

2016 – UK holds a referendum and votes to leave EU.

End of Chapter Questions

Think of an answer for each question and refer to the appropriate section for confirmation.

1. What is the BIS and what functions does it serve?
    Answer Reference: Section 1

2. What are the three pillars of the Basel II Capital Accord?
    Answer Reference: Section 1

3. What are the three primary areas of risk addressed by the BCBS?
    Answer Reference: Sections 1.1–1.3

4. Identify three types of credit risk and why they occur.
    Answer Reference: Section 1.1

5. Define operational risk and identify six factors that contribute to operational risk.
    Answer Reference: Section 1.3

6. Name seven elements that a global custodian will give attention to when conducting a risk review on a subcustodian.
    Answer Reference: Section 2

7. What is SEC Rule 17f-7 and what actions must be taken in order to comply with this rule?
    Answer Reference: Section 2.1

8. What is a depository risk report and what does it contain?
    Answer Reference: Section 2.1

9. What countermeasures are recommended in order to protect against safekeeping risk?
    Answer Reference: Section 3.1

10. What is relationship risk? What are the principal sources of relationship risk experienced by a global custodian?
    Answer Reference: Section 3.4

11. What is an ISAE 3402 report?
    Answer Reference: Section 4.2

12. What are the risks associated with failure to implement open trade reconciliation?
    Answer Reference: Section 6

Glossary

30/360

Calculation of accrued interest on bonds, assuming that the year comprises 12 months of 30 days each – used in the Eurobond market.

Audit and Assurance Faculty (AAF) 01/06

An independently audited record of the internal controls employed by investment services companies, including investment custodians. The AAF 01/06 reporting guidelines, issued by the AAF of the ICAEW, replace FRAG 21 reporting guidelines.

Accrued Interest

The amount of interest on a bond that has accrued since the most recent interest payment. Can be calculated using the 30/360 convention or the actual/actual convention.

Actively Managed Fund

A fund whose composition is managed actively by an investment manager – in contrast to Index Tracking Funds.

Actual Settlement Date Accounting

Accounting procedures by which the proceeds of a securities sale are credited to the seller's account, and the costs of a securities purchase debited from the buyer's account, on the date that a trade actually settles.

Agency Cross

An agency trade where the broker matches an order between two of its clients on its own books.

Agency Trading

Trading on behalf of clients in the capacity of an agent. Agency traders will typically not hold securities positions on their own behalf.

Alternative Investment Fund Managers Directive (AIFMD)

A European Union directive enacted in 2013 that regulates the activities of EU-based fund managers that manage and market alternative investment funds (typically hedge funds, real estate or private equity funds), along with non-EU fund managers that market alternative investment funds in the EU.

American Depositary Receipt (ADR)

A negotiable receipt issued by a US bank or trust company certifying that shares of a non-US company are held on deposit. The usual way for the shares of non-US companies to trade in the US.

Arbitrage

The process of buying the same or similar assets in one market and selling in another and then profiting from the difference in price.

Bank for International Settlements (BIS)

A Basel-based international organisation that serves as a bank for central banks and a forum for international monetary and financial co-operation.

Bearer Security

A security that has no facility for the issuer to register ownership of the security, such that the holder of the physical certificate (the 'bearer') is deemed to be legal owner. Income is typically payable upon presentation of the coupon, which may have been detached from the certificate.

Beneficial Owner

The true owner of securities; the person entitled to the benefits of ownership. The beneficial owner may or may not be the registered owner.

Bid Price

The price at which a dealer will buy securities.

Bilateral Netting

Offsetting trades between two counterparties in the same security such that there is only one transfer of cash and securities.

Bank of Japan (BOJ)

Bank of Japan, which also runs Bank of Japan Financial Network System (BOJ-NET) – a yen payment system.

Bolsas y Mercados Españoles (BME)

The Spanish stock exchange group.

Bond

A marketable debt instrument issued by a company, a government or a government agency.

Book-Entry Transfer

A system of transfer of ownership which entails only a change in the computer record of ownership. There is no movement of certificates and no new certificates are issued.

Bridge

An electronic link between Clearstream Banking and Euroclear Bank, across which settlement of trades is effected between the two ICSDs.

Broker

Brokers usually execute trades on an agency basis on behalf of their clients, finding buyers for securities that investors wish to sell and vice versa.

Broker-Dealer

Broker-dealers are licensed to trade on an agency basis on behalf of their investor clients (see Agency Trading, Broker), or on a proprietary basis on their own behalf.

Buying In

If the selling counterparty fails to deliver the securities necessary to fulfil its settlement obligations, the buyer (or sometimes the exchange) may purchase the necessary securities from an alternative source and pass any costs incurred onto the defaulting seller. This process is known as a 'buying in'.

Capitalisation

The issuance of additional shares by a company to its shareholders, free of cost, at a fixed ratio to the original shares held by the shareholder.

Cash Funding

Process whereby the buyer ensures that there will be sufficient cash in place to pay for the purchase of securities. Also called Positioning.

CASS Rules

Client Asset Safekeeping rules defined by the UK Financial Conduct Authority, a regulatory body for financial services in the UK market.

Central Securities Depository (CSD)

An organisation that holds securities in either immobilised or dematerialised form, thereby enabling transactions to be processed by book-entry transfer. Also provides securities administration services.

Central Trade Manager (CTM)

A straight-through processing (STP) solution provided by Omgeo.

Clean Price

Price of a bond excluding accrued interest.

Clearing House

An organisation operating a clearing system. Some exchanges act as their own clearing house, some depositories act as clearing houses and some clearing houses are entities separate from exchanges or depositories.

Clearing House Automated Payment System (CHAPS)

Clearing system for sterling payments between banks.

Clearing House Electronic Subregister System (CHESS)

Equities settlement system maintained by the Australian Stock Exchange.

Clearing House Interbank Payments System (CHIPS)

Clearing system for US dollar payments between banks in New York.

Clearstream Banking

Central securities depository (CSD) and clearing house for eurobonds and German stock – based in Luxembourg and Frankfurt.

Client Money

Money received from or for a client in the course of carrying on investment business.

Continuous Linked Settlement (CLS)

Real-time global settlement system for the foreign exchange market.

Consolidation

The amalgamation of multiple shares in a company into a single share.

Continuous Net Settlement

Extends multilateral netting to handle failed trades brought forward.

Contractual Settlement Date Accounting

Accounting procedures by which the proceeds of a securities sale are credited to the seller's account, and the costs of a securities purchase are debited from the buyer's account for value on settlement date (or an otherwise pre-agreed value date), even if trade settlement is not yet final and irrevocable on that date.

Convertible (Bond)

A bond that can be converted into shares of the issuing company on terms specified at the time of issue. Called a convertible bond (CB) or convertible unsecured loan stock (CULS).

Corporate Action

Any action by an issuer of investments, or by another party in relation to the issuer, affecting an investor's entitlement to investments or benefits relating to those investments. This includes, but is not restricted to, takeovers, rights issues, stock conversions, scrip dividends and redemptions.

Counterparty

One of the parties to a transaction – either the buyer or the seller.

Coupon

The physical coupon detached from a bearer certificate in order to claim a dividend or interest payment. The annual interest rate paid on a bond. The coupon rate is expressed as a percentage of the nominal (par) value.

CREST

The electronic settlement system operated by Euroclear UK & Ireland, the central securities depository for UK and Irish securities and for a small range of other foreign securities.

Crossing Network

An alternative trading system that matches buy and sell orders electronically for execution without first routing the order to an exchange or other displayed market which displays a public quote.

Custodian

An organisation that holds clients' assets in safe custody, ensures that they are not released without proper authorisation, and ensures the timely and accurate collection of dividends and other benefits.

Debenture

Another name for a corporate bond – usually secured on assets of the company.

Default Risk

The risk that the issuer of a bond will be unable to meet the payments of interest or the repayment of the capital.

Deferred Share

A class of share where the holder is only entitled to a dividend if the ordinary shareholders have been paid a specified minimum dividend.

Delivery versus Payment (DvP)

Settlement where transfer of the security and payment for that security occur simultaneously.

Depositary receipt (DR)

A negotiable financial instrument issued by a bank to represent publicly traded shares in a foreign company. The DR trades on the local stock exchange, but a custodian bank in the foreign country holds the underlying shares.

Depository Trust and Clearing Corporation (DTCC)

A clearing, settlement, central securities depository (CSD) and information service for US securities.

Depository Trust Company (DTC)

Depository for US equities. The US Central Securities Depository (CSD) is a subsidiary of DTCC.

Derivatives

A financial contract between a buyer and a seller, which is derived from the future value of an underlying instrument. Derivatives include futures, options, forwards, swaps and contracts for difference (CFDs).

Deutsche Börse

The group that owns the Frankfurt Stock Exchange and many other entities.

Dirty Price

Price of a bond including accrued interest.

Dividend

A distribution of profits to the shareholders of a company.

Domestic Bond

A bond issued in the domestic market by a domestic issuer in the domestic currency.

Entrepreneurs' Relief

Relief granted under UK capital gains tax against business assets. This allows individuals and some trustees to claim relief on gains made through the disposal of a company (or part of a company) or the assets of a company after it has stopped trading.

European Securities and Markets Authority (ESMA)

An independent EU Authority that promotes the stability of the European Union's financial system. In particular, ESMA fosters supervisory convergence both amongst securities regulators, and across financial sectors by working closely with the other European Supervisory Authorities competent in the field of banking (European Banking Authority (EBA)) and insurance and occupational pensions (European Insurance and Occupational Pensions Authority (EIOPA)).

Equities

Shares in a company that are entitled to the balance of profits and assets after all prior charges.

Euroclear Settlement of Euronext-zone Securities (ESES)

The settlement system employed to provide delivery versus payment (DVP) book entry for a wide range of securities in the Belgian, French and Dutch markets.

EUCLID

Communications system operated by Euroclear.

EUREX

German-Swiss derivatives exchange created by the merger of the German (DTB) and Swiss (SOFFEX) exchanges. The parent of Eurex Clearing, the CCP.

Eurobond

A generic name for bonds issued outside of the country of the issuer and denominated in a foreign currency.

Euroclear Bank

International central securities depository (ICSD) owned by Euroclear group, based in Brussels.

Euroclear France

CSD for French corporate securities and OATs.

Exchange-Traded Fund (ETF)

An instrument that tracks an index or a basket of assets, but is traded like a share on a stock exchange or Multilateral Trading Facility (MTF), thus experiencing price changes throughout the day as it is bought and sold.

Federal National Mortgage Association (Fannie Mae)

A government-sponsored organisation in the US that purchases eligible mortgages from lenders, packages these into new securities and sells them to investors, using the proceeds to provide further funding for home mortgages.

Federal Home Loan Mortgage Corporation (Freddie Mac)

A government-sponsored organisation in the US that purchases eligible residential mortgages from mortgage lenders, packages these into new securities and sells them to investors in the open market. The funds generated through the sale of these securities are utilised to support further mortgage lending. Fannie Mae and Freddie Mac have similar charters, regulatory structure and Congressional mandate, competing with each other in buying residential loans in the secondary mortgage market.

Foreign Account Tax Compliance Act (FATCA)

A US act requiring US taxpayers holding foreign financial assets that exceed given thresholds to report those assets to the IRS. Also, FATCA requires foreign financial institutions to report to the IRS information about financial accounts held by US taxpayers or by foreign entities in which US taxpayers hold a substantial ownership interest.

Financial Conduct Authority (FCA)

A regulatory body for financial services in the UK. The FCA sits alongside the Bank of England, the Prudential Regulatory Authority, the UK Treasury and the Financial Policy Committee in regulating financial services in the UK market.

Fixed Settlement

All trades within a specified period, called a period or a dealing period, are settled on one fixed day, a specified number of days after the end of the account.

Floating-Rate Note (FRN)

A bond whose coupon is refixed periodically in line with a benchmark interest rate.

Foreign Bond

A bond issued in the domestic market by a foreign issuer in the domestic currency.

Forward Rate (FX)

A foreign exchange rate for delivery at an agreed future date.

Futures Contract

An agreement to buy or sell a specific amount of a commodity, currency or a financial instrument at a specified price on a specified date.

Gilt Strip

An entitlement to a stream of income payments from a gilt security, without owning or having exposure to fluctuations in price of the underlying gilt. Gilt strips originated from the practice of separating coupons from the underlying bond and trading them separately. Hence, the holder could own the coupon (or 'strip') and be entitled to the coupon payment, without owning the underlying security.

Global Depositary Receipt (GDR)

A negotiable receipt issued by a depository bank certifying that shares of a foreign company that are listed and traded on a foreign exchange (or a number of foreign exchanges) are held on deposit. The GDR mirrors the shares of a foreign company, but can be traded in an investor's domestic market, in the investor's domestic currency, and according to the financial regulations operating in the investor's domestic market.

Globally Registered Share

A share that is quoted on more than one exchange.

Gross Settlement

Each trade is settled separately from any other. There is no netting. Also called trade-for-trade settlement.

Hedging

The use of securities and derivatives to protect a portfolio against an adverse movement in value. Also can be applied to one or more securities.

Herstatt Risk

The risk on an FX transaction where there is a non-simultaneous exchange of the different currencies.

High-Frequency Trading

Programme trading strategies that utilise powerful computers and high-speed fibre optic connections to trade multiple orders in a short time frame.

Iberclear

CSD for the Spanish market, owned by Bolsas y Mercados Españoles (BME), the Spanish stock exchange.

Index-Linked Bond

Bond whose interest payments and redemption value are linked to an index such as the retail price index.

Index-Tracking Fund

A fund that is run by a computer algorithm to track a particular set of stocks.

Initial Public Offering (IPO)

The first public issue of shares, that makes shares available for trading.

Institutional Investor

An institution that is usually investing money on behalf of others. Examples are mutual funds and pension funds.

Inter-Dealer Broker (IDB)

A firm that acts as an intermediary between market-maker firms, meeting the latter's needs for securities that they need to support their own trading requirements. An IDB also provides anonymity.

International Organization of Securities Commissions (IOSCO)

The worldwide association of national securities regulatory commissions, the national regulatory bodies for securities market activities around the world.

International Securities Identification Number (ISIN)

A system of unique code numbers developed by the **International Standards Organisation (ISO)** for use worldwide for identifying securities.

International Organization for Standardization (ISO)

The ISO promotes consistency of standards around the globe relating to goods and services, including the financial services industry.

In-the-Money (ITM)

An option or warrant with intrinsic value.

Jumbo Certificate

A certificate of deposit with a minimum denomination of $100,000. They have higher denominations than regular CDs and allow investors to deposit a certain amount of money and receive interest. These investments are considered low-risk, stable investments for large investors. They typically pay interest at a higher rate than lower denomination CDs.

Legal Entity Identifier (LEI)

A 20-digit, alphanumeric code, that provides a unique identification of legally distinct entities that engage in financial transactions.

Liquidation

The formal process of winding down a company. The assets are sold, the liabilities and preference shares are repaid, and any balance of assets is paid to the ordinary shareholders.

Liquidity (markets)

The ease with which shares can be converted into cash at close to fair value, or market value – ie, the ease with which they can be sold, or cashed in, and the speed with which the proceeds are received.

Listed Company

Company which has been admitted to listing on a stock exchange and whose shares can then be traded on that exchange.

Loan Stock

Another name for a corporate bond – usually unsecured.

Margin

Collateral paid to the clearing house or general clearing member (GCM) by the counterparties to a transaction to guarantee their positions against loss. Can also be paid over bilaterally between counterparties. Initial margin is paid when a position is first opened. Variation margin is paid or withdrawn daily as, respectively, daily losses and profits are made.

Market Capitalisation

The market capitalisation of a company is the market price per share multiplied by the number of shares in issue. The market capitalisation of a stock market is the sum of the market capitalisations of all the companies quoted on the exchange.

Market Identifier Code (MIC)

A unique identification code used to identify securities trading exchanges, regulated and non-regulated trading markets.

Market Maker

A securities trading firm that will buy and sell specified securities at published bid and offer prices and sizes.

Master Custody

A comprehensive custody service offered to investor clients holding assets with multiple investment managers and across multiple locations. This service combines the benefits of global custody and domestic custody, offering the investor consolidated reporting for their worldwide investments.

Maturity

Date upon which the principal of a bond or other securities instrument becomes due and repayable.

Markets in Financial Instruments Directive (MiFID)

The EU Directive that governs investment business within the European Economic Area.

MiFID II

An EU Directive that introduced revisions to the Markets in Financial Instruments Directive (MiFID) with the aim of making financial markets more efficient, resilient and transparent and strengthening protection of investors.

Mortgage-Backed Security

A type of asset-backed security that uses a single mortgage, or a pool of mortgage loans, as collateral. Investors receive payments derived from the interest and principal of the underlying mortgage loans.

Multilateral Netting

Trades between several counterparties in the same security are netted such that each counterparty makes only one transfer of cash or securities to another party or to a central clearing system. Handles only transactions due for settlement on the same day.

Multilateral Trading Facility (MTF)

Registered non-exchange trading venues which bring together purchasers and sellers of securities. Subscribers can post orders into the system and these will be communicated anonymously (typically electronically, via an electronic communication network, ECN) for other subscribers to view.

National Securities Clearing Corporation (NSCC)

Clearing organisation for US shares maintained by the DTCC.

Netting

Trading partners offset their positions, thereby reducing the number of positions for settlement. Netting can be Bilateral, Multilateral or Continuous Net Settlement.

Nil paid rights

(also known as 'non-renounceable rights')

Security that is tradeable but originally posed no cost to the seller.

Nominee

A person registered as the holder of a security who is holding it in safe custody on behalf of another person, usually a limited company that is a non-trading subsidiary of a parent company.

Nostro Account

One bank's foreign currency account with another bank.

Novation

When a CCP interposes itself between the counterparties to a trade, becoming the buyer to every seller and the seller to every buyer. As a result, buyer and seller interact with the CCP and remain anonymous to each other.

NYSE Euronext

Exchange created from the merger of the Paris, Amsterdam, Brussels and Lisbon exchanges. Now owned by the NYSE Euronext group.

Offer Price

The price at which a dealer will sell securities – also called the Ask Price.

Omgeo

Joint venture between Thomson Financial Services and the DTCC providing trade confirmation services.

On-Exchange

Dealing of securities through a regulated investment exchange.

Option

A contract that gives the holder the right but not the obligation to buy (or to sell) a specified quantity of a specified financial instrument at a specified price – called the exercise price – during or at the end of a specified period. A call option is an option providing the holder with a right but not an obligation to buy the underlying asset at a specified price within a specified time period. A put option is an option providing a right but not an obligation to sell the underlying asset for a specified price on or before a specified date.

Order-Driven Market

A stock market where brokers acting on behalf of clients match trades with each other either on the trading floor of the exchange or through a central computer system.

Ordinary Shares

An ordinary share gives the right to its owner to share in the profits of the company (dividends) and to vote at general meetings of the company.

Out-of-the-Money

An option or warrant with no intrinsic value.

Over-the-Counter (OTC)

The dealing of securities outside of an organised exchange or MTF.

Pari Passu

Latin meaning 'equal footing'. Describes situations where two or more assets, securities, creditors or obligations are equally managed without any display of preference. Treating all parties the same means they are pari passu.

Positioning

Positioning assets for settlement.

Preference Shares

Shares that are entitled to profits and assets in priority to the ordinary shares. Also called preferred stock.

Premium

The amount paid for a rights issue, or a warrant or other option.

Pre-Settlement

The term for the checks and procedures undertaken immediately after execution of a trade prior to settlement.

Primary Market

The market for new issues of securities.

Prime Broker

A one-stop clearing, settlement, securities financing and custody service, commonly used by hedge funds.

Private Investor

An individual who holds securities to realise investment returns for his or her own benefit.

Proprietary Trading

A trader that buys, sells and holds securities to make profit on its own account, not acting as an agent for investors.

Quote-Driven Market

A stock market where dealing is carried out with market makers.

Real-Time Gross Settlement (RTGS)

Gross settlement system where trades are settled continuously through the processing day.

Reconciliation

The comparison of a person's records of cash and securities positions with records held by another party and the investigation and resolution of any discrepancies between the two sets of records.

Record Date

For equities, the date at which shareholders on the issuer's register are identified for the purpose of distributing dividends and other shareholder entitlements. For fixed-income securities, the date at which the owner of the security is identified for receipt of income payments or redemption monies.

Redemption

The repayment of the capital of a bond.

Registered Security

A security where ownership is recorded on a register maintained by the issuer or registrar.

Registrar

The official with responsibility for maintaining the share register of a company.

Repo

Repurchase agreements are collateralised lending transactions whereby securities are sold with the agreement to buy them back. These represent a means of borrowing stock with cash provided as collateral, or a means of borrowing money with stock provided as collateral.

Rights Issue

A new issue of shares offered to the existing shareholders in proportion to their existing holdings.

Rolling Settlement

A trade is settled a specified number of days after the date of the trade. Usually denoted as T+n, where n is the number of business days. Thus T+3 means settlement three business days after the trade day.

Scrip Dividend

A scrip dividend involves companies offering shareholders a new issue of shares instead of dividends; similar to a (mini) rights issue.

SEC Regulations 17F-5 and 17F-7

In the US market, the Securities and Exchange Commission (SEC) has laid down strict rules governing the conditions under which a US-based investment company can hold its assets overseas. Under SEC Rule 17f-5 US investment companies can hold securities with any custodian that meets the SEC's eligible foreign custodian criteria, dictating that rigorous due diligence is conducted on any custodian before it can be appointed.

Secondary Market

The trading of existing securities on an exchange or MTF.

Securities Lending

Process by which a shareholder or bondholder lends securities to a borrower in return for a fee, in order to enhance the lender's return on its investment.

Selling Out

Process whereby, on failure by the purchaser to pay for securities, the seller sells to an alternative purchaser and any additional costs are passed on to the defaulting purchaser.

Settlement

The process whereby cash and legal ownership of a security are exchanged in order to fulfil the contractual obligations of buying and selling counterparties.

Share

The unit of ownership of a company.

Share Capital

The figure in the balance sheet representing the nominal value of the shares that have been issued.

Share Certificate

A certificate issued by a company to a shareholder stating either that a named person is the registered owner or that the bearer is the owner.

Shareholder

The owner of a share in a company – the part-owner of a company.

Short Selling

Selling of securities not owned by the seller.

Society for Worldwide Interbank Financial Telecommunication (SWIFT)

Secure electronic communications network between financial service providers.

Spot Rate

An FX rate for delivery in two business days.

SSAE 16

An internationally recognised auditing standard developed by the American Institute of Certified Public Accountants (AICPA) that succeeds the earlier SAS 70 standard. Like an AAF 01/06 report in the UK, an SSAE 16 report in the US verifies that a service organisation has had its control activities reviewed by an independent auditing firm.

Stock Exchange

An organisation that provides facilities for companies and governments to issue securities and for those securities to be traded among investors.

Stock Exchange Daily Official List (SEDOL)

A daily published list of values for UK shares, unit trusts, investment trusts and insurance-linked investment products traded on the LSE. A SEDOL number is a securities identifier issued by the London Stock Exchange or Irish Stock Exchange to provide unique identification of instruments traded in the UK, Ireland and on a global basis. It forms part of an ISIN.

Stock Split

A split of a share into a number of shares with a smaller nominal value.

Subscription

The process of an investor paying for, and taking up, a new issue of shares.

SWIFT Accord

An electronic trade data matching service for equity and fixed income trades.

Systematic Internaliser (SI)

An investment firm that, on an organised, frequent and systematic basis, deals on its own trading account by executing clients' orders outside a regulated market or a multilateral trading facility (MTF).

Systemic Risk

The risk that failure of a participant in a financial market to meet its obligations will cause other participants or financial institutions to fail to meet their respective obligations when required. Such a failure may lead to liquidity constraints or credit difficulties that may threaten the overall stability of the financial market.

Tap Stock

An issue of a bond that is not placed immediately with investors, ie, the issuer authorises the bond and makes it available, but holds it back until it needs or desires the cash flow that the sale of the issue would bring.

Trans-European Automated Real-time Gross Settlement Express Transfer system (TARGET)

TARGET2 is the RTGS system for the euro, offered by the Eurosystem. It is used for the settlement of central bank operations, large-value euro interbank transfers and other euro payments.

TARGET2-Securities (T2S)

A centralised settlement platform for the settlement of euro-denominated and some non-euro securities. Built and operated by the Eurosystem, CSDs will have the option of outsourcing their securities settlement activity to the T2S platform. CSDs will link to the T2S platform in a phased migration between May 2015 and 2017.

Trade Confirmation

Formal agreement of the details of a trade by the two counterparties prior to instructions being given for settlement.

Trade Date Netting

Multilateral netting, resulting in settlement of a single netted cash balance and a single netted securities balance calculated at close of business on trade date. This settlement of cash and securities relates only to trades presented for netting on that day, and will not include failed trades from previous days that have been brought forward.

Trade Matching

The matching by a clearing house of the trade details submitted by the two counterparties to a trade. Often combined with trade confirmation.

TRAX

Trade confirmation system for the Euromarkets operated by Xtrackter.

Treasury Bill

Money market instrument issued with a life of less than one year – issued by, for example, the US and UK governments.

Underwriter

Investment bank or other financial institution that will guarantee to buy unsold shares following an IPO or rights issue.

Warrant

An instrument issued by a company that gives the holder the right but not the obligation to subscribe for a specific number of shares in the company at a specific price (called the exercise price) during a specific period.

Withholding Tax (WHT)

Tax withheld by the payer of interest or a dividend and paid over to the Revenue Authority for the country of residence of the payer on behalf of the recipient.

Xetra

Dealing system of the Deutsche Börse, Austria, Bulgaria and Ireland (ISE Xetra).

Zero Coupon Bond

A bond which pays no coupon but which will be redeemed at a premium to the issue price.

Multiple Choice Questions

Multiple Choice Questions

The following additional questions have been compiled to reflect as closely as possible the examination standard that you will experience in your examination. Please note, however, they are not the CISI examination questions themselves.

1.   Deferred shares normally differ from conventional ordinary shares in which key area?

   A. Voting rights
   B. Dividend payments
   C. Tax treatment
   D. Shareholder perks

2.   What would an American depositary receipt (ADR) holder expect to receive when the issuing company makes a rights issue?

   A. Shares in the underlying security
   B. Nothing
   C. Proceeds of the sale of the rights
   D. Revaluation of the ADR

3.   An investor buys 100 call warrants for a premium of £0.40 each and a strike price of £1.00. Theoretically what will the share price have to reach for the investor to make a profit of £50?

   A. £50.40
   B. £1.90
   C. £1.40
   D. £0.90

4.   A buyer was due to pay £650,000 for shares on 1 July. Due to a computer processing error his payment arrived four days late. The seller incurred a 6% overdraft and discovered this on 28 July. The seller submitted a claim for interest on 2 September. Under ISITC guidelines, what is the likely amount of settlement of the sterling interest claim?

   A. Nil
   B. £254.82
   C. £427.40
   D. £433.33

5. What is short selling?

    A. A transaction where a broker delivers insufficient securities to settle a trade

    B. A situation where an investor delivers insufficient cash to settle a trade

    C. A strategy employed by an investor whereby the investor sells shares that it does not own, in anticipation that their market price might fall

    D. A term that describes all trading in covered warrants

6. Which ONE of the following activities is NOT regarded as a custody service?

    A. Tax reclamation

    B. Dividend collection reporting

    C. Safekeeping services

    D. Funds transference on trade settlement

7. Which of the following BEST describes the role of an agency trader?

    A. The lead client when creating an initial public offering of shares

    B. The supervisor of a group of junior traders

    C. Buys and sells shares on behalf of a client

    D. Buys and sells shares on behalf of his firm

8. A foreign exchange rate between currencies which is determined via the two currencies' respective dollar exchange rates is known as a:

    A. Bridge rate

    B. Cross rate

    C. Spot rate

    D. Split rate

9. What role does the CMU play regarding Hong Kong securities?

    A. It acts as a clearing house

    B. It acts as depository for corporate and government bonds

    C. It acts as CSD for equities and corporate bonds

    D. It acts as registrar for equities and warrants

10. One of the generally recognised advantages of rolling settlement, compared to fixed date settlement, is:

    A. A reduction in settlement costs

    B. A smoothing of settlement activities

    C. An increase in regulatory protection

    D. An improvement in tax treatment

11. A eurobond is:

    A. A floating-rate note denominated in euros

    B. A government bond issued by the European Central Bank

    C. A local bond issued in a European country

    D. An international bond issued in markets outside the issuer's domestic market

12. What is the main purpose of a request for proposal in the context of an institutional investor's custodianship needs?

    A. It serves as a draft agreement between the custodian and the institution

    B. It provides an initial indication of a potential custodian's capabilities

    C. It enables a consortium of custodians to be established

    D. It operates as a back-up should the chosen custodian default

13. Which of the following pairs correctly matches a country and its central securities depository for equities?

    A. UK and SETS

    B. France and LCH.Clearnet

    C. Germany and Euroclear Bank

    D. Japan and JASDEC

14. Typically an ICSD is established for what purpose?

    A. As a recognised clearing house for CCP-related activity

    B. To provide settlement and custody facilities over a range of security types and currencies

    C. As a clearing agent for the derivatives markets

    D. As an inter-dealer agent for the securities financing industry

15. Which ONE of the following is the best description of the electronic transfer of title (ETT) facility offered by the CREST system?

    A. The facility whereby all CREST eligible securities trades are instantly registered at the point of settlement following the acknowledgment of an actioned RUR

    B. The function of the positioning of securities post-matching but pre-settlement

    C. The instant legal registration of UK securities upon settlement

    D. The system that ensures full intra-bank cash settlement happens at the point of trade settlement

16. What is the settlement period for UK gilts?

    A. T+0

    B. T+1

    C. T+2

    D. T+3

17. TARGET2 is a payments system for which currency?

    A. GBP

    B. USD

    C. CHF

    D. EUR

18. What is the claims threshold under ISITC guidelines?

    A. US$100

    B. US$300

    C. US$500

    D. US$1,000

19. The primary difference between bilateral netting and multilateral netting relates to:

    A. Whether fixed date settlement or rolling settlement is used

    B. Whether the trades are on-exchange or off-exchange

    C. The number of counterparties involved

    D. The number of trades involved

20. A firm has chosen a new custodian to hold its safe custody investments. To comply with the regulations, how often must it carry out a risk assessment on this custodian?

    A. A minimum of once every six months

    B. A minimum of once every year

    C. A minimum of once every two years

    D. No prescribed minimum; it depends on circumstances

21. Under the substantial shareholder reporting rules, a company is empowered to:

    A. List its shares on a recognised exchange

    B. Initiate an investigation into ownership of its shares

    C. List its shares on exchanges outside of the UK

    D. Enter into a merger with another UK-registered company

22. If a broking firm is managing a private investor's portfolio and registers the client's shares into a nominee company name, the beneficial owner and the legal owner of the shares will be:

    A. The nominee company in both cases

    B. The client in both cases

    C. The nominee company and the client respectively

    D. The client and the nominee company respectively

23. An investment manager has a portfolio of invested assets with a market value of US$50 million. If the custodian charges an annual custody fee at 20 basis points, the annual charge will be:

    A. US$10,000

    B. US$20,000

    C. U$100,000

    D. US$1,000,000

24. A sweep account allows investors to:

    A. Transfer uninvested funds into overnight investments

    B. Secure special protection against money laundering

    C. Meet compliance requirements under Sarbanes-Oxley legislation

    D. Minimise foreign exchange transaction costs on cross-border investments

25. What is the electronic method by which Euroclear Bank communicates with Clearstream Banking?

    A. Bridge settlement

    B. ESES

    C. CreationOnline

    D. Link Up Markets

26. What is marking to market?

    A. Prioritising a block of trades for immediate execution by a broker

    B. Processing individual trades for prompt settlement

    C. Fixing the price of a security at a pre-agreed level

    D. Revaluing a securities position to its current market price

27. What is the basic rate of tax applicable, on a UK company dividend over £5,000 in value for a basic rate tax payer?

    A. Zero

    B. 5%

    C. 7.5%

    D. 10%

28. Withholding tax is tax deducted:

    A. Against revenues from safekeeping activities conducted by custodians on behalf of foreign investor clients

    B. In respect of capital gains generated by investors on their investment activity

    C. As a deposit by a jurisdiction's tax authorities against potential non-payment of tax by a foreign investor

    D. In the issuer's country of residence on income paid by issuers to investors

29. Operational risk is BEST defined as the risk:

    A. That an issuer may default on its obligation to meet interest payments and to redeem principal on redemption date

    B. Of loss resulting from inadequate or failed internal processes, people and systems, or from external events

    C. Of loss of earnings or capital arising from changes in the value of financial instruments

    D. Of material loss, liability or reputational damage resulting from failure to comply with the requirements of financial services regulators

30. An investor buys a gilt for £8,200 and sells it for £9,600. If this investor is a higher rate taxpayer who has exhausted his annual capital gains tax allowance, how much capital gains tax (if any) will be charged on this gain?

    A. Nothing

    B. £140

    C. £280

    D. £560

31. If the holder of a convertible preference share takes up the conversion option, what type of share will it usually become?

    A. Deferred share

    B. 'A' share

    C. 'B' share

    D. Ordinary share

32. Which of the following correctly describes a benefit extended by the process of listing securities?

    A. The issuing house will specify a minimum price for the share offer and invite offers from investors at prices of their own choosing

    B. Companies will be subject to detailed scrutiny designed to ensure that investors are buying securities in a bona fide company

    C. Unsold stock will be retained by the Debt Management Office and may be offered for sale at a later date

    D. The issuing company will sell shares directly to an investment bank or another sponsor, which will then sell shares to its preferred clients

33. The first two characters in an ISIN represent:

    A. Year of issuance

    B. Check code: confirming validity

    C. Country code

    D. Type of security: ie, equity, bond, mutual fund, ETF

34. A covered warrant is issued:

    A. By a company over its own underlying shares

    B. By a third party over a single asset or a range of possible underlying assets

    C. At a specified minimum price and investors are invited to submit offers at prices of their own choosing

    D. By government to applicants whose competitive bids are at or above a specified minimum price

35. A multilateral trading facility is:

    A. A regulated stock exchange that supports trading from broker members from multiple jurisdictions

    B. A registered non-exchange trading venue that brings together buyers and sellers of securities

    C. A share trading facility for the sole purpose of supporting trading of small cap equities

    D. An order-driven market where investors can route orders to the platform electronically or via a floor broker

36. Which of the following statements is TRUE regarding the execution of programme trades?

    A. It may be difficult to obtain all the required shares on the same day

    B. The operational risk and credit risk on programme trades will typically be lower than for single-security transactions

    C. Time from trade execution to trade confirmation will typically be shorter than for trades executed individually

    D. The trades must be settled at an ICSD

37. In their capacity as fiduciaries, pension fund trustees are required to:

    A. Manage subcustodian selection for pension fund assets held in overseas markets

    B. Ensure that withholding tax agreements are in place with tax authorities in markets in which the pension fund invests

    C. Ensure that pension fund assets are at all times sufficient to cover scheme liabilities

    D. Monitor and review the tasks that they delegate to custodians to ensure that these are discharged effectively

38. Which ONE of the following systems operates on a multilateral netting basis for the transfer of US dollar payments?

    A. CHAPS

    B. CHIPS

    C. Fedwire

    D. TARGET2

39. Contractual settlement date accounting works to the advantage of the seller because:

    A. The seller will receive funds on the original settlement date, even if settlement is delayed

    B. The seller will receive due funds three days after the proposed settlement date

    C. Delivery of requisite securities on the settlement date is guaranteed

    D. Settlement will take place free of payment

40. Due to internal problems, a firm is unable to carry out its periodic reconciliation of safe custody investments held with a nominee company within the required period. What action therefore must it urgently take?

    A. Obtain a written mandate from all the affected clients

    B. Obtain a written mandate from the nominee company

    C. Notify HMRC

    D. Notify the financial regulator

41. When securities are placed on loan, legal title to the securities lies with:

    A. The lender

    B. The borrower

    C. The securities lending agent

    D. The local central securities depository

42. Why might a cash lender enter into a repo agreement, rather than lending on an unsecured basis?

    A. It will typically earn a higher premium through repo agreements than through unsecured lending

    B. Unsecured lending is illegal in many European jurisdictions

    C. There is no possibility that the cash borrower may default on its obligations when a repo agreement is in place

    D. Repo agreements afford security by ensuring that the lender will inherit collateral if the borrowing counterparty defaults on its obligations

43. An investor buys 2,500 shares in a company at £9.00 per share. She sells the same number of shares later in the tax year for £10.25 per share. She incurs brokerage costs of £20.00 on buying the shares, and a further £20.00 on their sale. The amount potentially subject to capital gains tax will therefore be:

A. £3,085

B. £3,105

C. £3,185

D. £25,625

44. Which ONE of the following is considered to be a prime benefit of using a multi-currency cash account?

A. Faster dividend processing for multi-jurisdictional portfolios

B. More advantageous deposit rates

C. A reduction in the number of FX transactions

D. A bundled package of multi-currency accounting saves costs

45. A bonus issue is:

A. A release of new shares to existing shareholders provided free of cost

B. A cash dividend paid to a company's ordinary shareholders

C. A cash dividend paid to a company's preference shareholders

D. A decision to convert a single company share into a larger number of shares

46. An investor holds 5,000 shares in a company priced at £8.50 per share. The company subsequently makes a one for five share rights issue at £6.50. Nil paid rights on the share issue will therefore be worth:

A. £1.67

B. £2.00

C. £6.50

D. £8.17

47. One of the main reasons why custodians sometimes adopt a 'pooling' approach to client accounts is to:

A. Reduce taxation liabilities

B. Offset the credit risk

C. Benefit from arbitrage opportunities

D. Obtain more advantageous deposit rates

48. Credit risk is the risk:

    A. Of loss of earnings or capital arising from changes in the value of financial instrument

    B. Of loss resulting from inadequate or failed internal processes, people and systems, or from external events

    C. That a counterparty will fail to meet its obligations in accordance with agreed terms

    D. That an act conducted by a firm or one of its employees damages the reputation of the firm

49. Which ONE of the following is not a reason for failed settlement?

    A. A counterparty may have gone into liquidation

    B. The purchaser may have insufficient cash

    C. The purchaser may have initiated a buy-in of securities

    D. A corporate action may be in motion

50. Corporate actions typically present a high level of risk to the custodian because:

    A. It is not possible to automate processing of mandatory corporate events

    B. Operational errors in the corporate actions department at the custodian bank tend to rise sharply under conditions of high market volatility

    C. If the custodian fails to inform investors of an upcoming corporate event, it may be required to cover any financial loss

    D. Liquidity risk evaluation procedures for corporate events perform poorly in conditions of high market volatility

Answers to Multiple Choice Questions

1.   **Answer: B**   **Ref: Chapter 1, Section 2.1**

Deferred shares offer holders the same rights as ordinary shares with the exception that they do not rank for a dividend until specified conditions are met.

2.   **Answer: C**   **Ref: Chapter 1, Section 5.1**

ADR shareholders receive the proceeds of the sale of any rights.

3.   **Answer: B**   **Ref: Chapter 1, Section 4**

(£1.90 – £1.00 – £0.40) x 100 = £50.00.

4.   **Answer: A**   **Ref: Chapter 3, Section 4.4**

Nil, as the claim was submitted after 30 calendar days had elapsed.

5.   **Answer: C**   **Ref: Chapter 1, Section 6.5**

Short selling is a practice widely employed by hedge funds in anticipation that market valuations might fall.

6.   **Answer: D**   **Ref: Chapter 2, Section 2.1**

Transference of funds is part of the main function of clearing and settlement operations.

7.   **Answer: C**   **Ref: Chapter 1, Section 11**

Agency trading is when a firm acts as an intermediary, or agent, on behalf of a client.

8.   **Answer: B**   **Ref: Chapter 3, Section 3.3.7**

The cross rate can be calculated from the two dollar exchange rates.

9.   **Answer: B**   **Ref: Chapter 2, Section 3.3**

Central Moneymarkets Unit (CMU) operated by the Hong Kong Monetary Authority (HKMA) is the depository for corporate and government debt securities. The **Hong Kong Securities Clearing Company (HKSCC)** is the central depository for equities, and share certificates are immobilised at the Hong Kong and Shanghai Banking Corporation Ltd. All shares and most warrants must be registered.

10.   **Answer: B**   **Ref: Chapter 3, Section 3.3.6**

Fixed date settlement creates peaks and troughs of settlement activity.

11.   **Answer: D**   **Ref: Chapter 1, Sections 3.1.4, 8.4**

Eurobonds are issued in markets outside the domestic market of the issuer.

12. **Answer: B** **Ref: Chapter 2, Section 2.3**

RFPs are submitted by potential custodians as part of the early stages of the selection process.

13. **Answer: D** **Ref: Chapter 2, Sections 3.3, 3.4**

Euroclear UK & Ireland is the depository for the UK. Euroclear France is the French CSD. Clearstream Banking Frankfurt (owned by Deutsche Börse group) is the depository for Germany. SETS is not a CSD.

14. **Answer: B** **Ref: Chapter 2, Section 3.4**

International central securities depositories (ICSDs) came into being initially to meet the need for integrated clearing, settlement and custody services for international eurobonds. Subsequently, the ICSDs have now expanded the range of services that they offer and overlap in many areas with the custodian community. ICSDs can hold equities, eurobonds, government bonds, corporate bonds and many other types of financial instrument.

15. **Answer: C** **Ref: Chapter 2, Section 3.3**

For UK securities, the CREST record of its members' holdings is the legal record of title. When a transaction settles in CREST, transfer of title will happen electronically and simultaneously with settlement. CREST will notify the registrar of the transfer by issuing a register update request (RUR) so that the registrar can update its records. Under the electronic transfer of title regulations, legal title passes at the point of settlement even though the register may not reflect the change until later in the day.

16. **Answer: B** **Ref: Chapter 1, Section 14**

The settlement period for UK gilts is T+1.

17. **Answer: D** **Ref: Chapter 3, Section 3.2.5**

Trans-European Automated Real-time Gross Settlement Express Transfer (TARGET2) is the real-time gross settlement system for the euro.

18. **Answer: C** **Ref: Chapter 3, Section 4.4.1**

Netting and bulking of claims under US$500 are at the counterparties' discretion.

19. **Answer: C** **Ref: Chapter 3, Section 3.3.3**

Bilateral netting covers trades between the same two counterparties whereas multilateral netting covers trades by any number of counterparties.

20. **Answer: D** **Ref: Chapter 4, Section 1.4**

The frequency of the risk review should be dependent on the nature of the market and the type of services that the custodian delivers to the client.

21. **Answer: B** **Ref: Chapter 4, Section 2**

The rules give companies the power, following certain procedures, to investigate share ownership.

22.   **Answer: D**   **Ref: Chapter 4, Section 3**

The nominee company holds legal title whereas beneficial ownership continues to remain with the underlying client.

23.   **Answer: C**   **Ref: Chapter 4, Section 4**

20 basis points means 0.20%. Hence the charge US$50m x 0.20% = US$100,000.

24.   **Answer: A**   **Ref: Chapter 4, Section 6.1**

Sweep accounts avoid clients having funds sitting idle overnight in non-interest bearing accounts.

25.   **Answer: A**   **Ref: Chapter 2, Section 3.4**

Bridge settlement involves an exchange of messages between Euroclear Bank and Clearstream Banking across an electronic bridge.

26.   **Answer: D**   **Ref: Chapter 4, Section 7.5**

Marking to market means ensuring that exposures are valued at current market prices.

27.   **Answer: C**   **Ref: Chapter 5, Section 1.1**

Tax of 7.5% is due on dividends over £5,000 paid to basic rate taxpayers or non-taxpayers.

28.   **Answer: D**   **Ref: Chapter 5, Section 5.1**

Tax regulations in many countries dictate that income payments accruing to non-residents are liable to be taxed at source in the jurisdiction in which the investments are incorporated. This is known as withholding tax.

29.   **Answer: B**   **Ref: Chapter 6, Section 1.3**

Operational risk covers the four main areas of process, people, systems and external events.

30.   **Answer: A**   **Ref: Chapter 5, Section 3**

Profits generated from the sale of gilts are free of capital gains tax.

31.   **Answer: D**   **Ref: Chapter 1, Section 2.2**

If the preference share is convertible, the shareholder has the option, at some stage, of converting it into an ordinary share.

32.   **Answer: B**   **Ref: Chapter 1, Section 2.1.2**

Companies wishing to be listed will typically be subject to a detailed investigation to safeguard the integrity of the exchange and to offer a degree of protection to investors.

33.   **Answer: C**   **Ref: Chapter 1, Section 7**

The ISIN consists of 12 characters, the first two of which represent the country code.

34. **Answer: B** **Ref: Chapter 1, Section 4**

A covered warrant is structured by a bank or other financial institution over a range of possible underlying assets.

35. **Answer: B** **Ref: Chapter 1, Section 9.1.2**

MTFs are alternative trading systems which enable securities to be bought and sold.

36. **Answer: A** **Ref: Chapter 1, Section 12.1**

It may not be possible to complete the programme trade for the desired amount of shares on the day the order is raised.

37. **Answer: D** **Ref: Chapter 2, Section 2.3**

Legislation requires the trustees to take full responsibility for the appointment and monitoring of custodian actions.

38. **Answer: B** **Ref: Chapter 3, Section 3.2**

The Clearing House Interbank Payments System (CHIPS) is a computerised network for the transfer of US dollar payments and operates on a multilateral netting basis. CHAPS is an electronic credit transfer system for sterling payments; Fedwire is the electronic transfer of funds system for the Federal Reserve; and TARGET2 is a real-time gross settlement system for the euro.

39. **Answer: A** **Ref: Chapter 3, Section 3.5**

CSDA means that the seller does not suffer as a result of a settlement delay.

40. **Answer: D** **Ref: Chapter 4, Section 1.3**

A firm must inform the regulator in writing without delay if it is unable to comply with any element of the reconciliation requirements specified by CASS.

41. **Answer: B** **Ref: Chapter 4, Section 7.1**

Legal title to on-loan securities passes from the lender to the borrower for the duration of the loan.

42. **Answer: D** **Ref: Chapter 4, Section 7.5**

The cash lender under a repo agreement receives securities as collateral throughout the loan period.

43. **Answer: A** **Ref: Chapter 5, Section 3**

The net gain = 2,500 x (10.25 – 9.00) – 20 – 20 = £3,085.

44.   **Answer: C**   **Ref: Chapter 4, Section 6.4**

Multi-currency accounts are commonly employed by companies that need to process regular and sizeable payments and credits in a foreign currency. The **benefits** of multi-currency account structures include: securities can be settled on a DVP basis in foreign currency; these reduce the costs and risks incurred in maintaining multiple FX transactions required by a single-currency account structure; a global custodian may offer integrated custody and banking services, providing a one-stop shop for investors' cross-border service needs.

45.   **Answer: A**   **Ref: Chapter 4, Section 5.2.3**

Bonus issues involve existing shareholders acquiring new shares free of charge.

46.   **Answer: A**   **Ref: Chapter 4, Section 5.3.1**

Total value of investor's shares prior to the corporate event: 5,000 x 8.50 = £42,500. Subsequent to taking up the issue, the investor will have 6,000 shares in total. Adjusted price per share: (£42,500 + (1,000 x 6.50)) ÷ 6,000 = 8.17. Nil paid rights will be worth = 8.17 − 6.50 = £1.67 per share.

47.   **Answer: D**   **Ref: Chapter 4, Section 6.2**

Pooling is done in order to attract a higher rate of interest or to reduce the penalties incurred by some accounts being overdrawn.

48.   **Answer: C**   **Ref: Chapter 6, Section 1**

A is market risk, B is operational risk, C is credit risk and D is reputational risk

49.   **Answer: C**   **Ref: Chapter 3, Sections 4.1, 4.2**

Settlement failure may be caused by a number of factors, including **non-matching settlement instructions; insufficient securities; insufficient funds; corporate actions** and **counterparty default**. If a trade fails to settle on time, the exchange (or the other counterparty) may impose penalties, or may also seek remedial action by initiating a buy-in of securities. Therefore a buy-in is part of the solution to failed settlement, not a cause of it.

50.   **Answer: C**   **Ref: Chapter 4, Section 5.1**

The custodian will be responsible for losses resulting from failure to communicate in good time.

Syllabus Learning Map

Syllabus Unit/ Element		Chapter/ Section

For the purpose of this syllabus the 'selected markets' referred to herein are defined as:

UK; US; Japan; Australia; Euronext; Germany; Spain; India; Hong Kong; Singapore; Korea; Brazil

Element 1	Securities	Chapter 1
1.1	**Securities** On completion the candidate should:	
1.1.1	Understand the characteristics of ordinary shares: • ranking in liquidation • dividends • voting rights/non-voting shares • deferred shares • registration • bearer/unlisted securities • transfer restrictions	2.1
1.1.2	Understand the characteristics of preference shares: • ranking in liquidation • dividends • voting rights/non-voting shares • cumulative/non cumulative • participating • redeemable • convertible	2.2
1.1.3	Understand the characteristics of Depositary Receipts: • American Depositary Receipt • Global Depositary Receipt • Depositary Interest • transferability/registration/transfer to underlying • how created/pre-release facility • rights • stamp duty and conversion fees	5
1.1.4	Understand the characteristics of warrants and covered warrants: • what are warrants and covered warrants • how they are valued • effect on price of maturity and the underlying security • purpose • detachability • exercise and expiry • benefit to the issuing company and purpose • issue by a third party • right to subscribe for capital	4

Syllabus Unit/ Element		Chapter/ Section

1.1.5	Understand the characteristics of fixed-income instruments:
	• corporate bonds
	• eurobonds
	• convertible bonds
	• government bonds
	• discount securities
	• floating rate notes
	• coupon payment intervals
	• coupon calculations (may be tested by the use of simple calculations)
	• accrued interest calculations (may be tested by the use of simple calculations):
	  ○ actual/actual
	  ○ 30/360
	• clean and dirty prices
	• mortgage backed securities
	• asset backed securities
	• index linked bonds
		3

1.1.6	Know the uses of: • exchange traded products • mutual funds • tax transparent funds • hedge funds • investment trusts • real estate funds • private equity	6
1.1.7	Know how securities are identified: • ISIN • CUSIP • SEDOL • tickers	7

1.1.8	Understand how securities are issued:
	• equities:
	  ○ offers for subscription
	  ○ offers for sale
	  ○ introductions
	  ○ placing
	  ○ offer to tender
	• government bonds:
	  ○ auction
	  ○ tap
	  ○ tranche
	• eurobonds:
	  ○ lead manager
	  ○ syndicate
	  ○ underwriting
		8

Syllabus Unit/ Element		Chapter/ Section
1.2	**Principles of Trading** On completion the candidate should:	
1.2.1	Know the characteristics of the Regulated Markets and Multilateral Trading Facilities (MTFs)	9
1.2.2	Understand the differences between: • on exchange/MTF • over the counter	10
1.2.3	Understand the main characteristics of: • order driven markets • quote driven markets • principal trading • agent trading • systematic internalisers • dark pools	11
1.2.4	Know the roles of: • market makers/liquidity providers • sales traders • proprietary traders	11
1.2.5	Know the principles of programme trades, algorithmic trading and high-frequency trading	12
1.2.6	Understand the impact of high-frequency trading on the market	12
1.2.7	Understand the principles of multiple listed shares	13
1.2.8	Know the settlement periods for equities and bonds in the selected markets	14

Element 2	Main Industry Participants	Chapter 2
2.1	**Investors and Custody Service Suppliers** On completion the candidate should:	
2.1.1	Know the characteristics of the following types of participant: • individual • institutional • investment manager • prime broker • broker • inter-dealer broker • investment bank • central bank	1

Syllabus Unit/ Element		Chapter/ Section
2.1.2	Understand the advantages, disadvantages and purposes of the following types of custodian: • global • sub-custodian	2.1
2.1.3	Understand the purpose and provisions of custody and sub-custody agreements	2.2
2.1.4	Understand the purpose of a Request For Proposal (RFP) in the selection of a global custodian by an investor	2.3
2.1.5	Understand the requirements of a Service Level Agreement between an investor and its custodian	2.2
2.1.6	Understand how legislation can affect the appointment of custodians	2.3
2.2	**International Central Securities Depositories and Central Securities Depositories** On completion the candidate should:	
2.2.1	Understand the roles of ICSDs and CSDs generally for the selected markets: • depositories available • participation requirements	3.1
2.2.2	Understand the concepts of certificated, immobilised and dematerialised securities	3.2
2.2.3	Understand the roles played by Euroclear Bank and Clearstream Banking, including the Bridge	3.4
2.2.4	Know how securities and cash are held by ICSDs and CSDs	3.1
2.2.5	Know the range of custody and settlement services offered by the ICSDs	3.4
2.2.6	Know the purpose and functions of Target2-Securities (T2S)	3.5
2.2.7	Know the impact of CSDR on European markets	3.5.1
2.3	**Communications and Technology** On completion the candidate should:	
2.3.1	Understand the advantages of straight-through processing	4
2.3.2	Know the features and benefits of SWIFT and SWIFT messaging	5
2.3.3	Know the features and benefits of FIX Protocol messaging	4.4
2.3.4	Know the communication methods used with Euroclear Bank and Clearstream Banking	3.4

Syllabus Unit/ Element		Chapter/ Section
Element 3	**Settlement Characteristics**	**Chapter 3**
3.1	**Pre-settlement** On completion, the candidate should:	
3.1.1	Understand the data required for matching of settlement instructions	2.1
3.1.2	Understand the process of clearing (matching and the assumption of risk – trade for trade versus central counterparty)	2.2
3.1.3	Understand the role of third-party service providers in the pre-settlement process: • Omgeo • TRAX • Traiana • Swift Accord	2.5
3.1.4	Understand netting in pre-settlement	2.4
3.2	**Settlement** On completion, the candidate should:	
3.2.1	Know the role of the following types of financial institutions in the settlement process: • brokers • investment banks • investment managers • custodians • sub-custodians • Central Counterparty Clearing Houses (CCPs) and clearing members • ICSDs and CSDs	3.1
3.2.2	Know the characteristics of the following cash systems: • CHIPS • CHAPS • TARGET 2 • Fedwire • CLS	3.2

Syllabus Unit/ Element		Chapter/ Section
3.2.3	Understand the following settlement concepts: • trade for trade • netting – bilateral and multilateral • trade date netting, continuous net settlement • fixed date settlement • rolling settlement • free of payment transactions • delivery versus payment • book entry settlement • physical settlement • foreign exchange settlement	3.3
3.2.4	Understand the transfer of legal title: • bearer • registered	3.4
3.2.5	Understand Contractual Settlement Date Accounting (CSDA) and Actual Settlement Date Accounting (ASDA)	3.5
3.2.6	Know the main Giovannini Barriers to the creation of a harmonised market for Europe	3.6
3.3	**Failed Settlement** On completion, the candidate should:	
3.3.1	Understand the main reasons for failed settlement: • failure to match • insufficient stock • insufficient cash • counterparty default • corporate event	4.1
3.3.2	Understand the risks associated with: • buy-ins/sell-outs • counterparty risk • interest claims • settlement fines • matching fines • suspension of trading • short sale fines	4
3.3.3	Understand interest claims (ICMA rules on fixed-income and ISITC for equities)	4.4
3.3.4	Be able to calculate interest claims based on the ICMA rules	4.4

Syllabus Unit/ Element		Chapter/ Section

Element 4	Other Investor Services	Chapter 4
4.1	**Safekeeping** On completion, the candidate should:	
4.1.1	Understand the principles of safekeeping client assets: • to safeguard assets • to segregate safe custody investments • to reconcile safe custody investments • to maintain records and controls in respect of the use of mandates	1
4.1.2	Understand the requirements of substantial shareholding reporting	2
4.1.3	Understand the functions of nominee companies and the following concepts: • legal title • beneficial ownership • pooled nominee holdings • designated nominee holdings • nominee as bare trustee • omnibus accounts • segregated accounts	3
4.1.4	Understand how a custodian charges for the services it provides to its clients	4
4.1.5	Be able to calculate the cost of custody for a given portfolio given a value of assets held and the basis point price	4
4.2	**Corporate Actions** On completion, the candidate should:	
4.2.1	Know the characteristics of the following mandatory events: • dividends (cash and scrip) • interest and coupon payments • capitalisation issues • splits and consolidations • capital repayments/redemptions	5.2
4.2.2	Know the characteristics of the following voluntary events: • rights issue subscription • conversions • takeovers • exchanges • initial public offerings • proxy voting • exercise of warrants	5.3

Syllabus Unit/ Element		Chapter/ Section
4.2.3	Understand the importance of receiving timely and accurate corporate action data and the risks involved	5.1
4.2.4	Understand the following terms: record date; ex-date; pay-date; effective date; cum-benefit; ex-benefit and special-ex and special-cum	5.5
4.2.5	Be able to calculate corporate actions-related data on capitalisations, scrip and rights issues and the effect on the underlying share price	5.2, 5.3
4.3	**Cash Management** On completion, the candidate should:	
4.3.1	Understand the importance and use of cash management	6
4.3.2	Understand the advantages and disadvantages of operating single and multi-currency accounts	6
4.3.3	Know what is meant by the terms sweeping and pooling as they relate to base currency and settlement currency	6
4.3.4	Understand the importance of cash forecasting tools	6
4.4	**Securities Lending** On completion, the candidate should:	
4.4.1	Understand the role of a lending agent in securities lending and the risks and rewards to those involved	7.3
4.4.2	Know the definition, legal ownership implications and the advantages and disadvantages to the market	7.1
4.4.3	Understand the reasons for securities lending	7.2
4.4.4	Understand the reasons why loans might be delayed or prevented	7.2
4.4.5	Understand the use of repo agreements	7.5
4.4.6	Understand the lenders' and borrowers' rights (including manufactured dividends and voting rights)	7.1
4.4.7	Understand collateral and marking to market	7.3, 7.5
4.4.8	Know the role of a stock borrowing and lending intermediary	7.4
4.4.9	Understand the reasons why a loan might be recalled	7.1

Syllabus Unit/ Element		Chapter/ Section
Element 5	**Aspects of Taxation**	**Chapter 5**
5.1	**General** On completion, the candidate should:	
5.1.1	Understand the tax treatment of dividends	1
5.1.2	Understand the tax treatment of bond interest	2
5.1.3	Understand capital gains tax as it applies to equities and bonds	3
5.1.4	Understand the tax treatment of discount securities	4
5.1.5	Understand the advantages, disadvantages and uses of: • withholding tax • double taxation treaties • relief at source • tax reclamation • being an authorised US approved Qualifying Intermediary • FATCA rules • CRS rules	5
5.1.6	Understand transaction based taxes	6

Syllabus Unit/ Element		Chapter/ Section
Element 6	**Identifying and Managing Risk**	
6.1	**Concepts and Characteristics** On completion, the candidate should:	
6.1.1	Know the following major categories of risk: • credit • market • counterparty • issuer • settlement • operational • political • systematic	1
6.1.2	Understand the factors that should be taken into account when conducting risk reviews of market infrastructures, sub-custodian networks and outsourced functions	2
6.1.3	Understand the areas of global custody risk and appropriate countermeasures	3
6.1.4	Know the purpose of a ISAE 3402 report	4

Syllabus Unit/ Element		Chapter/ Section
6.1.5	Understand shareholder limits and restrictions	5
6.2	**Mitigating Risk through Reconciliation** On completion, the candidate should:	
6.2.1	Understand the risks associated with a failure to reconcile the following: • open trades • counterparty cash • corporate actions • cash accounts • custodian holdings • client assets • entitlements	6
6.3	**Regulation** On completion, the candidate should:	
6.3.1	Know the objectives and features of regulatory risk	7.3
6.3.2	Understand the risks associated with a failure to comply with regulation	7.3

Examination Specification

Each examination paper is constructed from a specification that determines the weightings that will be given to each element. The specification is given below.

It is important to note that the numbers quoted may vary slightly from examination to examination as there is some flexibility to ensure that each examination has a consistent level of difficulty. However, the number of questions tested in each element should not change by more than plus or minus two.

Element Number	Element	Questions
1	Securities	10
2	Main Industry Participants	11
3	Settlement Characteristics	11
4	Other Investor Services	11
5	Aspects of Taxation	3
6	Risk	4
Total		**50**

CISI Associate (ACSI) Membership can work for you...

Studying for a CISI qualification is hard work and we're sure you're putting in plenty of hours, but don't lose sight of your goal!

This is just the first step in your career; there is much more to achieve!

The securities and investments sector attracts ambitious and driven individuals. You're probably one yourself and that's great, but on the other hand you're almost certainly surrounded by lots of other people with similar ambitions.

So how can you stay one step ahead during these uncertain times?

Entry Criteria:

Pass in either:

- Investment Operations Certificate (IOC), IFQ, ICWIM, Capital Markets in, eg, Securities, Derivatives, Advanced Certificates; or
- one CISI Diploma/Masters in Wealth Management paper

Joining Fee: £25 or free if applying via prefilled application form   **Annual Subscription (pro rata):** £125

Using your new CISI qualification* to become an Associate (ACSI) member of the Chartered Institute for Securities & Investment could well be the next important career move you make this year, and help you maintain your competence.

Join our global network of over 40,000 financial services professionals and start enjoying both the professional and personal benefits that CISI membership offers. Once you become a member you can use the prestigious ACSI designation after your name and even work towards becoming personally chartered.

* ie, Investment Operations Certificate (IOC), IFQ, ICWIM, Capital Markets

Benefits in Summary...

- Use of the CISI CPD Scheme
- Unlimited free CPD seminars, webcasts, podcasts and online training tools
- Highly recognised designatory letters
- Unlimited free attendance at CISI Professional Forums
- CISI publications including *The Review* and *Change – The Regulatory Update*
- 20% discount on all CISI conferences and training courses
- Invitation to the CISI Annual Lecture
- Select benefits – our exclusive personal benefits portfolio

The ACSI designation will provide you with access to a range of member benefits, including Professional Refresher where there are currently over 100 modules available on subjects including Anti-Money Laundering, Information Security & Data Protection, Integrity & Ethics, and the UK Bribery Act. CISI TV is also available to members, allowing you to catch up on the latest CISI events, whilst earning valuable CPD.

Plus many other networking opportunities which could be invaluable for your career.

Professional Refresher

Self-testing elearning modules to refresh your knowledge, meet regulatory and firm requirements, and earn CPD.

Professional Refresher is a training solution to help you remain up-to-date with industry developments, maintain regulatory compliance and demonstrate continuing learning.

This popular online learning tool allows self-administered refresher testing on a variety of topics, including the latest regulatory changes.

There are currently over 100 modules available which address UK and international issues. Modules are reviewed by practitioners frequently and new topics are added to the suite on a regular basis.

Benefits to firms:
- Learning and testing can form part of business T&C programme
- Learning and testing kept up-to-date and accurate by the CISI
- Relevant and useful – devised by industry practitioners
- Access to individual results available as part of management overview facility, 'Super User'
- Records of staff training can be produced for internal use and external audits
- Cost-effective – no additional charge for CISI members
- Available to non-members

Benefits to individuals:
- Comprehensive selection of topics across sectors
- Modules are regularly reviewed and updated by industry experts
- New topics added regularly
- Free for members
- Successfully passed modules are recorded in your CPD log as active learning
- Counts as structured learning for RDR purposes
- On completion of a module, a certificate can be printed out for your own records

The full suite of Professional Refresher modules is free to CISI members, or £250 for non-members. Modules are also available individually. To view a full list of Professional Refresher modules visit:

cisi.org/refresher

If you or your firm would like to find out more, contact our Client Relationship Management team:

+ 44 20 7645 0670
crm@cisi.org

For more information on our elearning products, contact our Customer Support Centre on +44 20 7645 0777, or visit our website at cisi.org/refresher
er

Professional Refresher

Top 5

SCORM COMPLIANT

Integrity & Ethics
- High Level View
- Ethical Behaviour
- An Ethical Approach
- Compliance vs Ethics

Anti-Money Laundering
- Introduction to Money Laundering
- UK Legislation and Regulation
- Money Laundering Regulations 2007
- Proceeds of Crime Act 2002
- Terrorist Financing
- Suspicious Activity Reporting
- Money Laundering Reporting Officer
- Sanctions

Financial Crime
- What Is Financial Crime?
- Insider Dealing and Market Abuse Introduction, Legislation, Offences and Rules
- Money Laundering Legislation, Regulations, Financial Sanctions and Reporting Requirements
- Money Laundering and the Role of the MLRO

Information Security and Data Protection
- Information Security: The Key Issues
- Latest Cybercrime Developments
- The Lessons From High-Profile Cases
- Key Identity Issues: Know Your Customer
- Implementing the Data Protection Act 1998
- The Next Decade: Predictions For The Future

UK Bribery Act
- Background to the Act
- The Offences
- What the Offences Cover
- When Has an Offence Been Committed?
- The Defences Against Charges of Bribery
- The Penalties

Latest Modules

Bonds
- Definition, Key Terms and Characteristics
- The Different Types of Bonds
- The Advantages and Disadvantages of Bonds
- Rating Bonds

General Data Protection Regulation (GDPR)
- Understanding the Terminology
- The Six Data Protection Principles
- Data Subject Rights
- Technical and Organisational Measures

Human Trafficking and the Modern Slavery Act 2015
- Human Trafficking and Modern Slavery
- Definitions and Scale of the Problem
- Detection and Prevention
- Statements

Long-term Care
- Setting the Scene
- State Provision
- Planned Changes
- Funding Your Own Care
- Effective Structuring

Managing in the Regulatory Environment
- Regulatory Framework and Expectations
- The Conduct Rules
- Obligations on Managers
- Personal Responsibilities
- Responsibilities for Managing Others
- If Things Go Wrong

Operations

Best Execution
- What Is Best Execution?
- Achieving Best Execution
- Order Execution Policies
- Information to Clients & Client Consent
- Monitoring, the Rules, and Instructions
- Best Execution for Specific Types of Firms

Approved Persons Regime
- The Basis of the Regime
- Fitness and Propriety
- The Controlled Functions
- Principles for Approved Persons
- The Code of Practice for Approved Persons

Corporate Actions
- Corporate Structure and Finance
- Life Cycle of an Event
- Mandatory Events
- Voluntary Events

Wealth

Client Assets and Client Money
- Protecting Client Assets and Client Money
- Ring-Fencing Client Assets and Client Money
- Due Diligence of Custodians
- Reconciliations
- Records and Accounts
- CASS Oversight

Investment Principles and Risk
- Diversification
- Factfind and Risk Profiling
- Investment Management
- Modern Portfolio Theory and Investing Styles
- Direct and Indirect Investments
- Socially Responsible Investment
- Collective Investments
- Investment Trusts
- Dealing in Debt Securities and Equities

Banking Standards
- Introduction and Background
- Strengthening Individual Accountability
- Reforming Corporate Governance
- Securing Better Outcomes for Consumers
- Enhancing Financial Stability

Suitability of Client Investments
- Assessing Suitability
- Risk Profiling
- Establishing Risk Appetite
- Obtaining Customer Information
- Suitable Questions and Answers
- Making Suitable Investment Selections
- Guidance, Reports and Record Keeping

International

Foreign Account Tax Compliance Act (FATCA)
- Foreign Financial Institutions
- Due Diligence Requirements
- Reporting
- Compliance

MiFID II
- The Organisations Covered by MiFID
- The Products Subject to MiFID's Guidelines
- The Origins of MiFID II
- The Products Covered by MiFID II
- Levels 1, 2, and 3 Implementation

UCITS
- The Original UCITS Directive
- UCITS III
- UCITS IV
- Non-UCITS Funds
- Future Developments

cisi.org/refresher

Feedback to the CISI

Have you found this workbook to be a valuable aid to your studies? We would like your views, so please email us at learningresources@cisi.org with any thoughts, ideas or comments.

Accredited Training Partners

Support for exam students studying for the Chartered Institute for Securities & Investment (CISI) qualifications is provided by several Accredited Training Partners (ATPs), including Fitch Learning and BPP. The CISI's ATPs offer a range of face-to-face training courses, distance learning programmes, their own learning resources and study packs which have been accredited by the CISI. The CISI works in close collaboration with its ATPs to ensure they are kept informed of changes to CISI exams so they can build them into their own courses and study packs.

CISI Workbook Specialists Wanted

Workbook Authors

Experienced freelance authors with finance experience, and who have published work in their area of specialism, are sought. Responsibilities include:
- Updating workbooks in line with new syllabuses and any industry developments
- Ensuring that the syllabus is fully covered

Workbook Reviewers

Individuals with a high-level knowledge of the subject area are sought. Responsibilities include:
- Highlighting any inconsistencies against the syllabus
- Assessing the author's interpretation of the workbook

Workbook Technical Reviewers

Technical reviewers to provide a detailed review of the workbook and bring the review comments to the panel. Responsibilities include:
- Cross-checking the workbook against the syllabus
- Ensuring sufficient coverage of each learning objective

Workbook Proofreaders

Proofreaders are needed to proof workbooks both grammatically and also in terms of the format and layout. Responsibilities include:
- Checking for spelling and grammar mistakes
- Checking for formatting inconsistencies

If you are interested in becoming a CISI external specialist call:
+44 20 7645 0609

or email:
externalspecialists@cisi.org

For bookings, orders, membership and general enquiries please contact our Customer Support Centre on +44 20 7645 0777, or visit our website at cisi.org